Women as
Mythmakers

INTRODUCTION

Steps Toward a Feminist Archetypal Theory of Mythmaking

Much as a photographer seeks to stop action to reveal its structure and beauty, this book seeks to capture an ongoing process of re-envisioning our cultural mythology. Even after a century of studying myths, we do not know much about the processes whereby they are formed and altered. Scholars now generally concede that mythic thinking is a continuing process and not a stage that human beings passed through thousands of years ago when the dominant religions of the world were formed. But disagreement about the status of mythic thinking has prevented much serious investigation of contemporary processes of mythmaking in Western culture.

We do know a great deal about myths themselves from the multiple disciplines that have studied them: religion, anthropology, philosophy, literary criticism, analytical and psychoanalytic psychology, and sociology.[1] Their disagreements concerning the origins, functions, forms, and significance of myth have filled volumes, and I do not want to imply that their differences are unimportant. Still, it is possible to step back from the fracas and see that myth usually takes the form of an unusually potent story or symbol. Regardless of its origins (in group ritual or in the dreams of individuals), it is repeated until it is accepted as truth. Regardless of the specific purpose it serves (to charter a nation or to reconcile life-baffling oppositions), it often achieves the status of the sacred. Once a myth is in place, it is nearly impossible to dislodge it by exclusively rational means. It must be replaced by another equally persuasive story or symbol.

The continuing potency of myth remains something of a mystery. Many scholars have studied myth to triumph over it by reason.[2] They have regarded it as a "primitive" or even aberrant form of science or history—a form that is no longer necessary in an age such as our own with technological methods of validation at its disposal. Indeed, when we remember how the myth of racial superiority seized the German state in the 1930s, it is easy to wish that myths would disappear. Despite nearly a century of muckraking headlines, disparaging equations of myth with falsehood, and predictions of myth's demise, the phenomenon of myth remains intact. Myths are not like scientific hypotheses; they do not vanish when proved untrue. The myths of heaven and hell, originally based on the image of a three-storied universe, have not lost their power for many people who know from their exposure to modern science that no such "places" exist.

Perhaps we will find some day in studying the brain that myth is the product of the "old brain," or that it arises from unique conjunctions of hemispheric activity. Perhaps it depends on a kind of long-term memory we have not even begun to study yet—say, the memory of a point in our evolution when we could fly. Certainly it seems to depend on some other system of validation that is not fully responsive to the information gained from direct perception and cognition. Whatever it is, wherever it is rooted, it seems to be an integral part of our apparatus for structuring our lives. Far from being in opposition to science and history, it is intimately connected with them. Perhaps this is because myth is an aspect of our capacity to reason.[3] Or, according to current theory, perhaps it is because myth is an aspect of our language system.

Exactly how myth relates to other aspects of language remains unclear. Albert Cook posits that myth is both continuous and discontinuous with language: continuous in that it must be communicated in language, and discontinuous in that it "handles material that lies in some way out of the reach of natural language," providing a technique for "naming the unknown without offering a solution."[4] It is an act of storytelling whose source or motive (*raison d'être*) is the unconscious or the unknown. Myth is "the modality wherein we consciously mediate between fiction and belief, between language and whatever it is that lies beneath or beyond language."[5]

Eric Gould explains the relationship between myth and language somewhat differently, although he also sees myth as narrative and the unconscious as the "instigation" to myth.[6] For Gould, myth is synonymous with language and virtually indistinguishable from other fictions; it is a complementary class of discourse. Its special function is to express the inadequacy of language to close the gap between event and meaning, other and self, what-is and our desire to know it, outside and inside. Likewise, the archetype is a sign that serves to describe the site where inner and outer meet; it is nothing more or less than evidence of a linguistic transaction.[7] Myth and archetype are universal, however, in the sense of pointing to a condition that remains open to interpretation. Myth is an "expanding contextual structure,"[8] more concerned with the questions that arise in the gaps between nothingness and being than with final answers. It engages a persistent existential crisis and forges by means of metaphorical play a compromise which is always open to reconstruction. In a word, it is a "systematic protection against our not-knowing, against our 'soft inside.'"[9]

What implications do these concepts have for the critic? If myths are part of the dynamic of history instead of being one of its reservoirs; if they are structures that mediate between language and the unknown instead of being digests of beliefs; if they are structures that evolve in relation to existential crises instead of being revelations of reality; if they are part of an ongoing process of constructing a livable world instead of being records of a completed process, then how ought we to go about interpreting them?

Our first task is to identify them. While it is easy to do this from a distance of place, time, or culture (we speak comfortably of Greek myths or even Old Testament myths), it is not easy to identify structures that govern our own lives. Some structures are so pervasive and have been so fully described that we do recognize them despite our involvement with them: the story of the quest and the image of paradise are examples. Others, particularly those enmeshed in science (which has the status that myth and religion had in earlier phases of our culture), are less visible.

We usually recognize myths in our own literature and art by identifying familiar elements from traditional myths: the name of a hero or a god, the story of a famous exploit or gesture, a sym-

bol that has worked its way into the language carrying with it
forgotten mythic implications. We may also recognize the presence of a myth in a pattern of images or ritual gestures. If we
take seriously the concepts of myth just presented, we might also
consider stories that arise from existential crises, particularly if
they are repeated; for myth eventually differentiates itself from
other narratives by becoming a shared story.

Our task of recognizing contemporary myths is made doubly
difficult by the fact that we do not know what phase of the
myth-making process we are observing. It seems likely to me
that the full-blown story is a mature phase of myth, and that
both image and ritual are incipient and passing phases. I hypoth-
esize that the process of mythmaking starts with a tendency to
form mental images in relation to repeated experiences. I call this
tendency (which is like the tendency to form language described
by Noam Chomsky) the "archetype," and its manifestations "archetypal images." These images give rise to rituals and stories if
the experience is powerful enough, and these in turn become
mythic if they are widely shared. Once the images and stories
become "solidified" as symbols in language, they begin to
influence the experience of others (but I do not believe as Gould
does, following Jacques Lacan, that all experience necessarily becomes linguistic), and they may live on in ritual and language
long after they have stopped expressing the primary experience
of the individual. Thus the goddesses probably originated as images of the mother in response to the human experience of female
creativity in childbirth; and the multiple rituals and stories that
developed from these various sources gradually became the
highly articulated myths of Isis and Demeter—whose rituals and
images survived for centuries despite Christian efforts to negate
and then to absorb their mythic power. In the study of myths-
in-process, then, the repeated image or gesture may be just as
important as the repeated story or the symbol.

Once a mythic story has been identified, then it is possible to
examine the "bundles of relations" among elements in the manner described by Claude Lévi-Strauss. At such a point in our culture, a myth would be well enough accepted to appear in the
literary forms that are most responsive to societal conventions:
the novel, the Broadway play, the Hollywood film script, the
popular song, or any of the various forms of television storytell-

ing. The myth of the quest, for example, appears in all these media. For the less-developed or less-accepted phases of a myth, however, we must turn to modes of expression that allow more latitude for challenge to accepted cultural forms: poetry; experimental fiction, film, or theatre; dance; and visual art on the "fringe" of society.

There seems to be widespread agreement that literature, particularly poetry, continues to play an essential role in the evolution of myth, and vice-versa.[10] Albert Cook understands poetry as the primary strategy for getting back and forth from language to myth, and sees its bridging function as indispensable to other forms of human discourse such as philosophy and historiography.[11] Both Cook and Gould also recognize that the language of literature is only one of many language-like systems that carry mythic significance. (Gould says, "By limiting the subject to narrative, of course, we are not precluding dance, drawing, and the other arts of mythology, which have in common with the tale the nature of a semiotic or representational system."[12]) What they and others do not consider is that each of those systems may, in the current parlance of experimental psychology, "offer genuine alternative models for incorporating, storing and conveying information."[13]

The critic who is interested in mythmaking as an ongoing process can scarcely avoid turning to the arts for information. For at least a century in Europe, artists in several media have been expressing exactly the sort of existential crisis that Gould describes as generative of myth. The first wave of avant-garde artists (from Manet through the Cubists and the Expressionists) sought primarily to be free of formal and moral restraints embodied in aesthetic conventions so that they could express their own versions of reality. The second wave, beginning with Jarry and extending through the Surrealists to Artaud, abrogated reason along with convention and sought to inhabit a collective realm beyond the individual's consciousness. Later artists, following Duchamp and Cage, sought to transcend the perspective of the individual altogether, using the "languages" of art to achieve complete "objectivity," and apparently giving up the culture's hypothesis that there is something "inside" the human being for "languages" to represent.[14]

Although much of this art has been integrated into the symbolic system of Western culture, the crisis is by no means over. It disturbed the culture's premises and made us (in the late twentieth century) painfully aware of the effects of certain myths on our lives. We inherited from these art movements aesthetic forms that were highly suitable crucibles for myth: forms that tended toward ritual performance and toward the establishment of closer relationships between artist and audience. This restoration of art to the life of the group (after several centuries of rarefaction) has probably prepared the ground for the emergence of "new" myths. It remains to be seen, of course, how new they are.

The role of interpreter in this process requires care. Although our artists seem to have assumed the role of shaman in the absence of any other source of spiritual renewal, the critic need not assume the role of priest or priestess. Instead, we must balance our tendency to be skeptical with our willingness to suspend disbelief once again in the face of human imagining. Our chief job is to become conscious of the acts of mythmaking that occur and to establish viable relationships with the myths that result from them.

The problems of the feminist critic in this process are legion. The first is whether to investigate the role of women in mythmaking at all, since the enterprise seems to suppose a difference between women and men that has not been proved and may be detrimental to our health. Throughout history women and everything associated with the feminine have been relegated to second-class status. Why not confine one's studies to individuals without regard to their affiliation with a group?

The trouble is that *myths* are not made by individuals. To be sure, individuals do make *mythic* stories, but in order to become myths these require validation by a group. Myth is a collective agreement about some aspect of the unknown. Like it or not, female artists belong to the group called "women." No matter how individual we try to be, sooner or later we are singled out as women. The existence of a large female reading public in the nineteenth century created the opportunities for more and more women writers to be published. The existence of a strong feminist movement in the 1960's created pressure for the recognition of women's past achievements in the visual arts and opened doors for women to prove themselves in the seventies and eighties. Feminism also shaped the consciousness of the audience for literature and visual art so that strong female and feminist artmaking traditions could evolve. Without their various forms of allegiance to other women, individual women probably would not have the status they enjoy in the art world today.

Feminist scholarship has demonstrated other ways in which we belong to a group despite our considerable differentiation as individuals. Consider, for example, the effects of growing up in the nuclear family (a dominant institution in the West), where the mother and the father play different roles in child-rearing. The girl raised under such conditions, Nancy Chodorow claims, develops a more multidimensional internal "family" than does the boy. She remains attached to her mother, who is the first love object for both boys and girls, while she develops a secondary emotional attachment to her father. Because she never represses either attachment, she never develops the capacity that boys do for the denial of relational needs—a denial that seems to govern the world of work in Western society. Yet she has a capacity for rationality and distance that comes from having to forge an (unnatural?) erotic relationship with men in a heterosexual culture. Because women are emotionally more important to women than men are, she continues throughout her life to fulfill her emotional needs by creating personal bonds with other women. The result is that her "inner world" is more complex than that of men.[15]

Chodorow's theory also suggests that our physiological experience of the boundaries between ourselves and lovers or children differs from men's experience. Other studies suggest that our sexual response mechanism differs substantially. Still others support Mary Daly's hypothesis that women live on the boundaries of patriarchal culture, or that we live in two cultures at once: the dominant one and a "muted" one that is not yet entirely known even to ourselves.[16]

These commonalities, which seem undeniable, provide nearly perfect conditions for the development of myth. Even those who wish to deny or ignore them in order to focus exclusively on the also undeniable individuality of each woman cannot escape participation in a definitional struggle that is the stuff of mythology. (Indeed, one ironic possibility is that feminism is the last bastion of the myth of individuality.)

Another problem the feminist critic faces is the widespread belief that myths belong to a symbolic system that women did not create and that they use only at their peril. And it is true that Eric Gould's otherwise liberating description of what he calls "mythicity" rests on Lacanian psychoanalysis, which denies women a place in the symbolic. Likewise, Cook describes the contemporary process of mythmaking as relying on six or more previous phases of mythic development, each more sophisticated than the one before. Of these phases, only the first, embodying a unitary focus on one figure, the mother, precedes the creation of the symbolic, which Lacan describes as a prison of language that governs even the workings of the unconscious.[17]

One strategy for solving this problem apparently dates back to Freud. It involves combing the myths of the mother goddess for information about female experience that is untainted by patriarchal culture. If this strategy is undertaken with the notion that such myths reveal something essential and necessary about femaleness, however, it raises a new set of problems. Presumably we do not want to sanction a return to barbaric rituals in the search for female authenticity.[18]

In the midst of a culture that still wants desperately to define, once and for all time "what-is," it is difficult to establish an alternative mind-set that will allow us to move behind our cultural stage into the wings of female experience without claiming that we have found the essential nature of woman. I believe, however, that a feminist archetypal theory could help us to accomplish this task. If we redefine the archetype as a tendency to form images in relation to recurrent experiences and we acknowledge that women as well as men must have this capacity, we need only uncover enough images created by women to discover the patterns in our experiences. If we think of myth as a structure for dealing with shared crises of self-definition in the face of the unknown, we need only locate mythic stories created by women in order to know which of our experiences have been most critical or enduring.

The efficacy of this strategy depends on our willingness to redefine the unconscious (which at present seems to be a Freudian "text" rather than a human phenomenon) as the unknown within us instead of being simply a storehouse of repressed materials. It also depends on our willingness to challenge the prevailing idea that everything can be explained in terms of a semiotic model.

Jung found ample evidence that the unconscious "contained" materials other than those repressed by the child in the Oedipal stage of development, and we can respect those findings without committing ourselves either to his essentialist interpretations of them or to his desire to de-emphasize the role of sexuality in personality development. As for semiotics, the evidence is not all in. It is not clear that imagining, for example, is a linguistic process.[19] Nor is it clear that pictures, graphs, maps, and diagrams, to say nothing of music or dance, work on the same principle of representation as do words.

In fact it seems quite likely that women have used the various codes open to both sexes for nonpatriarchal purposes. The example of Hildegard von Bingen, whose illumination called "Cosmos" was published in a manuscript titled *Scivias* in about 1141, should make my point. According to the religious historian Anne Barstow, Hildegard's writings were thoroughly enmeshed in patriarchal values.[20] Her images, however, tell a different story. The vision presented in "Cosmos" apparently followed several others in an intense drama of light and darkness that culminated in

> a huge image, round and shadowy. It was pointed at the top, like an egg. . . . Its outermost layer was of bright fire. Within lay a dark membrane. Suspended in the bright flames was a burning ball of fire, so large that the entire image received its light. Three more lights burned in a row above it. They gave it support through their glow, so that the light would never be extinguished.[21]

The striking features of the image itself are the vaginal, labial, womblike qualities of the ball of fire which illuminates everything within the dark membrane. The image seems unlikely to have been dictated by the Holy Fathers.

We do not need to believe that such images define or determine woman's essential being in order to honor them as mythological nodes, if you will, of female experience. We find these nodes by locating images that seem unfamiliar in patriarchal usage, and we affirm their pertinence to female experience when we find them repeated independently in works by other women. The significance of our discoveries is open to interpretation. Suppose we learn, for example, that women thoughout the ages have had a tendency to resolve the human problem of relationship to the external world by means of female reproductive imagery. Depending on our willingness to articulate these images in narratives, these might become the basis of a new myth to rival the myths of dominance or husbandry articulated in Genesis. Then, depending on our willingness to establish a workable relationship with the myth, it might play a life-supporting role in our culture. The presence of such patterns of female sexual imagery in works by women need not mean that all women think through their bodies, or that women are more closely connected with nature than are men, or anything at all about Woman.[22] As long as they are seen as manifestations of female experience (in this case, of living in a female body), which is always open to change, they are merely expanding or contracting elements in a complex system of symbols.

With such a theory in mind, it makes sense to examine the relationships of women to myth in various media as carefully and thoroughly as feasible to see if any unusual images, stories, or patterns are rooted in female experience and whether they seem likely to sustain growth.

Two aspects of such relationships deserve particular attention. The first concerns the place women assume in the history of patriarchal mythmaking. As Cook describes it, this history has proceeded in a highly ordered fashion from its unitary focus on one female figure, to the binary extensions of its first stories in response to the dualities of human existence, and on to increasing levels of systematization and ironic scrutiny until, in the twentieth century, we finally achieved enough sophistication to be able to question, and at the same time to celebrate, the theoretical foundations of myth and language. Do twentieth-century women participate in this process as "team-members"? Do they engage in mythmaking practices that belong to earlier phases of our history or pre-history? Or do they establish a new phase?

The second aspect of women's relationship to myth that deserves our scrutiny concerns the *raison d'être* of myth. Granted that myth arises from our inability to close the gaps between language and reality, are those gaps the same for twentieth-century women as for men? Is "nothingness" the primary issue for women, as Gould contends it is for men?

Partial answers to these questions exist in feminist criticism; I believe that we will not have complete answers until many more studies have been completed across several disciplines. Nonetheless, we seem to have settled on the word "re-vision," following Adrienne Rich, as the term to describe our stance toward myth. Likewise, Rich, Sylvia Plath, and H.D. have emerged as key figures in our critical studies. But we need to establish now with greater clarity the nature, extent, and significance of our revisionary acts.

Susan Friedman places H.D., for example, in the center of the modernist mythmaking tradition that includes W.B. Yeats, Ezra Pound, T.S. Eliot, and William Carlos Williams. But H.D.'s experience required the construction of a new symbolic system that did not objectify her self as "other"—a system that involved her in a revision of patriarchal assumptions embodied in traditional myths. Friedman explains: "this negation ultimately involved a dialectical process that developed aspects of the old sources into antithetical myths which validated female experience, female quest, and female vision."[23] Revision, then, is a dialectical process. Karen Elias-Button, on the other hand, seems to imagine it as a process of leap-frogging patriarchal mythology to "claim" the archetypes of the goddess religions for expressing realities of contemporary female experience. Thus the figure of Medusa is revised to represent the "dark, but necessary, side of our own creative possibilities."[24] The "formal properties" of the archetype are dissolved. Along the same lines, Annis Pratt calls women's fiction a form of "unvention," an act of tapping a repository of knowledge lost from Western culture but still available to the author and recognizable to the reader as deriving from a world with which she, at some level of her imagination, is already familiar."[25] The archetypes Pratt describes in the forms of images or plots are products of rediscovery of lost knowledge through intuition and imagination.

Still another explanation comes from Alicia Ostriker, who sees revisionist mythmaking by women as a complex act of theft from virtually any mythological pasture, regardless of its place in history, followed by re-evaluation of the cultural values previously enshrined there, and re-presentation of the stolen elements in experimental forms to emphasize the poet's argument with tradition.[26] Sandra Gilbert describes the process of revision still differently, calling it "confessional." For her, it began with alienation from her own perspective through false identification with inappropriate mythological figures. After awakening to her own alienation, a moment of rejection and repudiation ensued, only to be followed by an appropriation and transformation of myth according to her own needs. She even sees the woman's "otherness" as something of an advantage:

> The outsider, the Other, the woman poet owns only her own vision and therefore she can steal into the house of myth, *see* everything, and say, for the first time (and thus with the dearest freshness) what everything means to *her*. While [the male poet] shores fragments against his ruin, she exults as the fragments join in her with their own music.[27]

Instead of being a thief stealing mythological elements from others' pastures, the woman revisionist imagined here breaks into the common house of myth in order to make it her own.

Rachel Blau DuPlessis describes women's critical engagement with myth in even more radical terms. She finds in some women's poetry a strategy of "defection" or "committed identification with Otherness," particularly those aspects of femaleness that are "taboo, despised, marginalized" in patriarchal culture. Another tactic is "displacement," or the "construction of the 'other side'" of a well-known plot in order to reinsert women into myth, thereby "rescuing culture from its own unexamined premises."[28] The most extreme tactic involves "deformation" or "safe-cracking":

> This is not simply a reversal of image, or a re-interpretation of events with different emotions. Rather deformation is a struggle with the stuff that makes a text into a text: adequate grammar, understandability, a known vocabulary, mandated sequences of events, speech itself as opposed to aphasia, stutter or the void.[29]

The point of the activity is to break into the myth to bring its ideological premises to the reader's attention. Since DuPlessis sees myth as the "repository of many layers of history," the rewriting of myth is a "drastically unorganic" choice—an act of "pretending to act as history itself."[30]

Impressive and exciting as this growing body of theory is, it may be unnecessarily limiting. *Does* all mythmaking directly engage earlier myths? Is it not possible to create new myths? And what is it anyway that leads to the creation of myths? Nearly all these critics see mythmaking as a project of self-definition. Is this always the case? Again, these questions will not be easily answered, and I hope we will not be satisfied until they are answered with reference to several media.

Although I summarize them below in the form of a continuous narrative to give the reader an overview of their content, chapters 1 through 6 of the present study were written independently of each other in response to more specific questions about each individual's relationship to myth. Chapter 7 concerns the potentially mythic dimensions of images created by many visual artists, and chapter 8 was written in response to those images in order to explore the possibility that poetry by diverse women has begun to articulate a "new" cultural myth concerning the place of humankind in nature. The conclusion suggests connections or patterns that emerge from all the previous parts of the study, returning to the broad questions I have posed here in order to evaluate the progress I have made toward answering them.

The chapter on Anne Sexton comes first for a number of reasons. In my view, Sexton's work records one of the central mythological struggles of our time—between the internalized father god of Judeo-Christian religion and the goddess who arises naturally and frequently in our dreams. Sexton rejected the goddesses of her dreams, I argue, primarily because the names she knew for them were fraught with difficulties that she could not surmount. After *Transformations*, in which she treated fairy tales as "fenceposts" surrounding heretofore hidden psychological truths, Sexton continued to hone what Alicia Ostriker calls her distinctive anti-authoritarian style[31] in the revision of other culturally loaded forms and figures: the New Testament parables and psalms, the bestiary, and the Greek Furies among them. In the process, she generated many images of the god[desse]s but none that was fully satisfactory—none that was powerful enough to overturn the story of the human fall from grace in the eyes of God the Father.

Far from remaining confessional (as Judith Kroll and others have contended),[32] Sexton's poems illustrate the phases of mythmaking that Sandra Gilbert describes—phases of being alienated from an accepted myth, recognizing her alienation, appropriating the myth for her own purposes, and passing into the reality of mythology. She does this most completely in "The

Jesus Papers" and in her psalms, "O Ye Tongues." In these and many other poems written during the last four years of her life, she assumes the role that Rachel Blau DuPlessis would call the "defector," taking the position of the "other" to illuminate our mythic assumptions in startling ways. She does this, apparently under pressure from her experiences as a mother and a lover, which generated images associated with "the goddess."[33]

Rarely, however, does she experience the exultation that both Alicia Ostriker and Sandra Gilbert describe as part of their own experience of revising myths; and so the process of transformation from the Christian story of the soul's journey to the Demetrian story she considered, was never completed. Regardless of what she achieved for herself in her mythmaking, however, she opens up possibilities (for those with theological needs) of moving beyond the asexual Christian story to a belief in gods who are both sexual and nurturing. She shows the necessity and the difficulty of creating a counterworld such as Mary Daly recommends, in which women believe in their own experiences.[34] And she offers a stunning reinterpretation of death as an icy baby that we carry within ourselves from our birth.

The chapter on Käthe Kollwitz is next because her imagination also dwelled on the figures of the mother and death. But Kollwitz did achieve the exultation that Sexton missed. She did so not by confessing her place in an old myth, but by evolving images for a new one. From her life-threatening experience of grief over the loss of her second son in World War I, she created a matriarchal figure who is capable of exercising her capacities for self-protection, self-assertion, and self-expansion (what David Bakan calls human "agency")[35] on behalf of others. In the images of the mother Kollwitz created after 1922, she fuses qualities of nurturing, militance and inspiration. In her depiction of death as a maternal figure during the same period, she warns that there is another aspect of the mother that can overwhelm the individual from within. The incipient story that informs Kollwitz's creation is articulated in the title borrowed from Goethe for her lithograph "Seed Corn Shall Not Be Ground"; that is, our children shall not be destroyed in war. But the fully realized story would concern the mother's role in bringing about a less coercive and aggressive society. Kollwitz's images become mythic, as Sexton's do, partly because of their psychological size—the magnitude of the issue they treat. But Kollwitz was involved, as Sexton (despite her popularity as a public figure) was not, in political movements with a scope of reference that makes her images likely bases for mythic development. Here is a story that begins in alienation from the myth that human aggression is natural and necessary, moves through rebellion against oppression and war, and continues on to the exultant creation of a mother who is liberated from her confinement to the personal sphere and capable of overseeing the development of a new order.

Margaret Atwood performs a similar task of transforming the image of the seductress, although her strategy is markedly different. In her "Circe/Mud Poems," she affirms the notion that traditional myths offer essential knowledge to free as well as to enslave us. She chooses the tactic DuPlessis calls "displacement," constructing Circe's story from the other side, Circe's side, which never appears in Homer's *Odyssey*. She even divides her poem into 24 parts, as if to assert her right to equal consideration with the great text. Circe turns out to be a sexual and nurturing witch—a poet, a would-be visionary, who disapproves of the masculine quest and would like to cure the hero of his disease. Men may find Circe seductive, but that is more a product of their own lust than of her intent to seduce. She emerges from the poem as a figure of the *seer*: the one who sees into, sees beyond, sees more than others do. Atwood makes us believe in this capacity by her poetic strategy of transcending the normal boundaries of time and space by means of her surreal images.

Circe is the model of an independent woman who uses her talent for assessing the needs of others for her own survival. Her story is that she stays on her island by choice and enters into liaisons with others by choice in order to provide an alternative model of the quest—one which does not require the triumph of one person over another.

Remedios Varo seems to pick up where Atwood leaves off, detailing in at least 27 paintings, completed over a nine-year period, the various phases of a female quest. She, too, convinces us of the authenticity of her vision by surrealistic techniques that break down the boundaries between the categories we normally observe. Although Varo uses details of several myths (concerning Psyche, Demeter, Athena, the Minotaur, the Grail, and so on), they are merely tangential reference points for her own vision.

Rather than beginning a recognizable myth over again by "de-
forming" it, as Rachel DuPlessis does in her "Medusa," Varo
begins over again by accepting the myth's skeleton and rejecting
its flesh. Her heroines, who resemble their creator, do *not* receive
a call, are *not* guided by helpers, do *not* engage in battles, do *not*
enter a sacred marriage, are *not* reconciled with the father and the
mother, and are *not* reintegrated into society upon their return.
They do experience a remarkable degree of union with nature, do
discover the Grail, do learn to distill the elixir from their experience, and do carry their own lamp of knowledge. The myth of
the female quest is a story of failure in success if we understand it
as having to do with individual achievement. But the "subtext"
of the paintings tells another story about the nature of female
creativity, which is imaged as the heroine's capacity to direct nature's genius toward creatures less fortunate than herself; to collaborate with the celestial bodies to create life out of art; and
finally to restore the vegetable world to life. In Western mythology, creativity involves individual genius, egotistical motivation,
personal achievement, and, finally, explicit recognition. The
creativity encoded here involves a sense of being in tune with
powerful nonhuman forces; of being fully conscious yet detached
from the concerns of the ego; of acting spontaneously without
selfconsciousness.

Varo's work suggests that the female protagonist as image or
person, in art or in life, may be required to reconnect human life
with the natural cycle of nonhuman life. Diane Wakoski, in her
struggle with the Western equation of woman with nature,
shows how a modern woman in an age of science might be able
to turn a potentially negative myth to advantage. Wakoski transforms the mythic formula "woman is to nature as man is to culture" by means of a complex combination of virtually all the
processes of revision I have noted so far. Her process begins not
with alienation so much as with identification with the moon in a
phase of archetypal imagining. After she realizes that in this
identification she has devalued herself, her strategy is not to reject
the identification but to revalue the moon through becoming
familiar with the scientific perspectives on it. She uses science for
her own positive ends as a means of revaluing her own internal
resources, which she uses on behalf of nature. The outcome of
her process is similiar to Varo's: she becomes a naturalist. In

learning to defend herself, she learns to defend the world. Wakoski's story involves the development of female strength to the point that she can take cultural responsibility for the condition of nature, which she insists is herself and yet is not her *self*. She successfully avoids two traps of Western mythology regarding women and nature: the tendency to separate nature from culture, and the exemption of women from culture.

In Wakoski's case we are dealing with a myth of a different order of generality from the story of Christ's birth and death or Circe's role in the quest of Odysseus. Like the image of the mother, the myth of woman's affinity with nature has developed from a set of specific stories into a cultural principle of categorization with no recognizable story. Wakoski's story does more than remythologize woman's role in nature; it creates a modern equivalent of the ancient mythic premises of a cultural category.

Léonor Fini performs a similar revelatory function *vis-à-vis* the category "human nature." She also goes through many stages of revision, beginning as Wakoski did with an identification with pre-Christian mythological figures—in Fini's case the sphinx, that riddling hybrid with a lion's body, a bird's wings, and a female bust against whom Oedipus was called upon to recognize man. She then represents a series of priestesses in a Demetrian religion, some of whom are also hybrids, but most of whom are asexual guardians. Apparently her vision required another sort of transformation, this time in the form of an underworld journey, because for several years her work shows explorations of the elements of earth, fire, and water. And then a new cast of characters emerges, different from the priestesses in their degree of sexuality, in their activities, and in their role. They are no longer protectors of the old order, but harbingers of a new one. The women of this new order stick together. They are beautiful and capable of ministering to others; but nurturing is no longer their primary function. Fini's images give us the chance to examine a world which is not organized according to the idea that woman equals love. The answer to the sphinx's riddle may still be "man," but the change in woman's relationship to the species envisaged here is profound.

These examples of individual relationships to mythmaking are intended to show the richness and variety of contemporary women's response to our troubles with Western mythology.

They help us to understand both why and how myths continue to take shape in a culture that mistrusts them. In summary, we might say that they arise because of the psychosexual inadequacy of traditional religion; because of life-threatening crises; because of the desire to tell the rest of the story; because of the need to validate nonprocreative female creativity; because of the desire to survive without being devalued; and because of the necessity to envision a new world in order to find one's rightful place. And these individuals tell us that myths take shape sometimes in collision with other myths, sometimes within them, and sometimes with only tangential reference to them—out of a pressing internal need whose mythological roots the artist may not surmise.

These essays tell us less, however, about the shape of the whole mythology that is being created by these and other means, for these and other reasons. As I said earlier, no individual *makes* a cultural myth, but many individuals working along the same lines may do so if their work becomes known to a receptive audience. In addition, one individual can tap this communal process by creating a summative text. In my chapters on the collective visions in visual art and poetry, I examine these two possibilities in relation to visual art and poetry by women.

The first step in assessing the coherence of a collective vision is to find the elements that are repeated most often and to try to ascertain why. In my survey of more than a thousand visual artists across the United States, more than two hundred were clearly concerned with a network of related images concerning the transformation of one form into another. In my interpretation, these images of transformation amount to a re-evaluation of nature—our own and the world's. Several aspects of this network or pattern of images relate to themes that I have described in Part One. Many of these artists accept the affinity between woman and nature as a starting point—in fact, creating hybrid images of woman/animal/earth until the old distinctions among the levels in the Great Chain of Being seem unimportant. Natural forms are used to describe the blooming of the female self and to re-evaluate the beauty of female sexual organs in the manner Judy Chicago has made famous, but they are also used to encourage us to reach beyond the realm of the human. These artists are concerned with the dimensions of the world that they believe must not be reduced to human terms. Insofar as a deity presides over the cosmic realm imaged in this body of work, it is the goddess. But the world envisaged is inextricably bound to the human and the human to the world. The images depend ultimately on a different concept of appropriate boundaries between forms of life—a concept which seems rooted in the female's experience of her own body in relation to significant others. But the images are also related to the newest insights of science concerning the ways our bodies assemble cells from other organisms and the way our present universe draws on the energies of the ancient past.

I am sure that many of the artists whose work I saw were unaware of their complicity in the process of mythmaking; yet many others showed in their titles or in the statements accompanying their work a consciousness of myth. No "story" emerges from this body of work. What does emerge, however, is an image of relationships among orders of being that is extremely fluid without being disintegrative. The movement from one level of reality to another (dream to ordinary waking consciousness, human to animal or vegetable form, the house to the universe) occurs without the sense of paradox, confusion, or *duality* that we experience in much twentieth-century painting. What we miss in terms of story, we gain in terms of stimulation to imagine a new way of being.

My concomitant search through contemporary poetry by women revealed a more extensive pattern of concerns with nature than I had expected when I began my study; and gradually it dawned on me that the prose poems at the end of Susan Griffin's *Woman and Nature* might serve a more summative function than I had thought when I first read her book simply as a critique of patriarchal attitudes toward women. Thus I decided to write this chapter as an investigation of the relationship between her work and the poetry of other women.

The key to the emergent myth I found is Griffin's term for the earth: "Sister." For although many women still understand the earth as "mother," the concept of the mother differs from the stereotype of the all-nurturing provider. She is more a vulnerable yet venerable person, worthy not only of our love but of our respect. Nature has a female form, but the human relationships with it need not be exploitative, if we regard it as *equal* to ourselves. We need not be overwhelmed by nature, nor should we put ourselves on a pedestal. We are akin to nature, not superior to it. The poets I examined see in the story of evolution evidence of our similarity to other forms of life. They are not antiscientific; quite the opposite: they are interested in the forms of animal communication science has discovered, and they are prepared to believe that the human brain contains vestiges of earlier phases of animal life. Neither the human nor the animal is devalued in this assessment. Instead, there is an acceptance of our groundedness in the earth, in the animal, in the body. To understand the earth as our sister means to be able to hail nature as Diane di Prima does: "Mother & Sister/myself."[36] Perhaps women were predisposed to this vision by centuries of identification with nature. Perhaps it is a strategy of survival to revalue the devalued world with which we have been compared for so long. Whatever the reason, a new story is taking shape.

In a final chapter, which takes its title from Griffin ("the light is in us"), I return to the questions I have raised here concerning mythmaking about women. And I advance the hypothesis that the incipient myth in the works I interpret here arises from the same distinctive aspects of female experience that also inspire a female epistemology.

Part One
Individual Visions

In what I am calling "creative" mythology
. . . the individual has had an experience of
his [sic] own—of order, horror, beauty, or
even mere exhilaration—which he seeks to
communicate through signs; and if his
realization has been of a certain depth and
import, his communication will have the
value and force of living myth—for those
who receive and respond to it of themselves, with recognition, uncoerced.

—Joseph Campbell, *The Masks
of God: Creative Mythology*

CHAPTER 1

Anne Sexton's Radical Discontent[1]

Between 1970 and 1974, Anne Sexton created an extraordinary, perhaps prophetic, body of poetry based upon images that have profound psychological and religious significance for our age. The brilliance of the images, her refusal to censor them no matter what kind of cultural challenge they contained, and her success in giving them significant form constitute a stunning achievement in poetry. This may come as a surprise to those who think of Sexton as a "confessional" poet seeking personal reconciliation with her parents and children, or seeking heterosexual love and psychological integration without concern for the larger issues of her time.[2] Her poems show, however, that by 1963 she understood her personal predicament as an "exile from God" (*WDY, Words for Dr. Y.*, p. 10), which would require a strenuous quest. Indeed, five of the six books containing poems she wrote after 1970[3] suggest that the original terms of her quest—the search for a viable relationship with the Father/Son/Holy Spirit promised by the Christian tradition—broke open under the pressure of her imaginative scrutiny. As she allowed her own images to matter, and they began to "leak" from her pen "like a miscarriage" (*BF, The Book of Folly*, p. 32), she began to inhabit a realm peopled by archetypal figures that could not be contained by the Christian story. Sexton was painfully aware that this new leg of her journey would be judged a folly by those who wanted her to spill her guts (*DN, The Death Notebooks*, p. 65), but *not* to "unlock the Magi" or to "bolt for the sun like a diamond" (*BF*, p. 4). Yet she could not stop; her desire to "dig" remained insatiable even when she found that "people pop off and/ muskrats float up backward" (*BF*, p. 34).

Sexton's quest is best understood, I think, in terms of archetypal psychology, as an act of "soul-making"—that is, the
effort to find the connections between life and the fantasy images
that are our "privileged mode of access" to the soul and to those
recurring worldwide figures who are tantamount to gods.[4] Yet
her search kept yielding unexpected results. Her poems, like the
bricks of gold God left when He walked out (DN, p. 46), seem
to have contained the treasure she sought without benefitting
her. Despite her innumerable encounters with her figures from
"the other world,"

> The soul was not cured,
> it was as full as a clothes closet
> of dresses that did not fit.
>   [AR, The Awful Rowing toward God, p. 63]

Unfortunately for us all, she could not accord full value to her
own visions. Apparently she persisted in seeing herself as the
loser in a rigged game with God,[5] remaining oblivious to the fact
that she had produced the richest body of god-images to appear
in some time.

I suggest that Sexton's difficulty in accepting the fruits of her
soul-making had much to do with her inability to name them—
particularly to know their feminine dimensions by name. I see
her last five books, then, as a tragic part of the process of revisioning prescribed by Mary Daly for women who find it impossible to live with theologies designed to serve patriarchal ends.[6]
Sexton's images raise questions about the premises of Christianity and show us one way to move beyond them; whether Sexton
understood the answers her images contained, she opened up a
process of encountering the soul which others may use.

In this essay, I sketch the contours of Sexton's later poetry to
familiarize the reader with her medium and her world before I go
on to uncover the psychological and religious dynamics of her
imaginative pilgrimage. Finally, I will place her discontent with
both the God of our culture and the alternative deities of her
visionary imagination in the context of archetypal psychology
and feminist theology in order to understand the implications her
quest may have for our lives.

I. THE FRUITS OF IMPUDENCE IN A WORLD THAT IS "UP FOR GRABS"[7]

The shift from the personal to the transpersonal in Sexton's quest is reflected in her aesthetic decisions regarding her tone, her figuration, her use of a *persona,* and her formal principles of design in her last five books. Suzanne Juhasz argues convincingly that *Transformations,* composed in 1970, marks a turning point in Sexton's poetry, and she notes an increased boldness in the figures of association which accompany Sexton's assumption of a "voice of power."[8] Sexton also renders her new boldness in a stance that I call "impudent" because its most important feature is a refusal to cover up, gloss over or withdraw from what she saw—a refusal to be shamed into silence. We hear it in the best-known phrases of all her later books: when she finds the gods "shut in the lavatory" (*DN,* p. 2), or remembers her mother's belly "big with another child,/cancer's baby, big as a football" (*DN,* p. 14), or flashes her buttocks to both life and death (*DN,* p. 62). Impudence is not the only stance she assumes; in *The Awful Rowing toward God,* it often gives way to a more defeated (p. 43), lost (p. 48), or deferential (p. 64) manner, and in *45 Mercy Street* it gives way to despair (p. 89) and fear (p. 96) as well. Yet even in these books, her ability to create strong poems out of her most self-destructive feelings may be one of the fruits of impudence. I speculate that Sexton had to create an alternative to the image of the "good woman" (the one who softens the truth) before she could express what she saw. Thus her new stance may have enabled her to move from simile toward metaphor; to adopt the mask of, or enter into dialogue with, extra-human figures; and to choose increasingly ambitious poetic forms.

In her last four books, Sexton relies less heavily upon her remarkable capacity for seeing likeness in the most diverse objects. This capacity is well-exemplified in the multiple similes of "The Break,"[9] where the heart is like the hip, and the hip is like crystal that explodes like a pistol, comes undone like a bag of dog bones and is wrapped like a nun. In *The Book of Folly* she often gives up the distance that simile always allows and steps into dramatic relationship with elements that previously would have been related only to each other. "The Silence" (*BF,* p. 32) is not *like* death; it *is* death, a white bird that comes to sit upon the speaker's shoulder. It is a presence, an embodiment of the whiteness of the environment contrasted with the blackness of the speaker's hair, eyes, words, and with the "vibrating" redness of her mouth. She refuses to put herself at a safe distance from what she sees or feels.

This refusal characterizes not only her use of language but also her "level" of imaginative activity. For example, "The Boat" (*BF,* pp. 44–45) is part of the sequence called "The Death of the Fathers," a subject that might have been handled in her earlier autobiographical manner, since the fathers are identified as her own biological and legal ones. But in this sequence, Sexton keeps pushing beyond her memories and beyond her fantasies to an archetypal realm. In "The Boat," she begins in her familiar autobiographical manner, placing herself with her mother and father in a mahogany Chris-Craft and recreating the scene as if it were happening now. This is an act of conscious imagination—graceful, authentic and inherently controllable. Then, the character of the poem begins to shift (line 20) as the poet-speaker delves more deeply into the fantasy life of her seven-year-old self wherein she is "riding/ to Pemaquid or Spain" instead of just outside the harbor. The waves seem as high as buildings, and the child feels like a kumquat tumbling in the boat. The speaker allows herself to experience the wave washing over the boat as if it were engulfing her and sending her under water: she becomes an actor in a heroic journey which she imagines that her father controls. But another shift takes place at line 33: all the characters in the boat become like "scissors" and they dare the sea by "parting" it, as Moses did. They experience the sea as a green room filled with the dead where an angel warns them *"You have no business./ No business here."* The father cries for "a sign," and suddenly, as if by magic, there is sky and air once more. The poem returns to the level of fantasy where the act of bailing the boat is seen as "dividing our deaths" and then as "closing out/ the cold wing that has clasped us." But from lines 33 to 45 we have inhabited an archetypal chamber, a non-human world where angels speak and humans are at the mercy of their signs.[10] It is a world that Sexton dared to frequent during the last four years of her poetry.

Sexton's choice of masks and her multi-partite poetic forms show her courage. Whereas in her earlier work the *persona*

"Anne" bore the closest possible resemblance to herself, in her last books Sexton adopts the masks of taboo figures (an assassin, for example) and God-figures (Jesus and Mary, among others) as a deliberate means of understanding experiences that lie beyond her own. Her late *persona* "Ms. Dog" becomes a way of extending the parts of herself to and about whom she can speak. Likewise, her forms become more complex and resonant with cultural significance. As if it were not enough to rewrite the fairy tales, she tackles the Christian parables and the Hebrew psalms, retells the creation and crucifixion stories, and adds a bestiary for good measure.

I am convinced that these artistic choices not only reflect her quest but make it possible. In her last books, Sexton's journey continues in response to a force within her which she knows through her embodiment of it in her poems. As she moves from one stage of her journey to another, she personifies that force variously. At first, she understands it as an "ambition bird" (*BF*, p. 3), and then as her alter-ego or imaginary twin named Christopher (*DN*, p. 84). In *The Awful Rowing* it becomes a rat (p. 2), a jigsaw puzzle image of God (p. 3), a fallen angel (p. 23), a crab (p. 28), and a dead heart (p. 36).[11] In *45 Mercy Street* it is a demon (p. 106). Sexton is alternately attracted to and repelled by these figures; they are both her salvation and her cross. Ironically, she could recognize such figures well enough to allow herself to be propelled by them, but as I will show in part three of this chapter, she could *not* accord her more positive discoveries the same degree of validity.

Still, we can appreciate what Sexton's poems did allow her to do. At the very least, they allowed her to inhabit every place she could imagine, from the interior of the earth (*AR*, p. 63) to "Floor six thousand" in the sky (*AR*, p. 18), long enough to know that none of them contained what she sought. Luckily for us, her poems allowed her to fulfill metaphorically some of the impossible demands of her vision, as when it required a destruction of the body more reminiscent of the dismemberment of Orpheus than it is of the Calvinist who probably inspired it. This metaphorical aspect of her journey seems to begin with her enumeration of body parts over which she takes control when she ousts the Doctor, that "seasick grounded man" (*BF*, p 6). In "The One-Legged Man," she assumes the *persona* of a man who has given away, planted, shipped off, and eaten his leg (*BF,* pp. 16–17). In "Going Home," she watches her loved one give an old crone her eyes, lips, and hands (*BF,* p. 20). In "The Red Shoes," she ties on the shoes of "All those girls" who tore off their ears, whose arms and heads fell off, and whose "feet could not stop" (*BF,* pp. 28–29). In "Killing the Spring," she identifies with a spring that refuses to live by drowning her eyes and nailing her hands "in training for a crucifixion" (*BF,* p. 37). In her sister's dream, she is laid out for the dogs and "loved" until she is gone (*DN,* p. 12). Indeed, the outcome of the dismemberment is a recognition of her kinship with Christ (*AR,* p. 41), when she eats herself and *then* receives mouth-to-mouth resuscitation from Jesus.

Impudence allowed Sexton to proliferate images of her God while exploring unsatisfactory aspects of His nature. Her images are extraordinarily rich, ranging across boundaries between inside and outside, female and male, animal, spirit, and human forms, and mythic or historical representations. In *The Book of Folly* we see God opening His teeth and saying "oh" like a witless old woman or a child (p. 8), or behaving like a magician, then a man, and finally a "pagan" demi-god (pp. 98, 101, 105). In *The Death Notebooks,* He is her grandfather (p. 21), but also a womb (p. 44), a casino owner who behaves like an unreliable washerwoman (p. 46), a dead fish (p. 53), and a mooner (p. 58). The poet boasts, "I am God la de dah" (p. 64). The lovers are God when they fuck (p. 37). Finally, in her psalms, Sexton prays to a playful God who plugs up holes in the sky with His finger, but who is also capable of digesting her (pp. 77, 81). In *45 Mercy Street,* He is Falstaff (p. 19), and a carrion (p. 107), as well as the One who decrees the death of "centuries of our blue mothers" (p. 110). In *Words for Dr. Y.,* He is a blue-faced tyrant (p. 47) or a heartless shopkeeper (pp. 48–49). The images in *The Awful Rowing toward God,* Sexton's clearest articulation of the "private God" she told her friends she found (*Anne Sexton: A Self-Portrait in Letters,* p. 390), are no less diverse or heretical. Perhaps the difference between this book and the others lies in her determination to put together the jigsaw pieces of God (the whore, the drunken old man, the man dressed up as a child "all naked,/ even without skin") into a "whole nation of God" (*AR,* p. 3). Her vision of Him at the end of this book as the winner in a crooked poker game is a sporting admission of defeat rather than a decisive renewal of the traditional Christian myth.

Sexton does not always stop short of mythmaking, although there are fewer full-fledged myths than one might expect in this mythic body of poetry.[12] Surely one of her most important poetic achievements is her image, in the final part of "The Death Baby" (*DN*, pp. 15–17), of death as an icy baby who has been with her from her birth. The cherub, one of those tiny nude angels familiar from early Renaissance paintings, is here envisioned as having the weight and size of the dough for a recipe of bread, soft golden hair, and glass eyes. In the act of rocking the cherub, chanting as she rocks, seeing in its glassy stare the essence of being, Sexton re-enters that archetypal space she saw in "The Boat." As she rocks and her vision enlarges, she sees the image of herself and the baby in stone, another *pietà* in the context of a world subdued and swallowed by war. Without breaking the rhythm of her rocking, she addresses us directly, admonishing us to beware of our tenderness for this "dumb traveller" who accompanies each of us through life.

In the context of Western iconography, where death is often figured as an adult skeleton posing as lover or monk, as if Lucifer were still engaged in the battle with God for souls, Sexton's image is stunning: an externalization of an ever-present, all-seeing eye within all human lives. This element is simultaneously the most private aspect of one's life (one's smell), and the most universal aspect (primordial eye). It is an aspect of self and world within the person that never grows and can elicit maternal tenderness in moments of despair. This act of imagining death as a still-born facet of life itself, rather than a power totally outside of life, belongs to a larger myth to which Sexton was drawn, outside the Christian frame of reference.

II. SEXTON'S JOURNEY TO THE SEA

> Ms. Dog stands on the shore
> and the sea keeps rolling in
> and she wants to talk to God.
> —*DN*, p. 71

Over and over again in the poems from 1970 to 1974, Sexton re-enters the archetypal space we saw in "The Boat" (*BF*, p. 41), but often her encounters are not effectively mediated by the father figure of that poem. Indeed, the essential drama of her work in these years lies in her repeated discoveries of the Father-God's inadequacy combined with her inability to give Him up in favor of the many gods whose faces and voices appeared in her poetry, but whose language she could not translate (*DN*, p. 73). I hope to set forth the terms of the conflict in my interpretation of "The Jesus Papers," Sexton's most ambitious attempt to work through her identification with Jesus,[13] before I uncover the alternative pattern that emerges in *The Death Notebooks, 45 Mercy Street* and *Words for Dr. Y.* in her psalms, prayers, dreams, and visions, which pulled her toward the gods in her lavatory (*DN*, p. 2).

The sequence of nine poems called "The Jesus Papers" (*BF,* pp. 91-105) clearly derives from the modern desire to know who Jesus "really" was, intensified by Sexton's desire for face-to-face conversation with his Father. The sequence expresses the fantastic quality of the New Testament parables on which it is based, while it preserves the vitality of the traditional cast of characters. Sexton achieves this delicate balance of mockery and belief by assuming different positions within the drama (the baby Jesus, the narrator, the dying Jesus, the poet-dreamer); by encountering the characters on several levels of imagination; and by envisioning them as presences, rather than as historical figures or figments of an ancient imagination. In other words, she uses all the resources of her later poetic style in order to salvage what is worthy of belief in Jesus' story.

Significantly, Sexton begins her exploration of Jesus in the sensory sphere of the mother in "Jesus Suckles" (*BF,* p. 93), speaking through the child directly to Mary about the experience of dozing, sucking, growing in her sea-like domain. From the perspective of the first stanza, Sexton can say "I'm a kid in a rowboat and you're the sea,/ the salt, you're every fish of importance." But this Jesus "grows" at an astounding rate, so that in the second stanza he rejects the previous stance of adoration and assumes a more moderate stance of gratitude for his mother's milk. In the third stanza, a still more truthful but less lovable Jesus says "I am a truck. I run everything./ I own you." In 23 lines, Sexton runs the gamut of possible attitudes toward Mary from worship to contempt. She draws at once on the myth of Jesus' impeccable honesty, on our common experience of the growing child's struggle to dominate the mother, and on our acknowledgment that our culture is run by the motor vehicle and dominated by the masculine symbol of the truck. She undercuts any sentimental attachment we may have for the mother-child duo at the moment she reveals how brutally the balance of power will be reversed.

In fact, "The Jesus Papers" can be read as a study of relationships between love and power. Thus, in "Jesus Awake" (*BF,* p. 94), the narrator reports that Jesus' penis is "sewn onto Him like a medal," all life and feeling *departed* from it, implying both that his sex organ is a reward and that he has *lost* his capacity for sexual feeling. Although he is shrouded in gold, he is like a house emptied of people. Sexton's concern with Jesus' sexuality does not stop here. In "Jesus Asleep" (*BF,* p. 95), she understands the symbol of the *Pietà* as a monument to his unfulfilled sexual desire for his mother. In her brilliant extension of Mary Magdalene's story, "Jesus Raises Up the Harlot" (*BF,* p. 96), Sexton focuses on the negative outcome of Jesus' "healing" Mary by lancing her breasts. He establishes a lifelong relationship of servitude. He "saves" her from being stoned to death; she is obliged to save his celibacy by giving up her sexual desire.

When Sexton turns attention to Jesus' power in the next two poems, she is no more reverent. In "Jesus Cooks" (*BF,* p. 98), she presents Jesus as a substitute short-order cook who is out of food. "The Lord" in this comic revision of the parable of the loaves and the fishes is an unskilled magician who has to supplement His one fish with advice about opening sardine cans on the sly. Here, Sexton's vision of Jesus as a human being applies to God as well. In "Jesus Summons Forth" (*BF,* pp. 99–100), her doubt about Jesus' capacity to raise Lazarus from the dead (and about Lazarus's attitude toward his restoration) is mitigated by her vision of the tenderness Jesus feels for Lazarus in a moment of artificial respiration. Here and in the next poem Sexton brings us as close to understanding what she wanted from the New Testament as we can get. Jesus is attractive to her in those moments when he expresses love physically.

Her desire for human love from the Father-God is never clearer than in "Jesus Dies" (*BF,* pp. 101–102), where she assumes the *persona* of Jesus once more—this time in order to envision what it is like for a real human being to die on a cross surrounded by others who think he has a special relationship with God. As Jesus, she desires the equality of a "man-to-man" bond, allowing affectionate teasing; the gift of heaven presented on a dinner plate; the enveloping kind of love that is most familiar to the child who is lifted out of a steaming bath by his mother; and privacy in death. This is the Jesus with whom Sexton identifies most clearly.

But not completely. She cannot forget Mary, even at the peak of her sympathy with Christ. Thus, in "Jesus Unborn" (*BF,* p. 103–104), she returns to the story of the "immaculate conception" and places us so close to Mary in the olive grove that we can see or feel the "pulse in her neck/ beating" in animal anticipation of her transformation. She shows us Mary's physical lethargy which stops any active expression of sexual desire and yet makes her receptive to penetration. The "strange" being who comes to take advantage of the moment is neither swan, bull, nor angel, but an "executioner" who deliberately "covers her like a heavy door/ and shuts her lifetime up/ into this dump-faced day." The poem shifts the responsibility for Mary's imprisonment from Jesus to God. Finally, it is with God and not with Jesus that Sexton must quarrel.

The final poem, "The Author of the Jesus Papers Speaks" (*BF,* p. 105), shows how the whole sequence is rooted in Sexton's struggle with God. She realizes her desire to "talk with God," at least in her dream. There she milks a cow, expecting "moon juice" or some magical mother-substance but receiving blood and shame instead, whereupon God appears to reprimand her for saying bad things about Christ's birth. Without succumbing to either the shame or the reprimand, she "went to the well and drew a baby/ out of the hollow water." Instead of punishing her, God (mercifully?) gives her a "gingerbread lady" to sacrifice as a surrogate for the beautiful women who must be eaten "When the cow gives blood/ and the Christ is born." God emerges as nothing more or less than a ruthless demi-god, and for the moment, the poet emerges triumphant.

"The Jesus Papers" is a wonderful act of *seeing through* God's power by means of her sympathy for Mary (and Jesus) and *seeing that* her own power lay in her ability to draw "babies" from the well of her own dreams. Although Sexton could identify with Jesus' need for his mother's nurturing and for his Father's com-

radeship, sustenance, and warm support, she could not live comfortably with his celibacy or with his eradication of female sexual
response in either Mary. Apparently Sexton's dissatisfaction with
these aspects of Christianity, coupled with her attraction to Mary
(Jesus' mother) and her growing faith in her own powers led her
into the realm of the archetypal mother often during the remaining years of her life. This was not a totally new direction for
Sexton. As Stephanie Demetrakopoulos has shown in her
definitive interpretations of Sexton's mother-daughter poems,
Sexton had long been preoccupied with the Demeter/Kore archetype.[14] However, her concern with it became predominantly
theological in the years 1970–1974.

Thus, in a poem I regard as crucial in Sexton's later canon, the
one Linda Gray Sexton chose to end 45 *Mercy Street*, Sexton
envisions the sea as "The Consecrating Mother," the one who
makes holiness or sacredness. The poet stands on the shore experiencing the rolling sea as if it were a woman in labor giving
birth to a handful of gods, and wishing she could participate in
the ritual. She wonders how the sea has borne all the ships of
trade, slavery and war, and then without warning she slips from
reverie into ecstasy:

> She should be entered skin to skin,
> and put on like one's first or last cloth,
> entered like kneeling your way into church,
> descending into that ascension,
> though she be slick as olive oil,
> as she climbs each wave like an embezzler of white.
>
> [45, pp. 113–114]

The poem offers an extraordinary combination of maternal images and explicitly sexual ones. As it continues, the moonlight on
the water suggests "flashing breasts made of milk-water,/ flashing
buttocks made of unkillable lust," and the poet wishes to participate in her "coming, coming,/ going" as the lover in The Song
of Solomon (p.114). The poem is not as polished as the ones
Sexton revised herself even in the galley stage of publication,[15]
but it is clear enough. In it, she desires sexual union with this
woman/ goddess/sea. Her image of worship is the antithesis of
the procedures she urged in "The Wall," in which her goal was
to escape the paradox of death in life. There she had prescribed:

take off your life like trousers,
. . .
then take off your flesh,
. . .
In other words
take off the wall
that separates you from God   [AR, p. 47]

By contrast, "The Consecrating Mother" would allow herself to
be entered "skin to skin."

III.   PART WAY THROUGH   Yet I'd risk my life
       THE PRIMAL CRACK   on that dilly dally buttercup
                                 called dreams, She of the origin,
                                 she of the primal crack, she of
                                             the boiling
                                 beginning, she of the riddle, she
                                         keeps me here,
                                 toiling and toiling.
                                             —WDY, p. 63

"The Consecrating Mother" belongs to a substantial group of
dreams, visions, and prayers concerning a female deity in three of
Sexton's last books: *The Death Notebooks, 45 Mercy Street*, and
Words for Dr.Y. Whereas her images of God in these books are
"impudent," her images of the female deity are ecstatic, even
when they are dark as in the epigraph above. Yet Sexton's relationship to the Goddess, whom she may have seen as multiple
figures, is no less complex than her vision of the Father God.
Perhaps by tracing the pattern of goddess images, we can gain
additional insight into the nature of Sexton's "radical discontent/
with the awful order of things" (*WDY*, p. 64).

As Stephanie Demetrakopoulos says, Sexton seems to have
reached a peak of self-affirmation in "O Ye Tongues" at the end
of *The Death Notebooks* (pp. 75–100), presumably written in
1972. The multi-partite poem, which begins as a revision of the
Biblical songs to the Father God, ends as a heroic act of speaking
in tongues which propels the poet "into the altitude of words"
(p. 98). Sexton's belief in her own power to create an inhabitable
world had never been greater, and rightly so, for in the "Eighth
Psalm" (pp. 93–95) she wrote an alternative to the Hebrew myth
of creation. In it, the source of life is the woman who "has come
through the voyage fit," carrying the "bagful of oranges" she

swallowed (p. 93). Her goddess-nature emerges as the poem continues. Forbidden, dangerous, lost, she is "a magnitude" ("each of us"). Sexton envisions her, Persephone-like, in a dark room under the earth where she hoards and tidies the things of the earth and in turn is nourished by darkness. Suddenly, her period of confinement ends and she becomes the creator of a "new dawn" in the world.

> For the baby crowns and there is a people-dawn in the world.
>
> For the baby lies in its water and blood and there is a people-cry in the world.
>
> For the baby suckles and there is a people made of milk for her to use. There are milk trees to hiss her on. There are milk beds in which to lie and dream of a warm room. There are milk fingers to fold and unfold. There are milk bottoms that are wet and caressed and put into their cotton.
>
> For there are many worlds of milk to walk through under the moon. [p. 94]

Sexton returns abruptly to a human scale, to a mother who jiggles her own baby on her knee, nurtures it without reservation and prepares to take the baby's alter-ego (Christopher, Christ?) with her when she dies. The Goddess, surely Demeter/Persephone, survives arduous human trials to give birth, nurture, and die, ordering the earth's treasures while she waits for her moment of power, removing sources of division in her death and, presumably, passing on her power to a baby girl. It is a vision that makes possible Sexton's positive relationships with her daughter, her art of words and death in the "Tenth Psalm."

In another poem called "Yellow," dated September 23, 1972, Sexton places herself in the Demetrian position she had envisioned, taking responsibility for the revitalization of the planet "when they turn the sun/ on again":

> I'll
> feed myself spoonfuls of heat and
> everyone will be home playing with
> their wings and the planet will
> shudder with all those smiles and
> there will be no poison anywhere, no plague
> in the sky and there will be a mother-broth
> for all of the people and we will

never die, not one of us, we'll go on
won't we?   [*WDY*, p. 45]

After the manic quality of her promises, the last line can only be described as wistful. The poem embodies Sexton's desire to be the all-nurturing goddess capable of preventing death, as even Demeter could not.

More often she casts herself as a worshiper. In "The Fury of Guitars and Sopranos" (*DN*, pp. 31–32), the poet recalls the mysterious, stirring song of a woman at whose breasts she drew wine, and at the mound of whose legs she drew figs. This figure is related to a recurrent dream-mother who floods her room with moonlight and olives. Surely this is an incarnation of Demeter in her most positive form; the votive ecstasy the poet feels in her presence is both "a kind of dying" and "a kind of birth" (p. 31). In the next poem, "The Fury of Earth," she assumes the voice of a prophetess speaking to a priest of the old religion: "The day of fire is coming";

You will have to polish up the stars
with Bab-O and find a new God
as the earth empties out
into the gnarled hands of the old redeemer.   [*DN*, p. 33]

Suspended between two world orders, she feels defiant of the old, and confident of the new. In "The Fury of Jewels and Coal" she is a priestess, recounting first how the miner has gone down into the pit and brought forth the spirit of Jesus; then she addresses the earth (moss, glass, and peat) directly in prayer:

dark mother,
brood mother, let the sea birds
bring you into our lives
as from a distant island,
heavy as death.   [*DN*, p. 34]

It is a call for the presence of the mother in place of the spirit of Jesus—for a maternal presence "heavy" enough to counter death.

The image of the bird bringing forth the mother is related to two more poems from 1972. In "Rats Live on No Evil Star," Sexton rewrites the myth of Genesis, having Eve come out of Adam's rib "like an angry bird":

> She came forth like a bird that got loose
> suddenly from its cage.
> Out of the cage came Eve,
> escaping, escaping.
> She was clothed in her skin like the sun
> and her ankles were not for sale.   [*DN*, p.18]

Reminiscent of the "woman clothed in the sun" from Revelations, Eve is the harbinger of a new order. She gives birth to a rat, itself a transitional figure (see note 11), and when it dies, she places it on "STAR," Sexton's alternative to heaven and hell, where even the "cursed" can be happy. In "The Death King" Sexton imagines herself released from death, dancing in her "fire clothes," and engaging in a bird-like flight,

> wounding God with his blue face,
> his tyranny, his absolute kingdom,
> with my aphrodisiac.   [*WDY*, p. 47]

The sexual dimensions of Eve's fiery escape from Adam's cage and Anne's "crematory flight" in the face of God are crucial to our understanding of Sexton's vision of the Goddess. In fact all her poems concerning female deity are imbued with sexual as well as religious energy. It may be that the Goddess Sexton dreamed of, prayed to and sought to emulate was the Aphrodite recently uncovered by Paul Friedrich—a figure whose twin powers are sexual and procreative. Or perhaps it was a predecessor of both Aphrodite and Demeter, as Friedrich's analysis suggests, who combined the double powers of generous sexuality and maternity so completely that she posed a threat to evolving civilization.[16]

Indeed, Sexton did make one attempt to embrace a Goddess like Sappho's Aphrodite[17] in a maternal form. In "To Like, To Love," again from 1972, the poet momentarily accepts a big-hearted "Cape Town lady" as Aphrodite even though she does not correspond to her dreams of the Goddess as "Nordic and six foot tall" or "masked and blood-mouthed" (*WDY*, p. 38). She even goes so far as to ask the Goddess to inspect her heart "and name its pictures," joining the circle of children around a campfire, sitting "like fruit waiting to be picked" (p. 38). When the Goddess herself becomes sick, however, the worshipers leave. They suddenly become aware that she is "no one" (p. 39);

in other words, they cannot identify her well enough to count on her. Even though they feel love for her, they become ineffectual, unable to nurse her back to health. This inability to *believe* in Aphrodite seems tragic in view of the fact that Sexton herself was the recipient of so much affection from her women friends. In the penultimate poem of *45 Mercy Street*, the one preceding "The Consecrating Mother," the poet sees herself as a house that has been swept back on to the beach by a sea "at war with itself" (p. 111) only to be rebuilt by "Barbara" with a generous adult love that carries no price tag.

Nevertheless, Sexton's impotence to believe prevailed. Perhaps it is expressed most poignantly in "The Consecrating Mother" because that poem renders her love for the nurturing and sexual deity most explicitly (see above, p. 34). The poet hears the sea reassure her that it has "a handful" of gods, and she hears the drowned voices call *"Deo Deo,"* but she is unable to accept the ocean's offer:

> I wanted to share this
> but I stood alone like a pink scarecrow.
> The ocean steamed in and out,
> the ocean gasped upon the shore
> but I could not define her.
> I could not name her mood, her locked-up faces.   [45, p. 113]

Sexton may not have known that "Deo" was an affectionate nickname for Demeter;[18] or if she did know, she may not have been able to reconcile that name with the nudity and lust she saw in the "flashing breasts" and "flashing buttocks" (45, p. 114) of the being she loved.

At any rate, the most compelling reason Sexton gives us for her discontent with the Goddess is her inability to name her in such a way as to reconcile her life-giving and death-accepting aspects, her maternal comfort and her sexual attractiveness, and her different faces or voices as she appeared variously in earth and sea, in real women or in dream women. As far as I know, Sexton tried only two names: Aphrodite, in the one poem I have presented, and Mary. "Mary" had more credibility because of Sexton's Christian background, but the name presented problems even when she used it unconventionally, as in "February 4th," written in 1971:

There I was dragging the ocean, that knock-out,
. . .
in and out. From my room I controlled the woman-of-war,
that Mary who came in and in opening and closing the door.
. . . .
All from the room I pray to when I am dreaming and devout.
[*WDY*, p. 66]

Here Sexton is reporting a dream, which has occurred twice, with the hope of advancing it, that is, using it to achieve control over the ocean, the unconscious, the source of the dreams that kept her "toiling and toiling" (*WDY*, p. 63). But nothing in the name "Mary" contains such force; nor does it offer leverage over other gods. As we saw in "The Jesus Papers," both the Virgin and Mary Magdalene were victims in Sexton's iconography.

Despite the inadequacy of the name, Sexton continued to pray to Mary in her conventional role as Intercessor:

Mary, Mary virgin forever,
whore forever,
give me your name,
give me your mirror.
Boils fester in my soul,
so give me your name so I may kiss them,
and they will fly off,
nameless
but named. [45, p. 93]

Unfortunately, Sexton could not use the name without being trapped again in the Christian story where virgin and whore are irreconcilable opposites, and where the best the mother can do is to cleanse the child of sin as established by some inscrutable other. As earlier poems and earlier lines of this poem reveal, Sexton could not invoke Mary without invoking the presence of her own mother, whose name was Mary—hardly a representative for her of either Demeter's or Aphrodite's bounty and certainly not a source of the wisdom she needed to salve her soul. As she says in another poem, "Mother,/ you and God/ float with the same belly/ up" (*DN*, p. 53). Both stink like dead fish in their insistence that she has not fulfilled their unknowable requirements; both belong to the religious perspective Sexton wanted to escape.

The problem of naming the force that seemed more and more

in control of her life was an acute one for Sexton. In "Demon"
she refuses to cover either her own mouth or the mouth of her
demon "even if it be God I call forth" (45, p. 107). It has become
a daimon, a spirit within her that she cannot renounce; but its
anonymity makes her an "anonymous woman/ at that anonymous altar" (p. 108)—painfully so, as we hear in this passage:

> My demon,
> too often undressed,
> too often a crucifix I bring forth,
> too often a dead daisy I give water to
> too often the child I give birth to
> and then abort, nameless, nameless . . .
> earthless. [45, p. 106]

To give birth and then abort is a strange and unnatural process,
but the image is appropriate to her feeling. It is akin to her growing sense that she herself is "no one" (AR, p. 28), even as she
becomes more intensely aware of the weight inside her.

Two horror stories reveal that the namelessness of her gods
continued to haunt her through 1974, the year of her death. "The
Ghost" (WDY, pp. 81–87) is told from the point of view of
Anna Ladd Dingley (Anne's mother's aunt who was her "Nana"
in childhood; Letters, p. 5), who spends her afterlife haunting her
namesake. She makes Anne mad as a punishment for her modern
ways (mainly her expression of sexuality) and reduces her to the
state of having "no name" to give to the officials at the mental
hospital (p. 86). The second story, "The Bat or To Remember,
To Remember" (WDY, pp. 93–101), is told by a bat who remembers taking part in the crucifixion of a "Miss No-Name" in
a previous life (pp. 98–100). Both stories seem to me to be efforts to conceive of a metaphysical framework in which Sexton's
anonymity made (macabre) sense.

"The Ghost" also contains a desperate attempt to assign responsibility for the mysterious voices Sexton had heard in the
leaves to some force outside herself that could be explained by a
familiar worldview. Apparently, she had reached a point where
belief in ghosts was more acceptable than belief in a pantheon of
unnamed gods—especially if they were goddesses. Here Sexton's
"green girls" (WDY, p. 29) become one of Nana's punishments
for her life of indulgence, imperfection, and sin. As the ghostly
narrator says:

Later, I tried lingering fevers that were quite undiagnosable and then when the world became summer and the green leaves whispered, I sat upon leaf by leaf and called out with a voice of my youth and cried, "Come to us, come to us" until she finally pulled down each shade of the house to keep the leaves out of it—as best she could. [*WDY*, p. 84]

As early as 1970 Sexton had written of her green girls as a sisterhood whose singing excited her to a "canker-suicide high" (*WDY*, p. 29). Always mysterious to her, the voices in the leaves were nevertheless comforting, seeming to promise a continuity of human and natural life. Although they encouraged her to "lie down whole in that green god's belly" (*WDY*, p. 29), their daily work was both death and life.

In "Leaves That Talk" (*45*, pp. 94–96), internally dated 1974, Sexton still wonders aloud who they are, thinking that they may be her whole past, "the generation of women, down the line" (p. 95). Yet she awakens with a scream from a dream about their disappearance to find that they have left her, unnaturally in midsummer, requiring her to "people" their cages. This poem should be read in the context of three others in *45 Mercy Street* that show how deeply disturbed "the order of things" seemed to Sexton in this period. Early in the volume, she recounts a waking dream wherein dolls fall from the sky and the poet, wondering who will catch them, catches ten of them herself, assuming the roles of the absent mother and father. She cannot save them all, whatever they are, and her questions about their nature imply ominously that they are the unnurtured aspects of human beings, "born but never fed" (*45*, p. 11). The image is like the ones about her demon, and it indicates the pervasiveness of her despair. In "The Love Plant" she experiences the pressure within her as a plant and wonders if she is "becoming part of the green world" (*45*, p. 76). She sees herself and anyone who might accept a rose that pops out of her mouth as a "pink doll" with "frantic green stuffing" (p. 76). In the course of the book, then, she has become one of the unattended dolls and her relationship with the earth is anything but comfortable. Then, in "The Sea Corpse," the ocean dies and she attends the funeral of "fifty tiny oceans" in their pink coffins. She reports:

I did not cry then.
I knew it was a natural order.

> The centuries of our blue mothers came
> and we spoke to them, adored their moods,
> immersed in their holy waters
> but one day they were dead.   [45, p. 110]

Having discovered the generation of women to which she belonged, Sexton finally had to accept its obliteration as "natural"! Her blasé attitude ("O.K. God,/ if it's the end of the world, it must be necessary," 45, p. 110) is further proof that she had put herself back into the hands of the Devouring Father, as Stephanie Demetrakopoulos argues.

Sexton had risked her life on the primal images in her dreams (*WDY*, p. 63). She had hoped to "cure the soul/ of its greed for love" (45, p. 105), and, in her ecstatic visions of female nurturing and sexuality, she had nearly succeeded in conceiving of a beneficent universe in which nursing and copulation, child and adult, love and power, life and death, soul and body were parts of a continuum—not irreconcilable opposites. She had "ousted" the doctor, that "seasick grounded man" (*BF*, p. 6), in favor of her own sea journey, escaped the tyranny of God the Father in the fertility of her dreams, and had begun to climb into her own "altitude of words" (*DN*, p. 98). But her desire to "ask and ask and ask/ until the kingdom/ however queer,/ will come" (*DN*, p. 74) was finally defeated by the anonymity of her goddess images. In the absence of other compelling names for them, she grasped at "Mary," thereby confusing them with the Christian motherintercessor and personalizing them by attributing their power to her dead mother and Nana. In so doing, she trapped herself again in her childhood feelings of sinfulness. Finally, as a "cracked orphan" (45, p.105), neither Father God nor Mother Goddess having sufficed, Sexton chose to end her own arduous voyage in death.

IV.   SEXTON'S AGON IN AN ARCHETYPAL FEMINIST PERSPECTIVE

At moments of affirmation such as those in "O Ye Tongues" (*DN*, pp.93–95, 98–100) or "The Consecrating Mother" (45, pp. 113–114), it is difficult to accept the fact that Sexton's visions failed to save her life. Ironically, two contexts that may help us to understand her predicament more fully were taking shape in

January 1973 when she wrote *The Awful Rowing toward God*. James Hillman was revising his Terry Lectures, wherein he had sketched the contours of a theology based upon the encounter with archetypal images of the human psyche; his book, *Re-Visioning Psychology*, provides an alternative theory of human questing that allows us to see the necessity of Sexton's journey. In the same year, Mary Daly argued in *Beyond God the Father* that the process of unfolding a God that was consonant with female being would require a painful exile to the "boundary of all that has been considered central."[19] Without these contexts, it is all too easy to discount Sexton's achievements in her last books by questioning their aesthetic value and by diverting attention from the poems to her suicide.

In interpreting Sexton's work, I find Hillman's perspective illuminating. If the purpose of life is to "make psyche matter"[20] in order to gain access to the soul, Sexton lived out that purpose "to the hilt" (*Letters*, p. 424). Hillman removes the stigma from both "craziness" and suicide; either may be required in a genuine encounter with the archetypal figures that lie at the roots of the soul. "Falling apart" breaks the soul free from its identification with the ego, and allows encounter with the deeper images. Other modes of soul-making are love, intellectual discipline, and death.[21] Apparently all these modes were necessary in Sexton's case; certainly she tried them all, substituting her imaginative discipline for the strictly intellectual kind.

Hillman also suggests a useful analytical procedure called "psychologizing" or "seeing through" one's images to locate the *idea* of psyche or soul that governs them. He points out, for example, that the "soul" has been variously defined as the life-principle, as "love" in Christian theology, and as a *tabula rasa*.[22] Unless we can see which idea frames our consciousness, we run the risk of being locked into one point of view, unaware that it is a point of view.

In this light, Sexton's predicament was that her soul-making involved antithetical ideas of the soul. In the Demeter/Kore myth, the soul is a life-principle whose body is developed anew in each fruitful season of life; in the myth of the crucifixion, the soul is attained in the sacrifice of the body and the identification with the Father. *The Awful Rowing toward God* reveals that Sexton chose the second pattern uneasily. But in the book's final

poem, she embraces the confidence man she had decribed as loaf-
ing around heaven desiring a body to house his soul (*AR*, p. 24),
because he outwits her in their decisive poker game (*AR*, pp.
85–86).

If Paul Friedrich is right that Aphrodite is a liminal Goddess[23]
who mediates between mortal and immortal life by means of her
sexuality and her nudity, we can imagine how Sexton's vision of
becoming the Goddess's lover in "The Consecrating Mother"
may have been a glimpse of a way to mediate her conflicting
ideas of soul. She had bravely acknowledged in "Demon" that
her quest might lead her to homeoerotic expression (*45*, p. 107).
If, again, Friedrich is right that Demeter and Aphrodite were
separated from each other in pre-history because together they
represented too great a concentration of power, and because the
incestuous possibilities that arise in the mingling of maternity and
sexuality were taboo,[24] then it is not surprising that Sexton re-
treated from this vision. No language has been invented to separate the kinds of love a woman may feel for her children, her
lovers, her mother, and her deity; until it is invented, the problem of maintaining life-supporting boundaries among these various figures will remain.[25]

In any case, Sexton's choice of God may have had less to do
with the merit of the Christian principle of soul than with her
inability to "translate the language" (*DN*, p. 73) of the deities she
discovered in her dreams.[26] She succumbed to the power of a
God whose requirement that the body be sacrificed was clear,
however unacceptable.

With 20/20 hindsight, we can speculate that in the 1970s Sexton
might have found in the explosion of writing about alternative
gods the clues that she needed to "unlock" the faces (*45*, p. 114)
she saw in her dreams. Perhaps not. Sexton was not a scholar. As
she cut herself off from many of her closest friends in the last two
years of her life and spent virtually all her time writing (*Letters*,
p. 390), her poems carried the entire burden of her soul-making.
As she said in a poem about pain as a medicine to cure the soul,

> One learns not to blab about all this
> except to yourself or the typewriter keys
> who tell no one until they get brave
> and crawl off onto the printed page.   [*45*, p. 104]

Mary Daly's warning that it is "*naïve* to think that healing can take place in isolation"[27] seems apposite in Sexton's case. If, indeed, the process of attaining wholeness involves for females an "exorcism of the internalized patriarchal presence, which carries with it feelings of guilt, inferiority, and self-hatred,"[28] then it would not be possible to accomplish this alone. Perhaps even the ancient herstories of the figures Sexton encountered would not have been enough to balance the weight of the internalized God of Sexton's childhood. As Daly says, only when women create a "counterworld to the prevailing sense of reality"[29] will we believe in ourselves.

Sexton's poems reveal, in a way that her *Letters* do not, that she had lived "on the boundary" of her culture for several years (at least from 1970 to 1974). With all her images of God, surely she was on the verge of seeing that the idea of god could not be contained by one name. Surely in *The Book of Folly* and *The Death Notebooks* she was on the verge of believing that her own power to draw images out of the well of her own unconscious was her "saving" grace. Mary Daly's notion of God as a "form-destroying, form-creating, transforming power that makes all things new"[30] is not so different from the complex of images Sexton gives us in her dreams, prayers, and songs concerning the female deity. But the possibility of reconceptualizing God as a verb, as Daly does, or of "seeing through" the nominalization of God, as Hillman suggests, did not exist for Sexton.

As a visionary poet who lived on the psychological and religious boundary between the desire for forgiveness for the "sins" of the flesh and the desire for sensual (if not sexual) nurturing love from her god(s), Sexton seems to me to be a prophetic figure. She shows us the psychological invalidity of the Christian idea of soul-separated-from-body for women who are finding a new comfort in their bodies (recall Sexton's words to her daughter, "there is nothing in your body that lies," *Live or Die*, p. 64). She also shows us the difficulty and enormity of the task ahead: the creation of a "counterworld" in which women can believe in the images generated by or appearing through their dreams.

I think we must be careful not to glamorize Sexton's struggle, and not to inflate the aesthetic value of her poems because of the difficulty of her quest. Yet I insist that many of her late poems are great. I mourn her death. And I cannot help but wish that her nameless deities had triumphed. If read in the context of archetypal psychology and feminist theology, Sexton's work is an urgent call to continue the process of soul-making until all possible deities are named. Beyond that, it is a call for a "new" myth of love in which those names may be effective.

CHAPTER 2

Käthe Kollwitz:
The Power of the Mother

(with Dominique Rozenberg)

In the course of her long career as a visual artist, Käthe Kollwitz chose most often to portray the human body in its female form, emphasizing the female's maternal aspects, but also treating her militant and inspirational potentials. In her works after 1921, she often combines these elements to render an archetypal mother whose caring transcends the realm of personal relationships, and whose insistence on the primacy of life and of relatedness defies the legitimacy of a social order based upon the heroic feats of individuals or nations. This chapter seeks to clarify the essential elements of the figure of the mother as she emerges in Kollwitz's later works in order to explore its potential psychological significance for other women. Recently, scholars in various fields have suggested that the task of differentiating the self from the mother is substantially different for women than it is for men, and that its successful completion is a crucial step in the development of the creative adult woman.[1] Thus, Kollwitz's artistic achievement is important partly because her struggle with the mother in herself allowed her, particularly in her later work, to chart a territory that lies beyond current maps of the feminine.[2]

In order to make this study broadly accessible, the argument rests on works that may be seen in the few books on Kollwitz that are readily available: Renate Hinz, ed., *Käthe Kollwitz: Graphics, Posters, Drawings*; Martha Kearns, *Käthe Kollwitz: Woman and Artist*; Mina C. and H. Arthur Klein, *Käthe Kollwitz: Life in Art*; and Carl Zigrosser, *Prints and Drawings of Käthe Kollwitz*.

I. THE DEVELOPMENT OF A MATRIARCH

Images of the human body in its female form dominate
Kollwitz's work from her girlhood drawings of her sister Lise in
1878 to her last work, a self-portrait in charcoal in 1943.[3] Males
do appear in her work, as fathers, as workers, as rebels, as
corpses, and occasionally as individual figures, but they do not
capture her imagination. Outside of her self-portraits, with few
exceptions,[4] Kollwitz presents the woman in one of three attitudes: as protecting another life with her arms; embracing or
reaching out toward another being; or fortifying herself by holding her hands against her head or over her eyes. Since Kollwitz
always sought to distill the essential qualities of a human form in
her work,[5] these recurring choices deserve interpretation.

The major exceptions to this generalization occur early in
Kollwitz's work in her studies of individual working women and
in her portrayal of women as fighters and revolutionaries. In the
most striking of these, Outbreak (Losbruch, 1903),[6] a woman
known as "Black Anna" appears in the foreground as the
catalyst, spurring the angry mob to action. In another, Uprising
(Aufruhr, 1899),[7] a transparent female figure flies above the peas-
ants who march from the burning castle brandishing scythes.
Stripped of clothing and released from the force of gravity, she is
an inspirational figure who both symbolizes and justifies the revolt. In The Carmagnole (Die Carmagnole, 1901),[8] peasant women
are shown dancing around a guillotine in a celebration of revolution. These works present an Amazon-like potential in women,
in addition to the "intelligence, courage, dignity, and compassion" Kollwitz herself characteristically portrayed.[9] But finally,
Kollwitz herself was not a revolutionary,[10] and it is not surprising that she explored a more maternal type of woman in the bulk
of her work. Nonetheless, this revolutionary potential does
gradually become a part of Kollwitz's maternal figures. In order
to see how this happens, let us examine her development of the
protecting, embracing, and fortifying attitudes in detail. In each
case, there is a progression from a personal concern to a transpersonal concern.

Let us look first just at her images of maternal protectiveness.
In her etching Woman with Dead Child (Frau mit totem Kind,
1903),[11] the seated mother seems to bury her head on the breast

of the child whose head is tipped back unnaturally. There is strength in the mother's muscular legs (the toes of one foot press against the other leg to brace her and express her tension), in her shoulder, and in her hand which is holding on to the child's limp shoulder. But the picture conveys her personal grief and its hopelessness, despite her strength. In *Woman with Child in Lap (Frau mit Kind im Schoss*, 1916),[12] the seated woman is using her lower body to cradle the sleeping child while her upper body protects and shields the child. The situation differs from the earlier one in that the child is alive; the mother's face expresses admiration and affection as she gazes at the child. The most striking difference, however, is in the way the woman's arms and hands are used not only to provide stability for her own pose, but also to surround and shelter the child. The arms become the most compelling element in the piece, and they make it convey the essence of maternal protectiveness (in the personal sphere) rather than simply maternal affection. In her sculpture *Mother with Twins (Mutter mit Zwillingen)* or *Mother Group (Muttergruppe*, 1937),[13] two children are huddled together as in a womb and the seated mother is protecting them with her whole body. Her legs are spread apart to form a shield for the baby on our left and a cushion for the toddler on our right. Her huge arms encircle them; her right hand holds the older child's arm in place while the fingers of her left hand rest lightly but purposefully on the ground. Her head is bent as if in contemplation of something within herself or beyond the present situation. The sculpture is only 30 inches high, but it has a massive appearance. The three figures form a block, a monument to the security offered by such a relationship. The sculpture no longer belongs to the personal realm where one individual mother protects a child. It belongs to an impersonal realm where such solidarity, such assertion of the value of nurturing, commands the respect of all who view it.

A similiar kind of shift takes place in her pictures of a single standing mother with a child or children confronting an aspect of death. In *Killed In Action (Gefallen*, 1921),[14] the woman reacts to the death of a loved one by covering her face with her hands and forearms, using her raised elbows to ward off any more blows from the world and to protect her grief. The two older children reach out and up to her for reassurance but with concern for her. The youngest child presses her face against her mother's abdomen and pulls on her dress, demanding solace. The mother must bear not only the grief of personal loss but also the responsibility of confronting the children. In *Death Seizes a Woman (Tod packt eine Frau,* 1934),[15] from Kollwitz's final series about death, the woman is caught by surprise by the personification of her own death. Even so, she uses her left shoulder and upper arm to protect her child from this force, and uses her right arm to support the child's head and upper back as she grasps him and puts her huge protecting hand over his face to shield him. Even as she stares at death knowing it is her own, her body protects the child. In Kollwitz's final lithograph, *Seed Corn Must Not Be Ground (Saatfrüchte sollen nicht vermahlen werden,*1942),[16] the woman confronts the impersonal threat to children of death by war. She is old and the children are not necessarily her own. Her gaze is fixed on the unseen enemy in a calm defiant way, while her arms and hands extend above and around the children as a symbolic enclosure which she will enforce, if necessary, even against the will of the child on the right who turns away from safety to satisfy his curiosity. Her clothing acts as a cape or even a cave, forming another shield for the children. The children are seeds that must not be destroyed before they have had time to bloom, regardless of the cause, regardless of their own child-like desires.

Kollwitz's development of the gestures of embrace is similiar. Compare her treatment of the woman in *After the Battle (Schlachtfeld,* 1907),[17] in which the woman searching among dead bodies after the battle with her flashlight finds and reaches down to touch her loved one, with *Woman Welcoming Death (Frau vertraut sich dem Tode an,* 1934),[18] in which she extends her hand to death in a firm handshake and lets her protective arm and hand begin to drop away from the children as she focuses her attention on her fate. This is not to say that Kollwitz completely transcends the personal realm of relationships with individuals in her later life. But even in the works where she used herself as model and where the impetus for the work was most personal, as in *Farewell (Abscheid,* 1940)[19] in which Käthe holds her husband's shoulders as he becomes passive and begins to slip away from her, she presents in her later work a "larger" image of the female human being as a force in a world of forces. The woman is a force to be reckoned and valued.

Seed Corn Must Not Be Ground (Saatfrüchte sollen nicht vermahlen werden), Käthe Kollwitz, 1942, lithograph, 14-½'' × 15-½''. Private collection.
Courtesy of Galerie St. Etienne, New York.

We see this progression toward the transpersonal again in comparing *Woman Thinking* (*Nachdenkende Frau*, 1920),[20] in which the woman is shown with closed eyes, drawn cheeks, and turned-down mouth, bracing her creased forehead against her broad open hand, with *Lament* (*Klage*, 1940),[21] the bronze relief Kollwitz did as a memorial for Ernst Barlach. In the lithograph, the hand is used almost defensively, to protect her thoughts from our gaze, and yet we are drawn into her anguish; we are asked to value her struggle. In *Lament*, we are asked to value something more abstract: the human capacity for enduring sorrow. One hand rests against the woman's cheek, her fingers touching the forehead as if to smooth it and ease the tension. The other hand, with its thumb pressing against the other cheek, is used to brace the chin and wrist, partly to cover and calm the lips as the mind's sorrow is absorbed into and steadied by the body.

Finally, let us look at the way Kollwitz combines these characteristic gestures of protection, embrace, and fortification in her complex rendering of mothers together. In her first treatment of them in *Mothers* (*Mütter*, 1919),[22] the women stand side by side, their bodies touching but not sustaining each other. The woman on our left has both hands cupped over her face to block any new information. The woman next to her holds a sleeping baby in one arm and holds her other arm over the shoulder and chest of another child as she gazes into the space before her, with all her energy consumed in the act of holding her children. The woman in the foreground clasps two older children with her arms and shoulders, her large hands resting limply over their arms and her eyes closed in an attitude of despair. The woman on the right looks out toward us, as does her toddler, as if to say, "How could you?" As always in Kollwitz's work,[23] the women are dignified, the children beautifully formed and innocent. We are asked to value their mothers' feelings and their lives. In the woodcut *The Mothers* (*Die Mütter*, 1922–23)[24] the women's bodies are joined to form a protected, even cavelike, space for the children, two of whom are peeking out from between their mothers. The pregnant woman on the left of the print faces left with her palms open to ward off the danger; her slightly downcast head suggests a defensive posture. The next woman covers her baby's head entirely with her huge hand as she looks past it with apprehension. The two terrified women in the center are locked in a protective embrace; the one on the right has her right hand on the other's baby and her left arm on the woman's shoulder, forming a barricade for the entire group. The pregnant woman on the far right expresses a stolid determination not to give in. The nature of the threat is not specified beyond the title of the whole series, *War*, but we can infer its human source from the direction of the women's eyes.

Kollwitz's image of the mothers in the woodcut differs from that of the earlier lithograph because of the way the women use their bodies together—to protect each other, to comfort and shield all the children, and to communicate their intent to resist being obliterated despite their terror. Whereas the lithograph asks us to value the women because of the children through our capacity for empathy, the woodcut asks us to accept the mothers' assertion of value.

In the *Tower of Mothers* (*Turm der Mütter*, 1937–8),[25] Kollwitz transforms the maternal image once again, in accord with the other transformations we have described, moving out of the personal realm altogether. The compact group is reduced to four adults and three visible children. Although the woman in the foreground is the most powerful, each of the women uses her entire body as an active force against the oncoming threat. The central woman has her legs spread and her knees bent in an extremely stable yet agile stance; she leans forward with her torso, thrusts her arms out from the shoulders and bends the forearms back to cover a child on our left and to encircle the back of the women on our right; her chin juts forward while her determined gaze is leveled directly at us. Although the sculpture is only 11 inches square and 10½ inches high, it transmits a huge image. (It could be translated into a sculpture 10 feet high without distortion of its meaning.) By contrast with the assertive but immobile mothers of the woodcut, the central mother in the sculpture gives the impression of being mobile, capable of moving outward to complete her act of protection. She is a matriarch— maternal in her concern for children, yet impersonal in her stance toward the world.

Mina and Arthur Klein suggest that Kollwitz's own concern for the welfare of children was the primary motive for her work.[26] Our study suggests that her portrayal of that concern shifted in the course of her work. In the *Tower of Mothers*, although the children are the motivating force behind their mothers' actions, they are no longer the focal point of their mothers' attention. In her denunciation of oppression, Kollwitz always chose to focus on the oppressed (the starving, the poverty-stricken, the bereaved), attempting to awaken our concern by showing their situation from the inside, by insisting on the strength and intelligence of her subjects no matter how downtrodden they are. But in her early work the children and the mothers are equally powerless; in fact, the mothers are particularly vulnerable because they care so much about their own

Tower of Mothers (Turm der Mütter), Käthe Kollwitz,
1937-1938, bronze, 11" sq. × 10-½" h.
Collection of Hans Kollwitz.
Courtesy of Max Jacoby.

children. Gradually, the mothers gain the strength first to protect their own children and then to assert their value publicly under siege. As that happens, the center of Kollwitz's work becomes an assertion of faith in the mother. The fact that Kollwitz also shows more scenes of maternal happiness in her later work[27] indicates that the emergence of a matriarch need not destroy the personal relationship between mother and child. From Kollwitz's point of view, the woman who becomes a force in the world to protect other lives does not become the "terrible mother" even when she holds individual children back against their desire. Instead she becomes a source of inspiration to others who can commit themselves to her primary value: cultivating the potential of human life instead of destroying it. Her attention is no longer fixed on the life of one child or a few children; it is fixed on the cultural value of children. The vision of the muse, the militance of the Amazon, and the caring of the mother are combined into one image. Let us call her a matriarch, leaving aside until my final chapter the question of her relationship to figures from our pre-history.

II. THE POTENTIAL PSYCHOLOGICAL SIGNIFICANCE OF KOLLWITZ'S TRANSFORMATION FOR MODERN WOMEN

Before we assess the significance of this transformation for ourselves, it may be useful to recount some accompanying dates and facts from Kollwitz's life. Kollwitz began to develop the theme of maternal grief and despair as early as 1896, at the time of the birth of her second son, Peter. She then became obsessed with the idea of a revolutionary female leader, between 1899 and 1905. This preoccupation gave way to her concern for the tragedy of everyday life in Berlin's working class, and that sense of tragedy culminated in an expression of her own intense awareness of mortality in *Death and the Woman* (*Tod und Frau*, 1910).[28]

The First World War cut her career in half and nearly ended it altogether. It disrupted her work at a time when she was already experiencing debilitating effects from menopause and when she felt degraded by her secretarial duties for the New Secession, the group of artists who supported her art.[29] The death of her younger son on the Belgian front in 1914 was devastating; she created no new works until 1916. In this interim, in her struggle with the unacceptable fact of Peter's death, she articulated the resolve that was to inform the rest of her work:

> I do not want to go until I have faithfully made the most of my talent and cultivated the seed that was placed in me until the last small twig has grown. . . . Since I am to be the cultivator, I want to serve faithfully. Since recognizing that, I am almost serene and much firmer in spirit. It is not only that I am permitted to finish my work—I am obliged to finish it. This seems to me to be the meaning of all the gabble about culture. Culture arises only when the individual fulfills his cycle of obligations.[30]

But in spite of such resolve, she did not resume work at her former level of confidence and productivity until 1922 when she did the series of woodcuts, *War*, in which she gave her grief its visual form.[31] From 1916 to 1921, she did several of the transitional works discussed above: the charcoal drawing *Woman with Child on Lap* (1916), the lithograph *Mothers* (1919), the lithograph *Woman Thinking* (1920), and the lithograph *Killed in Action* (1921). In 1920 and 1921, she did several self-portraits that reveal her effort to cope with her grief by turning inward,[32] and in 1921 she did a woodcut called *Death with Woman in Lap* (*Tod mit Frau im Schoss*),[33] in which death is herself a gentle maternal protector. The woman has removed her shoes and collapsed on the shoulder of Mother Death. The image of death as a female recurs twice in Kollwitz's later set of lithographs, *Death* (1934–35): in *Death with Girl in Lap* (*Tod hält Mädchen im Shoss*)[34] and *Death upon the Highway* (*Tod auf der Landstrasse*);[35] but never with the attractiveness of this woodcut. Indeed, Kollwitz identified her state of mind as an experience of "nothingness" in her *Diary* in the spring of 1921.[36] In the summer of that year she said that her work had become independent of her external experiences: "The readiness forms in waves inside myself; I need only be on the alert for when the tide at last begins to rise again."[37] She seems to have experienced a psychological nadir and regeneration.

The internal tide of Kollwitz's creative life did rise in 1922 and 23, and it kept a steady rhythm for 20 years, until the combined effects of war and age were too severe and she left Berlin for refuge at the age of seventy-six in 1943. During the second half of her career, Kollwitz did all her major works in woodcut and sculpture, made her famous posters for socialist political organizations, completed her largest work (the memorial to Peter, in process for seventeen years), and returned to the theme of death in a final series of lithographs. In those years, she was not oblivious to external experiences, but she showed remarkable resistence to them. Had she not developed tremendous personal strength, she might have been destroyed by them. Her memorial for the assassinated communist Karl Liebknecht was denounced because she was not herself a communist. Her posters were used by Nazis for purposes counter to her beliefs. Her works were removed from German museums by Nazis and destroyed. She was removed from her full professorship at the Prussian Academy of Arts. Still, she continued to work. From Agnes Smedley's description of her in 1925, we can see the qualities in her person that led her to develop her maternal image in the thirties:

> Her gaze is direct and her voice startlingly strong, and she sees far beyond those who bring her superficial, external tributes or who try to use her for their own propaganda purposes. She is a silent person, but when she speaks it is with great directness, without trimmings to suit the prejudices of her hearers. Many people, before meeting her, expect to see a bitter woman. But they see, instead, a kind—very kind—woman to whom love—strong love, however—is the rule of life.[38]

Kollwitz's achievement is the result of her talent, her education, her political commitment and social philosophy, and her decisions about how to develop those resources in extraordinarily difficult circumstances. Her life was unique. But the psychological and spiritual crisis she experienced in the years between 1914 and 1921 bears a resemblance to crises experienced by many other women—particularly creative women. Her resolution of that crisis, her development of the matriarch, has ramifications that extend well beyond the circle of women who share her specific experience of grief. In those years, Kollwitz encountered the possibility of being overwhelmed by maternal feeling.

In the symbolic language of the quest myth, the hero must overcome the female dragon who threatens to swallow him. But in female versions of the quest, it seems that the female quester cannot kill this dragon without killing something essential within herself; neither can she submit to it. In fact the analogous negative maternal or unconscious forces are not so easily identified in imaginative works by women. Stephanie Demetrakopoulos suggests, from her study of fiction, poetry, and autobiographical writing, that such forces may appear to women as the sea itself (a suggestion that corresponds with Kollwitz's verbal imagery), and that they may be either fatally attractive or regenerative.[39] In Margaret Atwood's novel *Surfacing*, which strikes responsive chords in a large audience of contemporary women, the protagonist heals her divided self after a sensational diving expedition and separate encounters with images of her own dead parents, by finding the mother within herself who can conceive a child (literally and metaphorically).[40] Her survival is hailed by critics because it is unusual. Annis Pratt finds in her study of novels by women that re-entry into society is difficult for a female protagonist whose quest results in rebirth or transformation. "She is met upon her ascent . . . with a forceful backlash, an attempt to dwarf her personality and re-accommodate her to secondary status. It is for this reason that so many women's rebirth novels are, at best, open-ended, the hero's precise place in society being left to guesswork on the part of the reader."[41] Thus, Kollwitz's survival of her psychological nadir, her subsequent survival of the "backlash" against the strength of her work, and her vision of matriarchal women are extraordinary achievements, both in life and also in the context of imaginative worlds.

But let us also look at the relationship of her life and work to the lives of more ordinary women. Modern psychology has taught us that one of our first tasks of individuation is to separate ourselves first from our real parents and then from the incorporated parents within ourselves. This task seems to be more difficult for women than for men because the woman's "final role identification is with her mother and women, that is, with the person or people with whom she also has her earliest relationship of infantile dependence."[42] Part of the difficulty lies in the societal requirement that she transfer any sexual attraction she may feel for females to males in order to become heterosexual. It now appears that this transfer is not and cannot be complete:

> Most women are genitally heterosexual. At the same time, their lives always involve other sorts of equally deep and primary relationships, especially with their children, and, importantly, with other women. In these spheres also, even more than in the area of heterosexual relations, a girl imposes the sort of object-relations

she has internalized in her preoedipal and later relationship to her mother.[43]

Other difficulties occur in the process of gender identification that make it difficult for women to develop self-esteem. Often, "feminine gender identification means identification with a devalued, passive mother," while rejection of the mother or of the feminine becomes an unconscious rejection and devaluation of the self because of the continuing "boundary confusion" with the mother.[44] In addition, "Women's biosexual experience (menstruation, coitus, pregnancy, childbirth, lactation) all involve some challenge to the boundaries of her body ego ("me"/ "not me" in relation to her blood or milk, to a man who penetrates her, to a child once part of her body)."[45] If a woman's confidence in herself is not firm, she is vulnerable to conflict arising from a challenge to any of these boundaries.

With these accounts in mind of the difficulties encountered by women, let us return to Käthe Kollwitz. Perhaps part of the power of her work for many women lies in her portrayal of vulnerability in female subjects who are physically strong and mentally capable, so that one cannot discount them as somehow unfit for the tests of life. Her encounter with death in the form of a mother in her woodcut *Death with Woman in Lap* at the turning point in her own life and work seems doubly significant, portraying the possibility of succumbing both to the mother in herself and to death. Kollwitz's work in the period 1916–1922 is transitional in her development of the image of the mother. It also marks a change in her attitude toward death. In five of the lithographs in her last series, the woman responds to death with equanimity or reverence, and in *Death upon the Highway*, death becomes only a tired old woman who needs rest. Kollwitz's new attitudes toward the death of adult women in no way altered her horror of death for children, which is still evident in *Death Seizes a Woman* and *Death Swoops* (*Tod greift in Kinderschar*, 1934).[46] Perhaps she saw that her grief, her identification of herself with that part of herself that was a bereaved mother, constituted the most dangerous of all threats to her life, precisely because it was an ever-present threat from within. Neither rejecting the mother in death, nor succumbing to it, Kollwitz forged an acceptance of both death and the mother that nurtured and sustained her art for twenty years.

Death with a Woman (Tod mit Frau im Schoss), Käthe
Kollwitz, 1921, woodcut, 9-⅜" × 11-⅜".
Courtesy of National Gallery of Art, Rosenwald Collection.

The result of her struggle is a powerful cultural image of a
maternal figure with highly developed confidence in herself, who
has made an active choice to care for children. Her existence is
not governed by an unconscious allegiance to Eros, in either its
nurturing or its transformative aspects. Nor is it governed by a
conscious or unconscious rejection of the feminine, as is sometimes the case in images of the Amazon. Instead, Kollwitz offers
an image of a fully-conscious adult woman who exercises her
"agency" (her capability for self-protection, self-assertion, self-
expansion)[47] to move society toward a less repressive condition.

The image of the mother embodied in *Mother with Twins, Seed
Corn Must Not Be Ground*, and the *Tower of Mothers* is a

ground-breaking achievement in what may be a lengthy process of liberating maternal potential from its restricted and often debilitating personal sphere and thereby revaluing an important aspect of the human potential we call "feminine."

CHAPTER 3

Margaret Atwood: Remythologizing Circe

In her sequence of poems entitled "Circe/Mud Poems,"[1] Margaret Atwood engages in a complex act of remythologizing.[2] That is, she steps back into the mythic realm of Homer's *Odyssey* to recreate and revise the story of the year-long sojourn of Odysseus with Circe from Circe's point of view.[3] Simply by refocusing our attention within the story, Atwood reveals a more essential power in Circe than her infamous ability to seduce and deform men[4]—namely, her highly developed capacity to see, see into, and see beyond her relationships to the persons, things, and events called "reality." Because Atwood shows how Circe exercises her capacity for insight, we are able to penetrate the masks and armor of the "hero with a thousand faces,"[5] and understand with her how the myth of the quest has become a disease in whose clutches the hero is helpless (p. 64). By adopting Circe's perspective within the quest myth, Atwood is able to revalue Circe positively; at the same time, she exposes the limitations of a myth that still dominates Western civilization. Atwood's strategy of participating in mythic thinking, instead of making the usual distinction between myth and truth,[6] allows her to suggest a surprisingly radical revision of the myth itself. She points out that we do not yet know the ending of Circe's story after Odysseus leaves her island,[7] and that in our visions of a new ending lie the possibilities for an alternative myth, in which there is no need to journey. Atwood's work has implications for those of us who are exploring alternative images of women, and for others who believe that mythic structures offer essential knowledge that can be used to free as well as to enslave us.[8]

I. CIRCE'S PERSPECTIVE

In order to involve us in her mythmaking process, Atwood has us enter the island landscape of a forest blackened by fire as we would enter a dream, in a boat that glides over land "as if there is water" (p. 46).[9] She explains through Circe's voice that she has not given us a full description of the landscape because she is quite sure that we live there right now and can see for ourselves. Atwood has Circe speak directly to a person who is never named, leaving open the possibility that she is addressing us. Since her awareness of Bronze Age rituals (p. 51) and modern steam-engines (p. 47) transcends ordinary boundaries of time and culture, we begin to believe that she can also transcend other restrictions that operate on our thought. Atwood reinforces this expectation of mythic behavior in her surrealistic images of bodies coming apart and crashing to the ground (p. 47) or trays of food containing "an ear, a finger" (p. 64).

In order to retain the degree of power Homer has assigned to Circe while she relocates its source and meaning, Atwood includes many of the trappings of Greek mythology: Circe has a temple where moon snakes speak of the future (p. 51), and she wears a withered fist on a chain around her neck (p. 57). But Circe knows the meaning of such symbols better than Odysseus or Homer did. As for her supposed power to turn her lovers into swine, she denies that she is anything more than a silent accomplice in the metamorphoses: she explains, "they happened/ because I did not say anything" (p.48). Actually, the men came to her in accordance with their own drives. She "decided nothing" (p. 50). They became animals because they allowed their skin to harden into impenetrable, armor-like hide, and because they failed to speak (p. 48).

Homer was misguided on several other counts. Circe was not superhuman in the sense of being above feeling love, pain, fear, and anxiety; she did not willingly grant Odysseus' request to leave her.[10] Nor was she rendered powerless during his stay. In Atwood's version, the lover unbuckles the fist on Circe's chain (p. 57); instead of gaining control over her, he frees her (p. 58) from a dehumanizing pattern of action. He frees her, not to be like the totally receptive and unfeeling surrogate woman made out of mud, reported in a story by another traveller (p. 61), but

to penetrate his armor because her caring for him enables her to
see who he is, what he intends, and how it will affect her life.
The nineteenth poem shows clearly who is in command of reality. In it, Circe says (in prose),

> You think you are safe at last.
>
> . . . .
>
> I bring you things on trays, food mostly, an ear, a finger. You
> trust me so you are no longer cautious, you abandon yourself to
> your memoranda . . . ; in the clutch of your story, your disease,
> you are helpless.
>
> But it is not finished, that saga. The fresh monsters are already
> breeding in my head. I try to warn you, though I know you will
> not listen.
>
> So much for art. So much for prophecy.   [p. 64]

Circe's power is not sufficient to transform her lover's story
without his consent, but her insight that the story continues to
happen partly because she has not revealed how she felt about it,
and partly because "fresh monsters" are "breeding" in her head
to test his mortal courage with more misadventures, suggests
that she may also have some unused ability to alter Odysseus'
script.

In Atwood's sequence, Circe does attempt to change her relationship to the quest myth by proclaiming her disinterest in
Odysseus' heroic gesticulations (p. 47). Her attitude toward his
infamous arrival on her island is scornful (p. 50). The merits of
his courage, pride and perseverance dissolve as she questions:
"Don't you get tired of saying Onward?" (p. 51). With Circe's
revelation of her boredom with the masks of heroism and of her
disgust for the greedy, deceitful, arrogant, oppressive, vain men
who have predictable desires for fame and immortality, Atwood
dislodges one of the reasons that the myth of the hero survives:
female approval of heroic behavior.

As the poems proceed, it becomes clear that the hero's dissatisfaction with mere material abundance has a deleterious effect not
only on his lover, but also on the landscape, which is burned
over, worn down, and strewn with skeletons. Since Circe states
at the outset her intention to search (without journeying) for the
"ones who have escaped from these/ mythologies with barely
their lives," and since she gives ample proof of her ability to love

those who will unmask, clearly she is not the source of the misery on her island.

By the final poem, we are convinced not only that Circe's position outside the framework of the quest allows her to see more than those who remain inside it can, but also that her boundary position is a source of hope. Her capacity for breeding new disasters to appease the hero's desire for action is easily converted into a capacity for creating valid images. In the final poem (pp. 69, 70), she "sees" two islands—one on which things happen pretty much as she has just recounted, over and over again like a bad film running faster and more jerkily each time it goes through the projector. The second island, independent of the first, exists only in her imagination. On the second, "we" walk together in a November landscape and are astonished by the orange hue of the apples "still on the trees." We lick the "melted snow/ from each other's mouths" without sexual passion, and we are free to notice the track of a deer in the mud beside the not-yet-frozen stream. On this island, which Circe says "has never happened," our delight in the November landscape does not require any journey; the birds are birds, not omens from the dead whispering "Everything dies" (p. 62); the gentle, sensuous caress between two people is enough; and mud is mud, not a symbolic woman to be fucked by man.

Circe's story remains unfinished in Atwood's sequence. We still do not know her fate after Odysseus leaves her island. We do know that she is not the seductress we thought she was. As an enchantress, her talents lay in gathering the syllables from the earth into healing words. Even without her magic powers, she is capable of imagining an alternative to the story that has imprisoned her. She emerges from the poem as an independent woman (perhaps a poet) who is capable of turning her considerable talent for seeing through others' stories into a strategy for her own survival—and perhaps the survival of all who are wise enough to trust her. Atwood's revision of Circe's story strikes us as true because it corresponds to centuries of partly-conscious experience of silent complicity in a myth we did not choose. Atwood's work raises important questions: How many other stories remain similarly unfinished? Should we finish them now? Is it really possible to change a myth?

II. MYTH AND TRUTH (OR, WHY WOULD ONE WANT TO
REMYTHOLOGIZE CIRCE?)

Atwood does not provide us with an ideal goddess so much as
with a believable woman, "by turns comic, cynical, haughty,
vulnerable and sad," as Sherrill Grace has observed.[11] But for all
her realism, Atwood does not "*de*mythologize" Circe.[12] In the
context of modern theological debate, that term is reserved for
the process of stripping away the fanciful layers of image and
story in order to penetrate to the (preferably historical) truth.
Since, we have no reason, apart from the say-so of poets like
Homer and Hesiod, to believe that Circe ever exsisted (she was
never an object of widespread worship, for example), the most
likely approach of the demythologizer would be to ignore or
discredit her. As scholar or poet, then, the demythologizer might
turn to the records of history for information about the lives of
Greek women, but she would not bother to retell Homer's story.

   In fact, of course, Atwood is sufficiently aware of Homer's
conventions to give her poem exactly the same number of parts
as Homer's book. She counts on our knowing the appropriate
section (book X) so well that she can alter the story without repeating it first (as a daring jazz musician might begin a piece with
an improvisation without stating the tune on which it is based).
In other words, Atwood assumes that Circe is familiar enough to
seem "real" to us before we begin reading her poem. Whether
this reality has accrued from aesthetic persuasion (the effectiveness of Homer's text) or from psychological persuasion (our
familiarity with women who seem to correspond with Homer's
story) matters very little. Atwood does not want to disturb our
belief; she wants to restructure it.

   The extent of her investment can be measured by comparing
her poem to Katherine Anne Porter's brief and charming essay,
A Defense of Circe.[13] Porter not only accepts but repeats Homer's
story, presumably in order to earn the right to reinterpret it.
Enthralled by the bard's "sunny high comedy," she exclaims,
"this is all pure magic, this poem, the most enchanting thing ever
dreamed of in the human imagination, how have I dared to touch
it?"[14] Indeed, she does touch it lightly, retelling all sorts of details
that Atwood omits: about Circe's immortal lineage and sunny
disposition, her lovely stone hall in the forest glade, her hand-

maidens, her loom, her song, the role of Hermes in providing the herb (moly) to disarm her, her oath that she will not harm Odysseus, her restoration of Odysseus' men to forms more beautiful than the ones they had, her advice about how to visit Teiresias in Hades, and so on.

Porter does point out several minor flaws in Homer's logic. She cannot quite believe that the immortal Circe would feel threatened by Odysseus' sword. She finds unfounded the hero's claim that Circe promised to send him and his companions safely on their way. She knows that Circe's "divine amiability and fostering care" could not save Odysseus and his men from their ordained suffering. She also wonders why Circe did not steal the moly to destroy Odysseus' power, or why she did not break her oath and turn him into a fox! She resolves these problems by accepting the text as given ("this is Circe") and by offering her own non-traditional interpretation of Circe's character: whereas Odysseus and Hermes are foxy by nature, Circe can be trusted completely. Her purity extends to other realms as well; she is a "creatrix," an "aesthetic genius," whose "unique power as goddess was that she could reveal to men the truth about themselves by showing each man himself in his true shape according to his inmost nature. For this she was rightly dreaded and feared; her very name was a word of terror."[15] This assertion of Circe's superior understanding is Porter's "defense" of Circe against those who fasten on her reputation for turning human beings into monsters.

Porter does not accept the theological distinction between myth and truth. She expects us to find her interpretation of Homer's story truthful, and she believes that *The Odyssey* is true in a way that "still hovers glimmering at the farthest edge of consciousness, a nearly remembered dream of glory."[16] For her, the story is a myth only in the sense of being something that was once believed, or in the sense of being an enduring fiction that continues to touch a sensitive nerve. Its truth is limited. Porter's main reason for not altering the fiction is respect for her venerable colleague.

Not so in Atwood's case. Although she shares with Porter the interpretation that the men turned themselves to swine, Atwood knows that no successful "defense" of Circe is possible within the framework of Odysseus' story. I speculate that she also knows how difficult it is to rid the human consciousness of a stereotype that has such a long and venerable history. She *could* have created an historical prototype, from Greece or elsewhere, to counter the myth;[17] indeed, many critics agree that her most successful book of poems to date is *The Journals of Susanna Moodie*, where she shows an uncanny ability to work with historical materials. She chose instead to *re*mythologize the figure of Circe.

If the reader is to believe that women's essential power is not to seduce (or shall we say influence?) men but to see through them and free them from their stories, then the poet must demonstrate this power in the figure who carries the image of seduction. The image must be transformed from within. Atwood chooses the surest way to convince us that her vision of Circe is true by letting Circe tell her own story in an authentic language. She counts on our natural desire to believe the stories that people tell about themselves—when the stories are good. But such a strategy alone would not suffice. The poet must preserve enough of the character of the original myth to give weight to her story; she must also extend it enough so that it stands on its own in the modern world. The *poet* must perform Circe's feats of penetrating vision with respect to the myth that has entrapped both of them.

Thus, Atwood has Circe describe her setting as the opposite of Homer's lush idyllic island. It is instead a burned forest which nonetheless spawns fireweed that splatters the air, symbolizing both nature's power of regeneration and Circe's verbal power over those who land within range of her voice. The voice, instead of singing seductive songs, asserts that Circe prefers self-effacing men who stand in humble relationship with nature to heroes who, like Icarus, regularly "swoop and thunder" around her island. She denies blame, or even responsibility, for the dismal fate of these "common" heroes; at the same time she admits her complicity. The fact that she "did not say anything" until now has meant that her words were wrecked along with their bodies.

In the fourth poem, Atwood begins to alter our image of Circe's role, presenting her as a healer (perhaps a psychiatrist?) whose people call upon her to soothe their pain, fear, and guilt with words from the earth they have assaulted. She is a hard-working witch who presses her head to the earth faithfully to collect the "few muted syllables left over." So depleted is her island that she can collect only syllables, "a letter at a time." Her wonderfully wry comment that she *is* a desert island (which she reports having quipped to the arriving hero) works on several levels at once. While she scores a point for clever repartee in the battle of the sexes, she also accepts the ancient identification of woman with earth as her source of power, and admits to the depletion of her own as well as the earth's resources.

In the next eight poems, a curious reversal of our expectations occurs as Circe "loses" the battle she initiates. The poems correspond to and replace about sixty lines of Odysseus' story about his "victory" over Circe which supposedly culminated in her invitation: "Come then, put away your sword into its sheath, and let us/ two go up into my bed so that, lying together/ in the bed of love, we may then have faith and trust in each other."[18] In Atwood's sequence, the battle between the two is more strenuous. Circe's part in it is largely verbal; she openly berates Odysseus for his lies, his passivity, his greed, and his delusions of power, interjecting that he need only inquire of the moon snakes at her temples in order to know the future. Her magic may be diminished, but she still knows "what is sacred" (p. 51). In the seventh poem, she includes us in the fray, taunting or chiding us to recognize this scene as part of our own landscape, but also revealing that it is a landscape of "ennui" that offers little satisfaction.

What is remarkable about this Circe is her consciousness of what is happening to her and her articulation of that consciousness at the moment of interaction with the "other." She watches Odysseus coldly as he approaches her for her sexual favors clothed in his shell of confident expectation. She anticipates that if she grants him his wish, she will either fear or despise him. Finally, she does capitulate, and she even allows herself some moments of generosity before she notices that he receives her gifts as his due without acknowledging them. Still, she protests his rough approach to her body, calling it "extortion" and pointing out the fine line between love and hate in such gestures (p. 55). She knows that underneath her own soft masks there is a face of steel to match his own, and she dares the hero to see his reflection in it.

Despite her consciousness and her protests, however, Odysseus "wins." Atwood invents her own symbol for Circe's magic power—a closed fist on a chain around Circe's neck—and presents Odysseus' conquest as a triumph of the hero's armor óver the fist's stuttering and muttering in the language of magic. Finding its foe unassailable, the fist gives up—even "renounces" Circe. So, far from graciously offering her body to achieve a fantasy of faith and trust (or to continue the struggle for power in a more "seductive" way), Atwood's Circe is overpowered. The prettiness of Homer's version is stripped away.

The surprising feature of Atwood's poem is that having "lost" the battle of wills, Circe is released from the mentality of battle. Circe "opens" like a hand cut off at the wrist clutching at freedom. The image is grotesque and not entirely successful.[19] It is not clear how a hand can open and clutch at the same time; and the arm that feels the pain of her absence (the goddess who surrenders to patriarchal force?) is not sufficiently defined. Still, the poem clearly asserts that Circe is released into the freedom of guiltless sexual enjoyment. The result is that she is able to see her lover's body for what it is—a scarred and flawed instrument—and to continue to feel desire for him, even though she knows that his body is not the essence of what she wants (p. 60).

At the same time, she suspects that her body is all he wants.[20] Extreme as the image of the "mud woman" is, in the story "told by another traveller," Circe is vulnerable to it. She has already acknowledged her affinity with the earth (p. 49), and in her present state of sexual responsiveness, she admits that it would be "simple" for her to give in to his desire, especially if Odysseus allows himself to be transformed into a gentle lover (as it appears he does later in the poem, p. 63).

Circe's "freedom" is short-lived. The lovers are assailed from all sides. Their pleasure offends "the suicides, returned/ in the shapes of birds" to warn or complain that "everything dies" (p. 62), who had not found the fruits of the earth sufficient, and who demand the lovers' death as vengeance for their own unhappiness. Circe still fears the goddess "of the two dimensions" (Hecate), who wants her to resist her lover, wants her to make herself "deaf as an eye,/ deaf as a wound, which listens/ to nothing but its own pain" (p. 63). Hecate would have Circe kick Odysseus out, and Circe knows that Hecate "gets results."

As for the hero, he becomes preoccupied with his own story,

and perhaps too trusting; as Circe becomes more servant than lover, her mind turns to the creation of "fresh monsters" to feed his heroic appetite. Whether these monsters are created to make him afraid to leave, or to keep him from leaving by giving him something more to write about, they have the negative effect of undermining the couple's newly found ability to value each other apart from their stories. That ability is also undermined by Circe's jealousy of Penelope, and her resentment of the fact (which she foresees) that Odysseus will believe Penelope's defense of her wifely honor.[21]

The hero's lack of contentment with the present, the only motive Homer provides for Odysseus' departure, is also an element in the disintegration of the lovers' relationship in Atwood's poem. Odysseus naively wants Circe to tell him the future. She responds caustically,

> That's my job,
> one of them, but I advise you
> don't push your luck.
>
> To know the future
> there must be a death.
> Hand me the axe.
>
> As you can see
> the future is a mess.   [p. 66]

Here, as elsewhere in the last eight poems of the sequence, Circe has powers that may be explained as psychological or cognitive rather than magical. Her ability to change the island's summer climate to winter in the twenty-second poem is presumably a correlative for the psychological state of coldness she must develop in order to let her lover go. Her knowledge and insight are more acute in relationship to others, however, than they are in predicting her own fate. She worries that when Odysseus leaves the animals "may transform themselves back into men" and threaten her life (p. 68). She questions whether her father, Helios, cares about her enough to restore her immortality. She wonders if Odysseus will give her back the facility with words that he released from her fist. In the face of her own fate, she is the vulnerable woman.

The final poem shows, however, that despite her worries Circe the woman retains her goddess-like capacity for envisioning the future. The first island that she sees would maintain the power of the story—revised, of course, so that she "is right." The second island seems more than anything to be a place where *neither story counts*. On it, the deer is not a stag to be killed for Odysseus' men, as it is in *The Odyssey*.[22] The birds are not disguised suicides and the snow is not a symbol of psychological coldness as they are in Circe's story. The landscape is neither idyllic nor burned. The lovers are not surrogates for the traveller and his mud woman. The image of the second island is too open to be quite convincing—but perhaps that is its source of power.[23] Since Circe does not articulate her dream fully, we are encouraged to dream it onward ourselves.

The Circe we see here needs no defense, although she is vulnerable. Certainly she is not pure, although she is no worse than Odysseus. Despite all the fanciful elements in the poem, we believe that Atwood has put her finger on a significant aspect of woman's power that was embodied in the ancient figure of Circe and needed only to be articulated clearly: the ability to see, see into, and see beyond the stories we tell about who we are. This is not exclusively a female power; traditionally it belongs to both Cassandra and Teiresias. But perhaps women have more often been consigned to the islands where such capacities flourish. Specifically, we have long had a different vantage point from which to view the male hero. Perhaps the delight that this poem produces in female audiences has to do with Atwood's success in modelling how to reveal the dark spot on the back of the man's head, without which, Virginia Woolf said, the man's portrait remains incomplete.[24]

Some will say that Atwood's Circe is ungenerous; Homer's Odysseus, after all, was capable of great sorrow and guilt, not to mention aesthetic appreciation. But Atwood knows, as most of us do, how often those capacities have been repressed in favor of rapaciousness. Others will say she is too generous—that men like Odysseus have no reason to change. Atwood presents the many difficulties we would experience in achieving a real partnership, but at the same time she holds out hope for change. Whereas Homer's Circe is a minor goddess whose power to seduce men is overcome by the superior connections of Odysseus with the pantheon of gods, Atwood's is a woman who had certain enduring goddess-like capacities.

Atwood herself might describe Circe as a Venus released from the "Rapunzel Syndrome" the poet described in her book of criticism, *Survival: A Thematic Guide to Canadian Literature*, published two years before *You Are Happy*. This literary pattern "for realistic novels about 'normal' women" includes Rapunzel, "the wicked witch who has imprisoned her," "the tower she's imprisoned in," and the Rescuer "who provides momentary escape." In the literary versions of the fairy tale, however, "the Rescuer is not much help. . . . Rapunzel is in fact stuck in the tower, and the best thing she can do is to learn how to cope with it."[25] Atwood speculates that although the Rapunzel Syndrome transcends national boundaries, it takes a Canadian form: the Rapunzel figures have difficulty in communicating, or even acknowledging, their fears and hatreds; "they walk around with mouths like clenched fists."[26]

Certainly Atwood's Circe symbolizes the release from such difficulties of communication. She has *not* become her own tower by internalizing the values of Western culture that would consign her to the role of cold seductress, *la belle dame sans merci*. Her enjoyment of sexual pleasure in the center of the poem identifies her as more Venus than Diana or Hecate, in the triple goddess figure from Robert Graves that Atwood uses to describe the possibilities for women in fiction. Circe is perhaps not a perfect Venus, as Atwood understands the figure, both sexual and maternal—unless we think of Circe's healing and serving capacities as products of maternal impulse. She is Venus with a difference: a Venus who finally does not lose her *self* in expressing her sexuality; one with the capacity to conceive of a new tower (island) in which she will not be imprisoned; one with the potential to be her own muse.

If the potential of this Rapunzel to liberate herself is not yet fully realized, we should not complain. It is up to us to do better. Whatever we might wish for Circe's future, we must admit that Atwood, through her knowledge of the psychology and history of relationships between males and females and through her brilliant use of literary precedents both ancient and modern, has restored her to the realm of living myth where there is no opposition between myth and truth. In this realm, myth is one kind of truth—a kind that retains its power long after philosophers and historians have revealed its impossibility, a kind that continues to glide through our dreams, fantasies, and even our gestures "as if there is water" (p. 46). Atwood gambles here on the possibility that myth can be transformed from within without losing its power.

Clearly the transformation worked for Atwood, as she demonstrates in the poems surrounding "Circe/Mud Poems."[27] The first section of *You Are Happy* is the record of relationships between men and women that are just short of violent in their outcome—where the only moment of "happiness" occurs when the woman, walking alone in sub-freezing weather, feels the images "hitting" her eyes "like needles, crystals" (p. 28). Then, "Songs of the Transformed," a contemporary bestiary (see chapter 8 for a full interpretation), ends with the warning song of the human corpse who hoarded both words and love until it was too late (pp. 43–44).

The section that follows the Circe poems, however, is markedly different. In these poems, enigmatically called "There Is Only One of Everything," the lovers make an honest attempt to inhabit their bodies instead of abandoning them "in favour of word games or jigsaw puzzles" (p. 72). The woman seeks to express both her anger (p. 75) and her desire (p. 92). They move from the experience of love based on need to an experience based on ripeness (p. 93). Together, they transform an ancient ritual of sacrifice into a ritual of love (pp. 94–96). Coming after the Circe poems and drawing on the same mythic elements, these poems have the effect of confirming Circe's vision of the new island and validating its essential truthfulness.

In turn, the presence of the Circe poems in the volume gives to the final sequence the status of myth. In it two people transcend both the powerful myth of the war between the sexes and its brutal history in order to participate in life organized by the values of Circe's vision. The lovers' responsiveness to each other and to nature, in a moment to be appreciated for its own unique *presence*, is sufficient to overcome all other imperatives—whether of life or of death. "There Is Only One of Everything" does not mean that the lovers submerge their identities to achieve the "oneness" promised in the traditional marriage ceremony, but that in sharing the uniqueness of each moment ("the tree/ we saw," p. 92), each opens him/herself and becomes whole (p. 96).

III. RE-ENVISIONING THE QUEST MYTH

In the poem "Is/Not," from the fourth section of *You Are Happy*, Atwood's female protagonist explains to her lover,

> This is a journey, not a war,
> there is no outcome,
> I renounce predictions
>
> and aspirins, I resign the future
> as I would resign an expired passport:
> . . .
>
> we're stuck here
> . . .
>
> where we must walk slowly,
> where we may not get anywhere
>
> or anything, where we keep going,
> fighting our ways, our way
> not out but through.   [pp. 75–76]

What kind of a journey has no outcome and goes nowhere? Unlike Circe's flippant dismissal of her powers in a moment of frustration ("So much for art. So much for prophecy," p. 64), this paradoxical formulation seems to be serious. But what does Atwood mean?

Furthermore, what should we make of the fact that "Circe/ Mud Poems" does not take the form of a journey at all? Indeed, one of its most intriguing features is that it does not propose an alternative form of the quest it criticizes so bitingly—not even the form Annis Pratt describes as the female rebirth journey.[28] Perhaps we could say that Circe's island itself represents a release from societal norms, or that Circe's rejection of Odysseus' story about her represents such a release. But this is more a matter of externalizing her private knowledge (splattering the fireweed) than it is part of an inward exploration—more an assertion of ego in defiance of patriarchal norms than a retreat from its concerns, as in other rebirth journeys by women. It would likewise be difficult to locate a green-world guide or token, unless it is the syllables from the earth that Circe gathers in her role as witch/ healer. But that is the substance of her reality, not a deviation from it. Odysseus never really becomes Circe's "green-world lover"; although for a brief period he does reveal his body beneath his armor,[29] he quickly returns to his own concerns. Perhaps we can see him as a catalyst in Circe's life, since he does undo the fist and release her capacity for passion. There is no overt confrontation with parental figures, although Circe does wonder whether her father, the sun, will rescue her. But her immortality is assured by language, not by Helios.

Circe's report of Hecate's desire for her relationship to fail, her jealousy of Penelope, and her spiteful creation of new monsters to inhibit Odysseus might appropriately be described as manifestations of self-destructive potential (or "shadow"). If she gives in to the part of herself that experiences Odysseus' love as an invasion of her privacy, she dooms herself to loneliness. If she derides Penelope's story, she devalues her own capacity for telling a believable story. If she creates new monsters for Odysseus to conquer, she becomes a participant in the quest she criticizes. Presumably she manages to overcome all of these impulses in order to envision the second island. But can we call these acts a "plunge into the unconscious"[30] for purposes of rebirth? This Circe seems to emerge from centuries in the unconscious to complete the cleansing acts of telling off the hero and admitting all sorts of other feelings she did not know she had.

It would be more accurate to see the whole poem sequence as proceeding from the inside out rather than in the usual manner of the spiritual quest. Circe says she "searches" for a certain kind of man. But it is more true to say that she opens herself to the possibility of a relationship that will develop that kind of man— and in turn will allow her to be the loving woman she would like to be. The poem is not so much a rebirth journey (there is no journey) as it is an exploration of what might happen if we *stopped* questing and made the most of the capabilities for relationship that we have "Right now I mean. See for yourself" (p. 52).

This is curious, for elsewhere in her work Atwood seems to be as committed to the idea of the quest as any modernist writer. Certainly *Surfacing* fits the pattern Annis Pratt describes, and many of her titles suggest a preoccupation with a psychological journey, usually in the form of a descent.[31] Robert Lecker suggests that Atwood uses such patterns to question their assumptions—even to prove them false. He points out, for example, that Atwood often makes use of the romance pattern

without its happy ending, return or ascent. In the case of *Surfacing*, he claims, "What Atwood really seems to be saying is that
the mythical pattern of separation, initiation and return must itself be seen as a sham in a culture where rituals have lost their
potency."[32]

I doubt this explanation. Clearly rituals have not lost their potency for Atwood. In *Two-Headed Poems*, she and her sister sew a
red shirt for her baby girl with every expectation of passing on to
her daughter the heritage or "birthright" of the world's mothers.
She says,

> It may not be true
> that one myth cancels another.
> Nevertheless, in a corner
> of the hem, where it will not be seen,
> where you will inherit
> it, I make this tiny
> stitch, my private magic.[33]

And the child, as innocently as Sleeping Beauty once received her
fatal prick from the wicked fairy, receives her mother's life-
supporting gift with joy. Atwood still hopes that one myth *does*
cancel another.

I think that what is finally mythologized in Atwood's poems is
the possibility of altering myths that are so basic that we can
scarcely dream of existence without them. Atwood knows that if
one myth cancels another, it happens slowly. "Circe/Mud
Poems," then, is part of a long process of rearranging the elements of the quest myth into a shape which may finally negate
the idea of questing, as we now understand it, in order to embrace an idea of self-acceptance and relationship quite different
from the traditional ideal of self-transcendence and attainment
perpetuated by the quest. Atwood's vision is not "duplicitous"
so much as it is double.[34]

Like Circe, she envisions two possibilities, and she sees that, at
least for the moment, "they do not exclude each other" (p. 69).
In the first, the quest myth is simply changed from within so that
the silent participants have their opportunity to "be right." In the
second, the image of the journey itself is transformed, so that it
becomes admirable to go through experience without going forward or getting anywhere. It is an image of movement "in

place." The challenge of this kind of "journey" is simply to "Be Alive" (p. 87). Eventually, the antinomy between self and other that informed the quest will appear quite different, as it does in a later poem:

> We do not walk on the earth
> but in it, wading
> in that acid sea
> where flesh is etched from
> molten bone and re-forms.
>
> In this massive tide
> warm as liquid
> sun, all waves are one
> wave; there is no *other*.[35]

Atwood's mythic sequence stands in a pivotal position in her work, looking back to the "power politics" of earlier volumes and ahead to her developing sense of fruitful relationship among forms of life she does not regard as totally separate from each other. Thus her title "Circe/Mud Poems," cuts both ways. On the one hand, it protests the vision of woman which reduces her to her sexuality and materiality without recognizing her consciousness. On the other hand, from that same woman's consciousness comes a vision of the satisfactions of material reality. Perhaps Atwood will be the "poet of earth" that Wallace Stevens wanted to be, to match the poets of heaven and hell of the great tradition.[36] As she says,

> So much for the gods and their
> static demands . our demands, former
> demands . . .
>
>   History
> is over, we take place
> in a season, an undivided
> space, no necessities
>
> hold us closed, distort
> us.   [p. 95]

Change is possible—even at the roots of our lives, in the myths that govern our experience.

CHAPTER 4

Remedios Varo: The Creative Woman and the Female Quest

Embedded in the works of a virtually unknown painter, Remedios Varo (1913–1963), are images of the creative process that deserve attention in this study of mythmaking. A consummate artist, Varo created an imaginative world rivalling that of Hieronymus Bosch in its visionary madness.[1] Whereas much that has been called "fantastic art" is the result of a "wilful" exercise of imagination for its own sake, Varo's paintings are not only internally coherent but also psychologically and mythically significant.[2] Her deepest images are fully accessible once we see the connections between her world and our own. Such connections are possible because recent research allows us to see that Varo's images of the creative process occur in the context of a female quest that differs substantially from the traditional models.[3] Thus, in addition to offering valuable insight into the nature of the visionary imagination, the paintings help to chart the undeveloped territory of female creativity. After a brief description of Varo and her world, I will explore her images of creativity and the quest in detail before I speculate on the significance of her vision at this moment in our history.

I. REMEDIOS VARO: PAINTER

Even though the information about Varo's life is sparse, we can be reasonably sure that her paintings were the result of her deliberate reworking of her own identity in response to the catastrophic events of civil and world-wide war that characterize our century.[4] Her career developed only after she fled to Paris from

Spain during the Spanish Civil War, and then to Mexico from Paris during the Nazi occupation of France. Born in 1913 in Spain, Varo travelled extensively with her father, a hydraulic engineer. Her youthful talent in drawing and mathematics earned her a place at the Academy of San Fernando in Madrid, where she married briefly at age nineteen to escape her conservative Catholic family. In 1936, she married the poet Benjamin Peret, and spent the years from 1937 to 1942 in Paris at the center of the Surrealist group. Throughout the thirties and the forties, she worked as a commercial artist, decorating furniture, designing costumes, restoring pottery, and even drawing insects for the Ministry of Public Health in Caracas, Venezuela. In 1953, after her divorce from Peret and her marriage to Walter Gruen, she began to paint works of such intricacy, maturity of style, and technical expertise that she achieved nearly immediate recognition. In the ten years of her career she completed more than 100 paintings. She won first prize in the Salon of Women Painters, and by 1962 her work had become sufficiently well-known to be included in the International Exposition in Tokyo. Varo died suddenly of a heart attack in 1963. Despite her success, we would not have access to her visions if the book based upon the retrospective exhibits of her work in 1963 and 1964 had not included texts by the internationally known figures, Octavio Paz and Roger Caillois. All of her works are in private collections.

As I mentioned, Varo's world is coherent in its own fantastic way.[5] Plants grow from table tops as if by spontaneous generation. People, animals, and spirits break through walls, chairs, or floors and erupt into ordinary reality without disturbing the protagonists. Animals and mythological creatures exhibit human characteristics, and human beings regularly become non-human in their clothing or bearing. The boundaries between interior and exterior space are exceedingly flexible, yet earthly life is bound to the planets by a thread.

Varo's commentaries on her paintings show that she was fully conscious of the psychological and spiritual "content" her work embodies. The comments on three paintings from the beginning of her career are particularly valuable because they reveal her starting point. For example, she has this to say about a painting called The Revelation (La revelación, 1955):

> The theme is time. That is why there is a watchmaker (which in a way represents our ordinary time), but through the window comes a "revelation" and he understands many things; I have tried to give him an expression of surprise and illumination. Surrounding him there are quantities of clocks, which show the same time, but inside each one there is the same character in very different eras or epochs that I manage through the costumes.[6]

Presumably his revelation has to do with the way in which an image or character can transcend its time or exist throughout time. In another painting called *Harmony* (*Armonía*, 1956),[7] a human figure of unclear gender who resembles Varo is seated before a metal replica of a musical staff on a table in a huge library. Varo says that the character is trying to find the invisible thread that ties everything together. The painter knows that "he" has in his possession a paper (on the middle line of the staff) that contains the mathematical formula which is the combination of all things; when he blows on the musical key supporting the pentagram, an "objective" music will be heard. The female figure above the table detaching itself from the wall is a collaborative fate from beyond the world of ordinary phenomena. Varo's belief in the occult could not be more explicitly stated, yet the paintings are beautifully realized—not mere ideograms. The notes show a remarkable capacity for reflecting the myth Varo participates in; the paintings show that such a double perspective can enrich rather than enervate art. A third painting identifies her mythic starting point even more precisely. In *Hermit* (*Ermitaño*, 1956) she shows us a single androgynous figure (with Varo's face, rendered in mother-of-pearl) in a primeval forest. "His" garments form the two intersecting triangles of a six-pointed star, and his chest opens inward to reveal a yin/yang symbol. Varo calls it the "most beautiful symbol of inner unity."[8]

II. IMAGES OF CREATIVITY IN A VISIONARY MODE

With these guidelines regarding Varo's world in mind, let us turn to the images of creativity. The earliest occurs in *Solar Music* (*Música solar*, 1955), in which a woman plays a stringed sunbeam with her bow, and her music releases the birds in nearby trees from their cocoon-like capsules.[9] Where illumination from the sun falls, it makes both the forest floor and her mantle green; but

Solar Music (Música Solar), Remedios Varo, 1955, oil on masonite, 35-⅞″ × 24″.
Courtesy of Walter Gruen.

it is her own music, rising in arcs from the point where her bow touches the strings, that releases the birds from their torpor. In this painting, the protagonist's resemblance to Varo is striking: she was a small woman with dark hair, huge eyes, and a "heart-shaped" face—wide at the brow, narrow at the chin, soft in contour—with a straight nose and a relatively small mouth. Thus the painting probably expresses a self-image rather than a vision of a goddess, even though the figure has been initiated into a cosmic realm. In Varo's world, it was not unusual for the human individual to affect the non-human environment by her action. In a lighthearted painting finished at about the same time, *Sympathy* (*Simpatía*, 1955), Varo shows a woman who caresses a disruptive cat when it jumps on her table, thereby creating a "very complicated electric astrology."[10] *Solar Music* is important among such images because it portrays a deliberately creative act of awakening life.

The creator in *Solar Music* has the power to affect her environment not by accident or by fate but because she is *attuned* to the sunlight. She must see the sun's rays as strings in order to play them, and she must play them well in order to affect the life of the birds so profoundly. The momentousness of her act becomes clear in the context of other paintings that portray the degree to which the planets control the lives of unsuspecting human beings.[11] By comparison with *Solar Music*, the otherwise marvellous image in *The Flautist* (*Flautista*, 1955)[12] becomes conventional. The music from the flute, in that painting, picks up the stones on the ground and lifts them into place to form an octagonal tower—a monument to the imagination and to the human ego as well. The flautist, whose face is also carved from mother-of-pearl, rearranges inanimate elements to give them the form he desires. The woman playing the sun creates no monument; instead she liberates one form of life from an imprisoning enclosure. Her unselfconscious consciousness and calm humility are among the most remarkable aspects of the painting.

Solar Music reverses several possible expectations and raises questions we will want to explore before we internalize its meaning. In poetry and life, the birds usually awaken human beings with their songs. In myth, the woman is associated with the moon, not the sun, and human beings do not traffic with celestial bodies directly without peril. We may wonder how the woman knows what to do with the rays, how she retains her composure, how many other birds must be freed. Without literalizing the painting by forcing it to answer our questions directly, we can engage in a reverie on the relationships among its elements.[13] The woman dares to play the sun. The sun responds by making the forest green. The music that she makes awakens and releases the birds who fly away. The woman knows what she is doing, enjoys it, feels no surprise at her results, and experiences no need to be observed or appreciated. We need only translate these relationships into psychological terms such as "genius, motivation, achievement, and recognition," to see how unusual the image is in the context of Western thought. Absorbing nature's genius (the brilliance of Apollo), she directs it toward creatures less fortunate than herself for their benefit. Her achievement is their flight rather than any permanent product. Ego-fulfillment has little or nothing to do with her motivation. She is comfortable in her solitude.[14]

Varo's next image of creativity repeats some of the elements of *Solar Music*—the female protagonist, her calm and solitude, her knowledge of how to use celestial resources; but *The Creation of the Birds* (*La creación de las aves*, 1958)[15] shows the woman as a full collaborator with the moon and the stars. In this painting, the protagonist has assumed the form of an owl in order to paint birds who will come to life and take flight for the first time. Her creative process is more complex than in the previous painting. She dips the brush, attached to her own violin (in the place of her heart), into paint from an alchemical alembic where the substance from the stars is stored. With her other hand, she holds a triangular magnifying glass to intensify the light from the moon. The birds she paints into life in this manner certainly equal the achievement of any alchemist, real or imagined.

Again Varo plays with our expectations. No one expects either a human being or an owl to create birds by any means. The owl in myth belongs to the patriarchal goddess Athena who would have been more concerned with preserving civilization than with creating birds (if we can believe Aeschylus in the *Oresteia*). What would "possess" a woman to become an owl? What alchemy would transform starlight into such a lifegiving elixir?

The image of creativity is both more radical and more conscious than the one presented in *Solar Music*. The woman/owl

The Creation of the Birds (Creación de las aves), Remedios
Varo, 1958 oil on masonite, 20-⅝'' × 24-⅝''.
Courtesy of Walter Gruen.

gives wing to *her visions* of the birds. By careful arrangement of
the violin, the alembic, and the glass, she enables the music of
her own life, the substance of the stars, and the light of the moon
to "feed" her paintings and confer life on them. The image differs strikingly from the related stories of Pygmalion and Pinoc-
chio. Their creators brought them to life out of a desire to be
loved. They did not make use of cosmic forces, nor did they
undergo transformation themselves. In this case, the self-
transformation appears to be crucial. The act is a collaborative
one. Her creation is the product of her love rather than of her
desire to be loved. The effect of the painting is to stress the
power of empathy with non-human forms of life.

In 1963, just before her death, Varo completed one of a very
few paintings that did not show human life. She called it *Still-Life*

Being Resurrected (Naturaleza muerta resucitando).[16] It shows plates of fruit being set in motion by a candle in the center of a table, and spiralling upward and outward until the fruit smashes to release its seeds, *which become plants and flower immediately*. Thus, the fruits which were regarded as *nature morte*, objects to be rendered beautiful in an artist's still-life, are brought back into the cycle of life. The image of spontaneous regeneration is complicated by the title which emphasizes the artist's role in arranging the harvested fruit and gives us the word "resurrection" to ponder. Clearly the artist is behind the renewal of life in this painting. She envisions life (in *presto* tempo) continuing its cyclical pattern from ripeness and stillness to the shattering of the old form, and the subsequent reseeding and growth of a new plant. At the center of her mandala image is the heat and light of the candle, the calm center in the eye of a force that lifts the objects into the air and ensures the process of regeneration. In the absence of a human protagonist, we may infer that the candle is the "artist." The source of illumination and energy is now in the painting itself. Instead of merely (!) awakening or envisioning animate life, Varo's creator must now resurrect vegetable life— not in some other world or time, but here on earth, now, right next to the table where it was to have been consumed by human beings. Perhaps this is the most radical image of human creativity we can imagine—this god-like responsibility for the continuation of inanimate life.

Why would Varo shift her focus from human and animate to inanimate life in her last painting? Why would she take on the task of resurrection? Why would she symbolize the creative force in the form of a candle (isn't that oddly phallic in this highly feminine body of work)? Possible answers to these and other questions I have raised emerge in the context of other paintings by Varo.

III.   VARO'S VISION OF A FEMALE QUEST

Among the 77 paintings by Varo that are known because of the extraordinarily fine book published by Ediciones ERA in 1966 as a result of a retrospective exhibit are at least 27 paintings involving a female protagonist in an explicitly psychological and

Still-life Being Resurrected (Naturaliza muerta resucitando),
Remedios Varo, 1963, oil on canvas, 39-⅜″ × 31-½″.
Courtesy of Walter Gruen.

spiritual quest. Paintings entitled *Rupture, The Tortuous Roads, Journey to the Sources of the Orinoco River, Born Again, The One Who Is Called* and *Emerging Light* leave little doubt as to Varo's intent. Her version of the quest involves the stages of separation, initiation, and return that Joseph Campbell has made famous,[17] but it differs from the traditional model so much that the psychological and social significance of the journey is altered completely. Recall, for example, "Amor and Psyche," the paradigmatic tale of the female quest in the traditional mode.[18] Because Psyche rivals Venus (Aphrodite) in beauty, Venus sets in motion a plan to have Psyche fall in love with "the vilest of men," and Psyche is sent away from her home in a funeral procession to accept her fate. Amor (Eros) substitutes himself for her intended monster-husband but will not allow her to know who he is. Her sisters frighten her into lighting her lamp to see him while he is with her at night; he awakens and punishes her by leaving her, even though she is pregnant, and by returning to his mother who is enraged by his betrayal. Eventually Psyche is brought to Venus, who first inflicts bodily punishment on her and then devises four "tests" of her worth. An ant performs the first task of sorting the seeds, peas and beans; a reed offers Psyche advice so that she can gather the gold fleece from a herd of sheep; a "royal bird" from Jove (Zeus) gathers icy water from the highest mountain; and a tower offers advice that enables Psyche to obtain a portion of Proserpine's (Persephone's) beauty from the realm of the dead. On her way home from the last task, Psyche opens the "casket" to partake of the beauty herself and is overwhelmed by sleep. She is awakened by Amor who enlists the aid of Jove to make her his immortal wife. She bears a divine daughter, instead of the divine son she had been promised if she had kept the secret of her husband's identity.

Although Varo uses some of the images from the Psyche myth (a lamp, a journey to find a goblet of water and an image of a woman opening a small "casket" are the most obvious), her vision of the quest is radically different. It involves no helpers, no perilous tasks, no union with the opposite sex, and no reconciliation with the father and mother figures. These are not whimsical alterations in the myth and we ignore them at our peril— especially since they correlate with similar changes wrought by other women, as I will show later in this essay. Although I will present Varo's images of the female quester roughly in order of their composition, we must not delude ourselves into thinking that they represent fixed stages of her own or any female's quest. In nine years, Varo envisioned a journey that many would not complete in a lifetime, and many of her images must have occurred to her nearly simultaneously.

One of Varo's first paintings is titled *Rupture*, (*Ruptura*, 1955).[19] It shows a cloaked and hooded female descending a walled flight of steps from an imposing building, under the ominous gaze of six human figures. She walks straight toward us with her eyes directed upward in anxiety or pain and her hands folded in resolution. She is on her toes. Her garment suggests that she is leaving a convent; its folds, however, suggest the vaginal shape that surrounds several questers in Varo's later work. Although the building and the steps remain solid, the walls appear to be vegetative, like the forest floor of *Solar Music*, done in the same year.

In this context, it becomes clear that *Solar Music* is an immediate initiation into a benign realm of nature which is already (at least intuitively) known to the quester. No one is present to tell her that she must play the sun to awaken the birds. If we think of this as a "test" at all, it is one set by the desire of the woman and not by some external power. The presence of the sun is felicitous and propitious, but we cannot impute to it an intention to help; it is not personified. The woman's achievement is a triumph of observation, intuition, and empathy—all forms of conscious orientation toward the world.[20]

Apparently Varo was not content to rest with her idyllic achievement in *Solar Music*, for in 1956 her face appears again with a different, more determined expression. The protagonist, called a *Star Huntress* (*Cazadora de astros*),[21] is elaborately dressed as if she were a Renaissance Queen, and she is equipped with a butterfly net which she has used to capture the crescent moon. Her garment is disintegrating into wings, making her seem more like a monarch butterfly than a strictly human creature. Her regal bearing and ethereal aspect coupled with the symbols of the moon and the hunt suggest an incarnation of Artemis/Diana. The painting implies both that some aspects of the quest require the assumption of a goddess-like power and that such power has a disintegrating effect, but it does not reveal why the quester would want to capture the moon.

In *Celestial Pabulum* (*Papilla estelar*, 1958)[22] Varo repeats the image of the caged moon, answering our question by creating an image of female nurturing with extraordinary power to move contemporary women. The protagonist is seated at a table inside an octagonal enclosure in the sky. She is grinding the food from the stars and feeding it to the moon in its cage. She is at once powerful and impotent. Because the moon is waning, it seems likely that she is saving it from death. Her sullen or dejected stance, however, belies the importance of this duty. A closer look at her setting reveals the source of her ambivalence: although there are steps leading from her enclosure, she could not take them unless she could walk on clouds. Although her house is open on several sides so that we can see inside, she is as caged as the moon. One can easily grasp why she neither rejects nor embraces her nurturing function. This is as close as Varo's questers come to a reconciliation with the maternal potential in their lives. It is clearly a stage to be passed through rather than an ending point, as it was in the myth of Psyche.

This painting is one of at least eleven treating the female quest in 1958 and 1959. Several of these, including *The Creation of the Birds*, involve a transformation of the female into a hybrid form. In *Character (Personaje*, 1958),[23] for example, she shows a female form with bat's wings, red mane, and goat's horns running barefoot through a forest (or escaping from a petrified forest, depending on how one sees the tree-like structure in the foreground of the painting). Her body is covered by a leotard made of a transparent substance like a cocoon. Again, the human face is very like Varo's, and it may express the development of a winged Pan within her. The image differs from the pattern it echoes, however; Pan is not a separate fertilizing power with whom the goddess must join in sacred marriage. Instead, the human female embodies the attributes of Pan.

A similar female figure appears a year later in *The Minotaur (El minotauro*, 1959),[24] clothed in an opaque blue cocoon that has begun to change into feathers, which may permit her to fly from her enclosure in the sky. She holds a key, but the door behind her containing the lock has already become permeable, so that the clouds are drifting into the room. Again, a mythological figure that is male by convention (the Minotaur) is rendered in female form; instead of being imprisoned inside a labyrinth to be found and destroyed by a hero, she is preparing to open the door to the sky.

The more familiar we become with Varo's vision of the quest, the more likely it seems that *The Creation of the Birds* is her image of what will be required if human creators wish to make a world in which all the species of life can survive. Her choice of the owl, always a figure of wisdom, is clarified by the information that the pre-Hellenic, Cretan Athena was a patron of the arts and a goddess of renewal whose other major symbols were the pillar and the serpent.[25] Only the alchemy, the transformative power, of the goddesses of wisdom and renewal could suffice if our creative task is to be the revival of a dying moon. The creator must assume the aspect of the goddess in order to act.

During the same period in Varo's work, several of the protagonists who remain unconventionally human encounter immobilizing difficulties. In *Encounter* (*Encuentro*, 1959),[26] for example, Varo portrays a woman seated before a table in a disintegrating dress somewhat like the Minotaur's cocoon. She has just opened a chest (like Psyche's casket) only to find her own head, and she looks appropriately despondent. In *Mimesis* (*Mimetismo*, 1960),[27] the woman begins to take on the shape of the chair's arms and legs, while the furniture begins to reach out in human fashion to open drawers or grasp objects. As Roger Caillois observes, "The being has no resistance: a simple chair conquers her nature, transforms her to its image and likeness by osmosis and contagion."[28] These are the primary dangers of the quest as Varo conceives it: finding what one already possesses (in a form detached from the body), or becoming so susceptible to transformation that one loses one's identity altogether, achieving metamorphosis without meaning.

Other difficulties seem less serious, although they involve conflict with a male figure. In the case of the *Unexpected Visit* (*Visita inesperada*, 1958),[29] a nude woman who is accustomed to seducing her guests is surprised and frightened, at her intimate table set for two, by the sudden appearance of a machine-like being. A hand emerges from the wall behind her in response to her desire for help. In another painting with a similar title *Unexpected Presence* (*Presencia inesperada*, 1959),[30] a male seducer emerges from the back of the woman's chair as she works at her table. In *The Tortuous Roads* (*Los caminos tortuosos*, 1958),[31] a woman on her bicycle, who is trying to fly by means of insect wings extending from her arms, is detained by an old man who grabs one arm with his mustache. Insofar as the male appears in the female's quest in these paintings, he does so as a nuisance, not as a helper or as a significant adversary.

In the midst of all these images of the transformed or the stymied quester is Varo's most explicit image of a journey. In *Journey to the Sources of the Orinoco River* (*Exploración de las fuentes del río Orinoco*, 1959),[32] an Amazon dressed in army fatigues and a bowler hat navigates a womb-like egg-shaped vessel which is no less a hybrid than was the Minotaur. It is both ancient and modern, mythic and technological; it has angel wings, fish-like fins, and tuxedo-like lapels, but it is riveted together and equipped with modern instruments for navigation. The journey has ended in a primeval forest which has drowned in the water that spouts from a goblet-fountain on a table in a hollow tree-trunk. A bird looks on from a nearby hollow in another tree. This may have been a sacred place of origins, but now it is nothing more than another landmark of civilization. If Jove himself were to offer her a goblet of this water, it would not suffice. The woman looks remarkably calm, or perhaps she is stunned.

The moment of discovery in Varo's rendition of the quest occurs in *Born Again* (*Nacer de nuevo,* 1960).[33] It is the discovery of the grail, which eluded all but three of King Arthur's knights. The naked female breaks through a wall into a sacred space that contains the grail, miraculously full and containing the reflected image of the crescent moon. This time the moon is discovered rather than captured. It is an ecstatic moment, and a highly sexualized one, but it is entirely feminine because of the ancient association of the woman with the vessel and the moon, and because of the vaginal imagery presented in the tearing wall. If we compare this image with the image of fate in *Harmony* (cited above), it becomes apparent that the protagonist has become her own fate.

Surely Varo herself experienced the full measure of her protagonist's discovery and might have rested with that attainment. Varo's paintings were neither intellectual contrivances nor surrealist abandonments of reason; her images, however fantastic they may seem, have the quality of things seen. To see a vision of the grail might have been enough for some artists, but Varo's images of the quest continued.

In *The Calling* (or *The One Who Is Called; La llamada,* 1961),[34] the quester is dressed in an incandescent flame-like garment. Her

Born Again (Nacer de Nuevo), Remedios Varo, 1960, oil on masonite, 31-⅞″ × 18-½″.
Courtesy of Walter Gruen.

red hair reaches up to and wraps around the largest celestial body in the dark sky. She moves forward swiftly, carrying a vial of precious fluid and wearing an alchemist's mortar around her neck.[35] The citizens, so immobile that they have become part of the city walls, indicate no awareness of her presence. No one acknowledges her triumph, her apotheosis as a goddess of fire or as a spiritual alchemist who has produced the elixir of life.

Another painting from the same year elaborates upon and clarifies the difficulty of the quester's return to society. In *Woman Coming Out of the Psychoanalyst's* (*Mujer saliendo del psicoanalista*, 1961),[36] the woman, wearing a green cloak, holds her father's head by the beard and prepares to drop it into the well. Her hair has turned white and has begun to form horns in addition to taking the shape of the crescent moon. Her vision has enabled her to discard her father's head (the most powerful embodiment of all that is threatening to her) along with other elements (a clock, a key, a pacifier) that Varo labels "psychological waste." Part of her mask has slipped in the process, but her mouth is still covered.

Thus, Varo's final vision of the female quester shows a woman who is still emerging rather than one who is fully visible. *Emerging Light* (*Luz emergente*, 1962),[37] is one of the most compelling visions of female wisdom ever rendered. The woman's right hand precedes her body through the vaginal space in a burlap-covered wall; it holds the lamp of knowledge. She carries her own source of illumination now instead of merely playing or collaborating with a source outside herself. Her face is alert and calm; it is only a matter of time before the space will open naturally of its own accord to allow her birth.

Returning to *Still-Life Being Resurrected* now, we can see that the source of illumination has indeed been drawn into the work of art, and we may infer that it embodies all the accumulated wisdom of the quest. Varo effaces herself from the work and concentrates her illuminative power in the candle, in order to reverse centuries of images of fruit plucked without compunction for our pleasure. In view of her death shortly after this painting was completed, we may speculate that she chose to use all of her remaining life-energy to sponsor the regeneration of nature as she had come to understand it—nature that was not merely dying but already dead. The candle is the torch of Demeter; the offspring in this vision is not a human son but a new cycle of vegetation.[38]

This image of the artist as one who has mysterious power to restore life appears in Varo's work after a complex examination, on her part, of the scientist's relationship to nature. In *The Non-Submissive Plant* (*Planta insumisa*, 1961),[39] she shows a botanist who is perplexed because one of his plants insists upon producing a flower instead of branches in mathematical figures. In her *Discovery by the Mutant Geologist* (*Descubrimiento de un geólogo mutante*, 1961),[40] she satirizes the geologist's attempt to study the one flower that is left after an atomic holocaust; she finds his elaborate instruments and his dispassionate attitude preposterous. In the *Phenomenon of Loss of Gravity* (*Fenómeno de ingravedad*, 1963),[41] she presents a strait-laced astronomer who is astonished to find himself with his left foot in one dimension and his right foot in another. In *Vegetarian Vampires* (*Vampiros vegetarianos*, 1962),[42] three male figures, whose disintegrating garments recall those patrons of science Hermes and Apollo, greedily consume the rose, the melon, and the tomato through straws.

Varo's antipathy for these scientists emerged during the years when her visions of female attainment were at their peak, and they illuminate the content of her own commitment. She had begun her career as a painter with the idea that unity or harmony exists outside human life to be discovered by the philosopher or the mystic. Through her paintings, a commitment to regeneration developed—not to human rebirth or transcendence, but to regeneration of the fruits of the earth.

IV. THE CREATIVE WOMAN AND NATURE: A SPECULATIVE CONCLUSION

For Varo and for her female protagonists, the quest requires a rupture with the values that confine them within ordinary life situations. The quest takes place in a primeval forest or in strange enclosures suspended in the sky, but these realms are not dangerous. Instead of confronting and battling monsters or outwitting gods, the quester learns to embody mythic powers within herself. She learns to capture and feed the moon, to fly from the forest as she desires, to create new life, and to unlock the door leading to the sky. She confronts the dangers of solipsism and assimilation. Perhaps the nadir of her journey comes when she discovers that the fountain of life has been pre-empted by civilization. Her victory is an ecstatic breakthrough into a space where the grail, itself a feminine vehicle, reflects the moon. Rather than being a formula for achieving unity, it is an affirmation of the feminine in its ancient, permanent, cosmic form. Her discovery does not come about through union with a male; rather it presupposes an androgynous starting point. Although it is sexual in character, it does not result in an interpersonal act of love, nor does it produce a child. Her experience is shareable; she may distill from it an elixir. She may attain spiritual greatness. Her chances of gaining recognition from those who are embedded in the walls of the city, however, are slim indeed. Far from achieving atonement with the father, she must dispose of his head and assume the ultimate task of creation, the resurrection of nature, by herself. No one stands ready to be the midwife to the birth of her body; no one stands ready to take her lamp of knowledge. Her atonement is with nature, not with us. But she makes the Demetrian torch available to us. Through these images, Varo seeks to awaken the capacity for visionary imagination in those of us who may share her desire for the renewal of earth.

A few years ago, Varo's paintings might have seemed not only subjective but bizarre. Now, with our increased understanding of the omnipresent image-making that goes on in human thought and our increased familiarity with works by other women, the paintings seem profoundly communal. While remaining her own unique visions, Varo's paintings correlate with other images of the quest created by women. For instance, Annis Pratt has found in her study of 300 years of fiction by women that female questers are neither called upon nor chosen to be heroic; they embark on a journey, as Varo suggests in *Rupture*, without societal sanction.[43] If they find an elixir, it is not likely to be valued by the society they rejected, so the possibility of a successful return is even smaller than it is for the male; *The Calling* is a tragic image of this rejection. Pratt has also noticed that the journey envisioned for the female protagonist in fiction is often accompained in its early stages by a "naturistic epiphany" which may either lead her away from any union with a male or may precede a fulfilling sexual union.[44] *Solar Music* presents a momentous symbol of such an epiphany. *The Creation of the Birds* presents the choice of a natural rather than a human collaborator.

As I have found in my own studics of twentieth-century poetry and painting by women, Varo has struck another chord in her presentation of the female's "confinement" to nurturing; it appears that the female hero must transcend the traditionally maternal use of her powers in order to continue her quest.[45] Of Varo's works, *Celestial Pabulum* is often the most compelling to an audience of women. Her *Woman Coming Out of the Psychoanalyst's* correlates with other renunciations of the Apollonian bias of our scientific culture.[46] *Born Again* correlates with images of the birth of an adult female from female genitalia.[47] *Emerging Light* correlates with a growing body of images of female wisdom and illumination.[48] Nor is Varo alone in her belief that even "dead" nature contains life within it; Georgia O'Keeffe says, speaking about her famous paintings of skulls and bones, "I don't see death in them. To me they are alive."[49]

Far from being private visions, then, Varo's paintings tap images that are shared by many women. I do not know the extent to which they are shared by men; that is for someone else to discover. I do not rule out the possibility that they are shared— that the feminine protagonist as image or person, in art or in life, may be required by both men and women to reconnect human life with the ancient natural cycle of non-human life. At the very least, Varo's paintings alert us to a strong undercurrent in the sea of modern technological images of "man's relationship with nature."

Certainly Varo's paintings offer all of us powerful images for aspects of the visionary processes of creation which have been difficult to articulate in "scientific" terms. In *Solar Music* we find an image for the sense of being in tune with powerful non-human forces; of being fully conscious, yet detached from the concerns of the ego; of acting spontaneously on behalf of others without self-consciousness. In *The Creation of the Birds*, Varo shows us the degree of self-transformation and collaboration with forces beyond ourselves required if we aspire to bring something new into the world. Finally, in *Still-Life Being Resurrected*, she shows us the Demetrian energy it will take to restore the nature we have destroyed.

Seen in the context of the female quest, Varo's final image has a tragic dimension. If the quester's return from her visionary atonement with nature could be acknowledged, even acclaimed, one wonders if Varo's final intense concentration of creative power in a symbolic act of resurrection would have been necessary.

CHAPTER 5

Diane Wakoski: Disentangling the Woman from the Moon

Perhaps Diane Wakoski's interest in the moon stems from its association with her given name. Whatever the reason, she transforms that coincidence into a remarkable exploration, over a ten-year span, of women's relationship to nature. In turn, by tracing the contours of her relationship with the moon through eight books of poems, I want to explore here some of the attitudes twentieth-century women might take toward nature.[1] Specifically, I will argue that Wakoski effectively escapes two traps set by our cultural mythology: the radical separation of the human species from nature, which allows us to oppose culture to nature; and our curious exemption of women from the human category, which allows us to devalue women and all "things" feminine.[2]

Diane Wakoski is known, and sometimes devalued, as a confessional poet whose primary concern is her relationships with men: her absent father, her (probably imaginary) suicidal brother, her several lovers, and her mythic images of masculine power—George Washington or fantasy figures such as "the King of Spain." But the term "confessional" is problematic. Wakoski's work reveals less about her life than it does about her imaginative confrontations with beauty and pain, love and rejection, greed and generosity, sacrifice and reward, or loyalty and betrayal.[3] To name her "subjects" is to place her in a long line of Romantic poets who have mythologized their lives by relating themselves to aspects of the world with symbolic importance. Her poetry is valuable to us here precisely because she reveals her thought processes in an accessible, engaging style that allows her to connect the factual and the mythical, the mundane and the visionary, in the same poem. She holds our interest in the most ordinary aspects of our common experience by placing them in unexpected, often mythic, perspectives.

Wakoski not only relies heavily on nature for her imagery, but she makes its cosmic aspects (sun, moon, planets) a primary concern—even to the point of identifying herself with the moon at times. Thus her work raises questions for the feminist critic that extend well beyond the scope of poetry. She allows us to think about what happens when a woman raised in a scientific age identifies with nature, the object of science, and to ponder whether a woman can use the traditional equation of woman with nature for her own purposes.[4] How does she, as subject, as creative agent, overcome centuries of efforts to domesticate nature and strip it of its mysteries?[5] Such issues are difficult to resolve at present because we know so little about the world-views that actually inform women's lives. While we wait for the accumulation of significant biographical and autobiographical materials[6] and for the philosophical attention that will reveal the shape of women's contribution to Western thought,[7] the questions press and multiply. My strategy here is to turn to a poet who, while eschewing the politics of feminism, nonetheless gives access to processes that may enable a collective re-envisioning of relationships between women and nature.

Wakoski's explorations began in her fourth book, *Inside the Blood Factory*,[8] with a personification of the moon as a menstruating woman. The figure is at once stereotypic and bold, playing on masculine romantic-erotic visions of the inconstant female, but insisting on the presence of blood in the image. Wakoski pictures the moon bathing, breastfeeding her children, and sending messages to her lovers, but allowing herself to be taken away at the beginning of each day. The moon is a model of amicable separateness between lovers. Particularly in the poem's final lines, "she" becomes the "Virgin" figure that Mary Esther Harding describes[9]—the female who, despite her attachments to men or children, defines her own purpose in life. Wakoski's speaker says:

> Oh how can I tell you, she loves you,
> but wants to be alone,

> wants to be in your wrist,
> a pulse,
> but not in your house. See,
> she is outside the window now.
> You look at her.
> It does not mean you should try
> to bring her inside.   [*IBF*, p. 73]

"She" is also the speaker herself. The role of the moon in the poem is to justify the speaker's stance in a troubled relationship with a lover: "What we never speak of is that/ I love too many men/ and would not be unfaithful to myself" (*IBF*, p. 72). The moon is an utterly feminine model (both motherly and erotic) for the speaker, who asks "to be rebathed/ in thick plasma each night," yet desires to be independent by day.

The poem under consideration is called "3 of Swords—for dark men under the white moon," and it appears in a series, based on the Tarot cards, that announces Wakoski's desire to "unlock" the sun and moon (*IBF*, p. 67). The card, however, portends sorrow, separation, absence of a loved one; thus the poem is an attempt to avert such sorrow by explaining the kind of love the speaker bears. She begins by sharing fragments of her dreams with her lover, claiming that his sleep is only a "ghost sleep" because he is so constantly in her dreams. In her plea for him to dream of her, she claims willingness to be totally submissive, even masochistic in her love; but she is *not* willing to be permanently domesticated. In return for granting her the love that would restore him to his own sleep, he will remain free by day to pursue his own sword-like activity. The poem is an extended image of desired reciprocity, but one wonders how, starting from such an accomodating base, the woman can possibly win her bid for freedom. Only the inexorable logic of the final image drawn from nature saves the reader from incredulity. Just as the moon maintains both her independence and her "love," so will the speaker.

Inside the Blood Factory also announces Wakoski's interest in Isis (p. 95), the Egyptian goddess who is mother, virgin, wise woman, and creator, all in one.[10] The context is a modern ritual, the patriotic cocktail party where the melting eagle in the punch bowl becomes a symbol for the speaker of how men treat nature (in the form of the eagle), out of "fear of that great mystery/ the veiled woman, Isis/ mother, whom they fear to be greater than all else" (*IBF*, p. 95). "The Ice Eagle," which Wakoski considers one of her best poems,[11] clarifies one starting point in her thinking about the relationship between woman and nature: she understands that men prefer the beautiful surface of both and that they will allow the substance of both to disappear unnoticed into oblivion, like melting ice.

As if to accept a challenge, Wakoski moves into the slippery realm of Isis in her next book, *The Magellanic Clouds*.[12] She briefly inhabits a mythic realm where human and non-human forces meet and merge, where the moon is "Queen of the Night," and the speaker *is* Isis (*MC*, p. 30) in search of the sun god.[13] Wearing the mask of a falcon, she watches over the course of history (p. 30), burns through the veil that separates her from others (p. 32), and navigates a porpoise under the ocean (p. 34) as if these were ordinary acts.

In the first of these energetic poems, "Reaching Out with the Hands of the Sun" (*MC*, pp. 28–31), the speaker insists that she can attest to the effect of beautiful women on men because she has watched men through the masks and statues of Isis. In "The Queen of the Night Walks Her Thin Dog" (*MC*, pp. 32–33), the speaker becomes the queen who walks the dog, "passing through every house," penetrating each "veil" by acts of drinking, seeing, touching, turning a key, and finally by burning through it, but primarily by "singing." Presumably each "house" is a body, and the speaker imagines that, as Isis, she is able to run through bodies with her "song" much as the moon traverses the sky. In the next poem, "The Prince of Darkness Passing through this House" (*MC*, pp. 34–35), the house is under water, and it is a place where the Prince (Osiris) comes to be with the Queen (Isis). The navigator and her porpoise also come there to be initiated into love by "burning suns, moons, stars, meteors, comets, into our earlobes and eyelids/ making our hands hold the live coals/ of commitment. . . ." (p. 35). The poem ends with a non-human pact that gives the participants the "power of fish/ living in strange waters" (p. 35).

In these poems, perhaps the moon is simply intended to symbolize a degree of passion that transcends the boundaries between male and female selves; Wakoski may be covertly describing moments of sexual orgasm and longing for them to be the rule rather than the exception in human relationships. But if so, her language and her imagination gain the upper hand, taking her into a realm where consciousness of differences within the order of things is transcended by images that eradicate those differences.[14] The significance of this for our purposes is that the customary separateness of the human and the natural dissolves, as surely as the ice eagle did. Instead of using nature as a reference point, Wakoski becomes inseparable from it, as in the book's title poem, "The Magellanic Clouds"(*MC*, pp. 110–112), in which the speaker imagines herself taking the place of the clouds. The dangers of this stance become apparent in her next book.

By *The Motorcycle Betrayal Poems*[15] the speaker and the moon are interchangeable, so that she can say:

> I am thinking about myself
> now,
> the moon,
>
> . . . .
> Moon,
> is what I am thinking about   [*MBP*, p. 55]

Even though Wakoski returns to a conscious mode of imagining, the book shows traces of her "underwater" journey. For one thing, the poems reveal her discovery of the shadow or negative side of her personality, presented in these pages in images of herself as a shark (p. 41), a tiger (p. 139), a rock (pp. 66–68), and in her desire for vengeance against those who have wronged her (dedication, pp. 16–18, 67, 158). Out of these experiences emerges the *persona*, "Lady Bank Dick" (pp. 93–97),[16] a tough cop who seduces the con men she chases, paying her own price in battered emotional health (p. 96). This is the underside of her more ideal *persona*, Diane, who is part virgin goddess and part moon, but not fully reconciled to the exigencies of her human life; to her sorrow, she "must stand alone, for any effect at all" (pp. 117–118).

In this book it is as if the scientific image of the moon has possessed Wakoski's consciousness;[17] several poems show Diane grappling with its "negative" aspects—its deadness, lack of gravity—and accepting them as descriptions of herself. In "Caves" (*MBP*, pp.116–118), for instance, she understands herself as a stony crust out of which empty cold caves have been carved. But in the poems where Wakoski allows herself to look directly at the equation of self and moon (*MBP* pp. 49–57, 62–65) instead of letting it shape her language, she finds in her own images the equivalent of "a new element" for the scientist. The moon within her then becomes "only a dead crust/ that I've learned to lift/ in each foot" (*MBP*, p. 49). By contrast, the heavy new element (potassium in her blood), which creates an internal pressure and gives her poetry, bathes her in its own blue light. The outward form (dead crust) of the moon becomes relatively unimportant (a mere sliver) compared with its unknown interior.

Each of the three poems on the moon in this book repeats the same process, starting with an equation of the woman with nature, so that the new element the scientists look for is heavy enough to drag her heart down (*MBP*, p. 49); arriving at an acceptance of the negative emotional valence of this act; and circuitously finding within the equation a way to revalue some aspect of the self. The revaluation is tentative and minimal compared with the weight of the traditional images, which dominate the book (as in "My rock doesn't crumble," p. 68; or "I am the mountain/ A frozen ocean/ behind my eyes," p. 138). But it is a potential source of strength nonetheless. Thus, near the end of "The Moon Being the Number 19"(*MBP*, pp. 49–52), the heaviness within the woman becomes nothing less than the power to create, to become the "Superior Man" [*sic*] recommended by the *I Ching*.

In "The Moon Has a Complicated Geography" (*MBP*, pp. 53–57), the speaker explores the more mundane fact that the moon disappears from view in daylight, calling it a murder, and uses it to explain how one life is superceded by that of another or by thinking about life. Her own process of thinking not only reveals to her that she is dry and invisible (like the moon by day) to her lover, but also that she and the moon have a complicated geography, which continues to exist without the light of the sun. Although the poem ends with the desire for the moisture and coolness of the nighttime relationship among the planets, a liberating idea has emerged: the moon's geography may be interesting in its own right without reference to the sun.

"I Lay Next to You All Night, Trying Awake to Understand the Watering Places of the Moon" (*MBP*, pp. 62–65) carries this line of thought a step further by imagining that the moon's geography includes "watering places," a position held by scientists long enough to cause the dark areas of the Moon to be called *mares* or seas. The speaker's daylight voice, which chides others to "burn like the sun," becomes at night a call for water; her arms try to gather the water, even though she knows

      there are no Li Pos left
  to drunkenly fall into a river
  attempting to hold its radiant face
  all night.   [*MBP*, p. 65]

These are painful, brave poems, seeking to recognize the devalued internal potential of the moon and the woman at moments when the sun-man no longer serves to highlight their complicated geography.

  The one poem in *Smudging*[18] that is focused on the moon, "The Moon Explodes in Autumn as a Milkweed Pod," (*S*, pp. 78–80), continues the exploration of the self. It begins with a rhetorical question:

  Is there a moment when the moon explodes in autumn
  as a milkweed pod
  wet wings of membrane unfolded
  clinging to the polished seed,
  sends light particles into the air
  flying to some secret reunion
  with the hidden parts of a man, woman
  keeping her secrets   [*S*, p. 78]

The "moon" that does explode in this poem is a metaphor for multiple aspects of the self: on one level, a memory of the speaker's lover; on another, an image of herself under the lover's pillow; on yet another, the development of old wings behind her own eyes; and finally, of the self who cannot fly yet (p. 79). The poem concerns an awakening of vision that gives the speaker the power to be alone with herself. She can no longer be found where the lover expects to find her. He must gain the secrets released in the explosion in order to bring her to the place of his expectations; he must follow her into the world of dreaming, where she is now comfortably alone with herself.

  "The Moon Explodes . . ." marks a turning point in Wakoski's relationship with the moon. She had personified it as a woman in order to dignify her claim to loving independence as a *modus vivendi*, and she had entered its nighttime space to form a mysterious pact. She had sought her own inner "moistness" by penetrating beneath the astronomer's descriptions of the moon's surface and by insisting on the presence of a new element within her. The object of her quest, however, remained her lover's affection. The explosion (release of new life, shower of light, revelation of secrets deep inside herself) changes her attitude toward both her lover and herself. Neither the moon nor the self can any longer be encompassed by the lover's conventional descriptions. Both explode into secret parts.

The title poem from *Smudging* (pp. 9–13), which Wakoski also identifies as one of her best, suggests that her changing sense of the moon (and nature) is indeed part of a psychological shift in her attitude toward herself. Granted that we must be careful not to assign a speaker's attitudes too literally to the poet, the changing feeling-tone of the poet's imagery is too marked to ignore. In "Smudging," Wakoski embeds an autobiographical story about her childhood fear of unruly laborers, who tended the smudging pots at night in the orange grove next to her flimsy house, into a poem that celebrates her ability to transcend that fear. The method of her transcendence is her identification with the orange prevented from freezing by the fire:

> That year
> I sought sunshine,
> looked for men who could work in a foundry,
> who were not afraid to touch hot metal.
> And I was the orange
> who began to love the dark groves at night,
> the dewy shake of the leaves,
> and who believed these burnings in the night
> were part of a ritual
> that might someday be understood. [S, p. 12]

Her transcendence is not so much a matter of renouncing her fear (of men, of fire, of disorder) as it is a matter of allowing fear to co-exist with her orange-like need for warmth, and with the meteor-like fire within her head that allowed her (both figuratively and imaginatively) to get out of her house in the orange grove initially. In seeking ordinary sunshine and identifying with a mortal fruit, she grounds herself on earth. She trusts her imagination to prevent her from getting stuck there as she was stuck in her identification with the negative moon. As she says near the end of the poem, "Thank god for our visions./ That in our heads/ we play many roles" (S, pp. 12–13). The tone of this book is as full of pleasure in possibility as the previous one was full of anger in denigration.

Dancing on the Grave of a Son of a Bitch[19] contains, in addition to the strident but also joyful poem that gives the book its title, a series called "The Astronomer Poems" which carry us further in our inquiry into possible relationships between women and nature. Wakoski's *persona* still identifies herself with the moon and claims to be in love with both the sun and the astronomer, "who defines her life" (DG, p. 20), but the identification is more conscious and playful than in *The Magellanic Clouds*. The poet has an intonation that suggests a sense of power: the nonchalance apparent in the opening of "Sun Gods Have Sun Spots" ("I don't care if you are/ the sun god,"DG, p. 38) comes from her secret knowledge that

> I am
> also a ruler of the sun,
> I am the woman
> whose hair lights up in a dark room,
> whose words are matches
> who is a lion
> on fire,
>   burning in the woods,
> at night. [DG, p. 38]

The necessity for vengeance that arises from feeling oppressed is gone. The poet can turn her wit to clever reversals of stereotypes, as when she makes women the tenders of home-fires on the *sun* and then asserts that "The first man to land/ on the sun/ will scorch his feet" (DG, p. 38). Her *persona* also has far more freedom, tentatively defined as being alone without having anyone notice (p. 29), or as not being afraid of the dark (p. 30). Now she can look for "a poet, an astronomer" (p. 24) to study *her* moon (or the contents of her overflowing trunk, p. 31). She would *like* a man who would "locate" her when she is lost in her own ideas, which glow in the dark at night (p. 34); she would like to be opened up. Some astronomer *should* love her (p. 47). Yet she also understands that "All the light in the world/ will not penetrate my darkness" (p. 47).

It may be the case, as the parable called "The Dream of Angling, the Dream of Cool Rain" suggests, that Wakoski's boat called "Diane," or her more secure sense of self, came to her through the love of a man at a time when water flooded her life and she could not swim (*DG*, p. 49). But I think it would be as true to say that her newfound sense of ease with herself and the world of this book comes from the increasing conviction that her imagination (or the kind of perception that arises when she fixes her attention on the sun or moon or smells the fragrance of flowers) is sufficient to the task of living (see especially pp. 31, 52–3). There is also just the slightest suggestion that her sense of belonging may relate to the discovery of another female figure who stands in a supportive relationship to her, an Isis who exists outside herself:

> There is
> an ancient priestess
> whose tears make the spiderlilies grow.
> She knows my name is darkness.
> We are sisters. [*DG*, p. 23]

But more of this figure later.

For the moment, it is enough to note that Wakoski's habit of thinking about herself in celestial terms produced the possibility of understanding that she too is the sun (with the capacity to scorch and singe others). There is also a new clarity about reality that comes from shifting her focus, so that the sun is simply an "old fire ball" with no intention of hurting the humans who would nonetheless melt on its surface (*DG*, p. 18). Significantly, her newfound sense of power and equanimity occurs in a volume of ritual chants stemming from her first sun poem in *Inside the Blood Factory*, where she was still looking for a key. Including poems in (mock?) celebration of the Buddha's birthday and outrageously imaginative psychological fables, *Dancing* restores the surreal image to the center of Wakoski's poetry.

In *Virtuoso Literature for Two and Four Hands*,[20] Wakoski's requirements for the astronomer go up, and the moon becomes interchangeable with the poem rather than the poet (*VL*, p. 8). The astronomer, whom she still hopes to find, must be not only a reader of poetry but also a "magician who understands/ what is invisible" (p. 25) and can turn the text of a poem into a "handful of silver,/ something solid and real" (p. 26). This occurs in a poem called "Story," in which the poet sees that the stories of her life (all lives) are like mushroom spores "dancing over the ground" (*VL*, p. 25). In another extraordinary image of the woman moon, she remembers that

>   all stories are one story,
>   leaving a woman with a handful of silver
>   that turns to moonlight
>   slips away as air,
>   disappears with the sun,
>   she standing with her own hands open
>   and poetry which is music,
>   a song which haunts us all
>   is what she has left,
>   her reality mysteriously,
>   perhaps microscopically, gone
>   to appear in some other patch
>   of damp ground.   [*VL*, p. 25]

Both realities (moonlight and woman) disappear only to appear again mysteriously, presumably in the poetry that the magician must *realize* in "a new kind of garden" (p. 25). Woman, moonlight, and poetry together become synonymous with the mysterious force that assures the continuation of life, but not with materiality itself.

Indeed, this is a book of survival stories—of Wakoski's resolution, after Richard Maxwell's death, never to fall apart (*VL*, p. 6); of her "second chance" after receiving an electric shock from a defective lamp (p. 9); of her pleasure in playing Chopin (badly) after fifteen years of not having touched piano keys (p. 17); of her reconciliation with the necessity of being alone (pp. 22, 83); of love that endures in spite of the imperfections of the body (p. 54); of mushrooms growing out of the earth (p. 60)—each survival as important as the other. They are poems of the conscious imagination, expressive of Wakoski's love of beautiful things; like Katherine Anne Porter's emeralds, they are "what comes out of life, not life itself" (*VL*, p. 35).

In *Waiting for the King of Spain*,[21] Wakoski has so loosened the ties binding her to the devalued moon in *The Motorcycle Betrayal Poems* that she can say "I once thought I was the moon./ Named Diane, I fought all day with the sun/ which was trying so hard to obscure me" (*WKS*, p. 109). For the first time, she refers to the moon as male, remembering Harry Moon from her childhood anthology of verse (*WKS*, p. 107), walking his dog much as the Queen of the Night walked hers in *The Magellanic Clouds*. And she writes fifteen poems for an unseen lunar eclipse (*WKS*, pp. 73–92), which turn up images for the moon that are separate from the self. Thus, the poet wishes the moon were more like the firm tomato, not like the old, mushy decaying one (p. 75). Or she sees it floating on the ocean in her dreams and thinks "surely salt/ kills moon creatures" (p. 92). Or it is an audience who sometimes applauds for a singer, but mostly sleeps (p. 82). These images co-exist with a poem that reaffirms the moon as one of the poet's many names (p. 86), but not as her sole identity. Somehow, without heroic acts by an astronomer or anyone else, the silver coins the poet wished for from the moonlight in *Virtuoso Literature* pile up in mounds to her knees. *Waiting for the King of Spain* is full of poems that present the poet as throbbing with life:

> In my wrists
> the salmon return every spring
> and lay their shining eggs.
> We are faithful always
> to ourselves,
> those leapings and slidings which take us
> somewhere
> we feel
> we must go.   [*WKS*, pp. 122–123]

She no longer seeks fulfillment outside herself, although she waits patiently for the manifestations of the sun to appear in others as well as in herself (pp. 26–27, 44–46).

At this point, Wakoski returns to the goddess imagery of her first books. She addresses "Daughter Moon," one of her most beautiful poems, to a woman whom she sees as Penelope, "in the version of the story which gives her/ power over dark seduction" (*WKS*, pp. 137). In Homer's *Odyssey*, Penelope uses her art as a ploy to keep her suitors at bay, weaving her tapestry by day and undoing her work at night. Wakoski steps into the myth, as Margaret Atwood did in her "Circe/Mud Poems,"[22] in order to imagine what Penelope does with her nights after the ritual unweaving is accomplished. In Wakoski's version of the story, Penelope moves, with the moon, to "a shrine of eucalyptus"

(*WKS*, p. 137) where Hecate takes Penelope's head in her hands (p. 138). Dressed in silver before an altar, like yet unlike the moon, the woman in the poem stands alone, worshipping simply by learning to "see in the dark" (p. 138). In so doing, she touches reality in a way that terrifies her suitors who hope to catch her off guard. From her perspective of reverence and contentment, marriage would seem like "a struggling fish" (p. 138), and all lovers would be interchangeable. The poet sees Penelope—and herself in the act of imagining her—as a witch (pp. 137, 139), and she sees her poem as a means of re-establishing a "Broken line of contact" (p. 137). She identifies with Penelope's love of that "golden invisible man" (her Odysseus, Wakoski's King of Spain) whose mysterious light is "Only shown to women slip-ping down/ soft silver stairways/ of themselves" (*WKS*, p. 139). Again the image depends on the fact that the light of the sun is reflected by the moon at night and so is known then only through the moon. The attitude of worship celebrated in the poem is a withdrawal into the self, from which vantage point both darkness and light are known. The figure of the witch re-establishes the broken line of contact between the female self and her inner source of light at night, just as the poem establishes a line from Hecate to Penelope to the poet and her friend to the female reader. In its title, the poem also affirms the scientific theory that the moon was "daughter" of the earth.[23]

In spite of Wakoski's negative pronouncements on the woman question, this is a feminist poem. That is, without denying the ultimate worth of the masculine principle (Odysseus or the King of Spain), but with no illusions about the general run of men, Wakoski creates a bond of sisterhood with the protégée of Hecate who sees in the dark and is confident of what she sees. The qual-ities she worships are no longer projected onto men but are visi-ble in herself and in the world she observes when men are absent. The power of illumination the poet has attained in her quest is generalized to *women*—or at least to those women who are will-ing to slip down the "soft silver stairways/ of themselves" (*WKS*, p. 139).

In a section of *The Man Who Shook Hands*,[24] Wakoski narrates a literal journey in search of bald eagles in Wisconsin. The climax of the story is her arrival at the Mississippi River where the eagles are perched on the ice floe. On one level, the poet appears to be freer than ever before to turn her remarkable powers of observation outward to the external world. But her journey is mythical as well, taking place as it does astride another of her improbable beasts: a black camel "heavy-coated against/ the winter snow" (*MSH*, p. 79), born perhaps in the convivial aftermath of a Lebanese dinner. She writes as one of the "new Americans," whose job it is "to invent new animals,/ new elements" (p. 79). She is, by her own admission, "a good navigator/ thru any world where I can ride/ those magical beasts" (*MSH*, p. 79). The reins she uses to steer them are her intimate knowledge of nature's rhythms (p. 80). And the objective of this, as of all her journeys, is

> to find
> like some mythical goddess
> a satisfaction,
> a fulfillment,
> a partner, another rider
> of black camels
> for these trips.   [*MSH*, p.80]

Instead, she finds only the eagles. And within the narrative, she becomes a magician or goddess, showing the birds two tableaux of the moon. To her sorrow, the landscape of the moon is no more real to this endangered species than it is to the American for whom the birds serve as totem. Nor do all the capsules of the space program seem likely to *realize* the moon; that is the poet's office—to offer "an un-/ traditional/ Ride" to an unknown realm. If we had wondered what she would do with the power she gained in her trans-human explorations, Wakoski lets us know her intent to use it on behalf of the non-human elements of the landscape.

To sum up Wakoski's progression on her journey to the moon and back, after the explosion of the moon-pod, the poet/*persona* became capable of surviving without the affection of a lover. As she began to understand the depth of her own mystery and realized that no one would be able to penetrate her darkness completely, she began to understand the darkness within her as the source of her power, her light, her poetry. As the pulse of life within her became stronger, the illumination more radiant, the sense of connection with other women more compelling, she became more free to observe the world and her fellow creatures with compassion.[25]

We might say that she learned to value herself by identifying deeply with the moon. She learned to value both the moon and herself less romantically by adopting the perspective of the astronomer. She learned the limits of astronomy in the veritable explosion of the goddess-like imaginative source within her. She also felt the limits of her desire to shine alone in the empty sky. She resumed her mortal lineage, retaining the magician's and the poet's facility of making the invisible visible. She acknowledged her female ancestry as a source of strength. She became a naturalist—a defender of nature—for the sake of defending herself.

This was not an easy journey. Her first strategy, evident in "3 of Swords," combined two characteristic ways of viewing nature in our culture: the "romantic" idea of moon as a lovingly feminine force, and the "materialistist" view of it as a physical phenomenon with no special power over human life. The strategy was destined to fail because the male lover to whom she addressed the poem had nothing to gain from accepting this compound of loving independence.

Her second strategy, that of imagining herself to be a nature goddess, may have produced a momentary sense of power, but it did not produce a permanent change in her sense of self-worth. She still had to deal with the problems of living a human life in a cultural setting. Not the least of her difficulties was having to live with the devalued aspects of nature after she had admitted her identification with them.

Wakoski got herself out of this predicament by mining science and by playing on the possibilities it offered for revaluing nature. In the case of the moon, she countered the image of the moon's unappealing surfaces with the image of water, drawn from the historical controversy over the origins of certain sea-like features of the moon. She used the disagreement about the moon's origins and its present composition for her own purposes, denying the theory that it is cold and dead, and affirming the possibility of its embodying a new element not known on earth.

At first, she embraced the information from the early space missions without giving up her identification with the moon. This position had its dangers. It is one thing to say, somewhat vaguely and poetically:

I am a cloud
dust on the desert,
fog over the waters,
gases in the sky   [*MC*, p. 112]

It is quite another to say,

Oh the caves of cold iron ore
I'm made of are so
empty/   [*MBP*, p. 118]

A less brave woman might have shrunk from the specificity science offered her, fearing its negative implications. A less clever poet might have taken fewer liberties with scientific hypotheses. But Wakoski used the idea of a "missing element" to sponsor a search for the missing element in herself.

Her next step was to explore the complicated geography or unused potential of herself, using the multiplicity and productivity of natural phenomena as touchstones. This exploration led to her insistence on her equality with the sun and with the men who had devalued both the moon and herself in their failure to notice what lay beneath the surface. With equality came responsibility. Thus she made herself responsible, through the medium of poetry, for the perpetuation of life in nature.

Wakoski did manage to use the traditional equation of woman and nature for her own purposes. At first it was little more than a crutch to develop a concept of herself. Later, however, the balance shifted completely, and she became a "naturalist," interested in preserving endangered phenomena outside herself through her imaginative powers of revealing reality to others. The transformation in her perspective took place because she dared to immerse herself in that endangered reality called "nature," challenging both the separateness of "man" from nature and the exclusion of "woman" from the human realm.

CHAPTER 6

Léonor Fini: Re-envisioning La Belle Dame sans Merci

In an extraordinary set of three paintings completed in the years 1968–1971, *Capital Punishment (La Peine capitale), The Sending (L'Envoi)*, and *The Strangers (Les Étrangères)*, Léonor Fini shows a red-haired goddess, naked and accompanied by priestesses, receiving a sacrifice, wrapping and tying a child-sized cocoon-shaped bundle, and peering into a large bowl of human body parts. Seen by themselves, the paintings must be horrifying to many, belonging as they do to pre- or post-Christian ideas of appropriate activities for gods. Even within the context of Fini's *oeuvre*, they are mysterious and jolting, bespeaking destruction in a way that her earlier goddess figures do not. Through her earlier work, however, we can begin to understand Fini's visionary meaning. By tracing the development of her images in this essay, I hope to show how the paintings in question may prepare us to meet the strangers of the new "world" currently under construction by feminist thought—a world no longer based upon the principle of sacrificial love.

Although Fini is virtually unknown in the United States outside of the small circle of art collectors,[1] the quality of her painting needs no defense. Always independent, in her life and her work, she nonetheless participated in group shows with the most famous surrealists and received acclaim from European artists and intellectuals throughout her career. No doubt her preoccupation with the human figure prevented American critics entranced by Op, Pop, and Minimal styles from noticing her. Whatever the reasons for their neglect, her story now deserves to become part of our standard repertoire of knowledge about the arts. She is one of the most talented and productive women in the art world.

Fini was born in Buenos Aires[2] of a cosmopolitan mother and a Latin father, whose tyrannical behavior soon sent Léonor and her mother to the home of her maternal grandparents in Trieste, where they remained despite her father's attempts to kidnap her. At age five, she drew a chicken laying an egg in a casserole,[3] but she received no special training in art. After a bout with rheumatic conjunctivitis in her teens, during which her eyes were bandaged for two months and pictures flooded her mind, she made drawings, paintings, sculptures, and marionettes so obsessively that her mother conceded to her desire to be an artist.[4] In fact, she was kicked out of school at about that time, age fifteen,[5] and was subsequently self-educated in the context of the very rich environment provided by her mother's family and their friends. As a child, she had rummaged the Adriatic coast for skulls and skeletons. As an adolescent, she frequented the morgue to draw cadavers. In art, she developed a taste for the pre-Raphaelites, Gustave Klimpt, and fifteenth-century German and Flemish painters. At seventeen, she participated in her first show in Milan and received her first commissions for portraits. Apparently she moved to Paris in the mid-thirties,[6] became associated with the surrealists immediately, and began to show her work: in New York at the Julian Levy Gallery (presented by de Chirico and Paul Eluard) in 1937, and in Paris the following year. During the period from 1943 to 1946, when she left Paris first for the island of Giglio and then for Rome, she began to illustrate books. In 1945 the first of many monographs entitled *Léonor Fini*, a work by many hands, was published in Rome (Ediziones Sansoni). In 1947, after she had returned to Paris to form a commune, she began to design scenery and costumes, including masks, for ballet and the theatre. In 1951, a film based upon her work appeared, and during the next few years she added costumes for films to her long list of credits. From 1952 to 1957, she participated in another communal living situation near Anzio in Italy, camping on Corsica in 1954; there she began the paintings of female "guardians" for which she is famous. After 1957, she returned to Corsica for several months of each year, eventually establishing a residence there. Her works continued to be exhibited in Paris, London, New York, Brussels, Lausanne, Hamburg, and

other cities. In 1972, a retrospective of 100 works took place in
Japan, while fakes of her paintings began to appear on the streets
in Paris.[7] In her interview with Nina Winter, Fini comments that
she understood at an early age that she would have to "revolt" in
order to live as she wanted, that it would be better to make her
own money than to depend upon someone else, and that she
could not live with just one person[8] or in just one place. Since the
early seventies, she has divided her time among Paris, Corsica
and a country home in the Loire valley.

A list of her associates over forty years reads like a *Who's Who*
in European literature, theatre, visual art, and criticism.[9] It is a
measure of her originality that her *oeuvre* resists all their labels.
For example, in a public letter to Fini, Jean Genêt complimented
her on her perfect draughtsmanship and advised her imperti-
nently to take her place in the Louvre alongside Dürer, Cranach,
and Holbein by becoming a classical portrait painter. In the final
paragraphs of his letter, he praised her portraits of shaven con-
victs (whom he sees as possible projections of what he would
have liked to become) for their "cruel kindness," their embodiment of the "deep melancholy of men for whom nothing is left
but to organize as a *fête* a life which stands on the far side of
despair."[10] Genêt was a powerful writer and an influential critic; a
less daring and original artist of either sex might have taken his
advice. Fini did not. Instead she moved on to create her series of
guardian figures, scarcely human in their demeanor (certainly not
portraits), who reverse Genêt's expectations in their explicit presentation of women in connection with the symbols of rebirth.

Neither Genêt nor any other of Fini's admirers succeeded in
containing her feminist vision. Gloria Orenstein has shown how
she departed from the idea of woman held by the male surrealists,[11] and Silvio Gaggi has effectively demolished the wishful
positions of Marcel Brion and Constantine Jelenski that her work
is feminine but not feminist.[12] Nevertheless, in their oblique
way, Genêt and other friends understood the tensions in Fini's
work. Consider this comment by Genêt:

> If you hold so fast to the bridle of the fabulous and misshapen
> animal that breaks out in your work and perhaps in your person, it
> seems to me, Mademoiselle, that *you are highly afraid of letting your-*
> *self be carried away by savagery*. You go to the masked ball, masked
> with a cat's muzzle, but dressed like a Roman cardinal—*you cling*

> *to appearances* lest you be invaded by the rump of the sphinx and driven by wings and claws. Wise prudence: you seem *on the brink of metamorphosis*. [emphasis mine][13]

There can be no doubt now, looking back on Fini's career, that she was indeed on the brink of metamorphosis in 1950. And I will argue that in her work over the next two decades, Fini went well beyond the kind of *sauvagerie* or wildness Genêt had in mind as she penetrated the world of appearances in three distinct stages of her painting. First, however, I must quickly sketch in the stage that preceded this metamorphosis.

Silvio Gaggi says of Fini's first phase, the most derivative and surrealistic, that the women who dominate her paintings are protagonists in unexplained ritual activities, while the men are passive, even asleep.[14] What no one has said, however, is that several of these figures (for example, *Small Guardian Sphinx, Petit Sphinx gardien*, 1948) belong to an easily identifiable tradition of goddesses who preside over animal life and are often represented as animals. "The Lady of the Beasts," as Erich Neumann calls her, is a goddess of a matriarchal era in human history close to its early instinctual phases; but she symbolizes a purposive, active ordering of multiple drives.[15] She stands between the "manna" figure, who dominates Fini's work in the mid-fifties, and the chthonic figures (goddesses of darkness, night, water and earth) who appear in the first phase of her work (notably in *Chthonian Deity Espying the Slumber of a Young Man, Divinité chtonienne guettant le sommeil d'un jeune homme*, 1947). The lifegiving quality of the ancient chthonic goddess is epitomized in the swamp, while her permanence is symbolized in stone.[16] Thus both the famous *Sphinx Regina* (1946), which shows a decaying marsh, and *The Ceremony* (*La Cérémonie*, 1938), in which two young women tend a stone altar or oven, belong to goddess worship in its earliest phase. They are tributes to fertility with little consciousness of human concerns. The paintings of the sphinxes are different in that they are images of the emerging power of consciousness. In *The Shepherdess of the Sphinxes* (*La Bergère des Sphinx*, 1942), the beautiful but dependent sphinxes must be herded by a woman who has risen above them. In *Small Guardian Sphinx*, however, the sphinx is a powerful figure in her own right, surrounded by symbols of the Great Goddess (the tree, the triangle, the sistrum, and so on), regal and proud. As Fini's self-portrait *The Ideal Life* (*La Vie idéale*, 1950) makes clear, Fini imagined that she was assuming some of the powers and responsibilities of the Goddess herself. In that painting, now familiar from Karen Petersen and J. J. Wilson's *Women Artists: Recognition and Reappraisal*,[17] she wears the horned headdress of Hathor/Isis (later identified with Demeter and, by extension, Aphrodite), and is attended by cats. The dark circular image behind her has twelve radii or branches, suggesting the tree of life from which both the sun and the phoenix are born in Egyptian myths concerning Hathor (see frontispiece).

If it is true, as Fini told both Gloria Orenstein and Nina Winter, that she always worked directly from the unconscious without conscious thought of symbols, then the first stage of her painting is a remarkable testimony to Neumann's idea that an individual may recapitulate human history in her personal development. For Fini seems to emerge from the realm of the goddesses who supported human life, in the hunting and agricultural eras of our pre-history to a psychological realm dominated by the goddesses of spiritual transformation, which immediately preceded the Christian era. The psychological portraits that Genêt valued so highly belong to a transitional period from 1949 to 1952.

From 1952 to 1958, in what I call her second stage because of the changes in her imagery, Léonor Fini was preoccupied with the bald priestesses who assume positions of authority within the pictorial space as manifestations of Isis/Demeter/Ceres—guardians of the egg and the phoenix, bearers of human life, spinners, seamstresses, and custodians of the veil of illusion. A painting of *Cérès* (1954) is the only one that shows the female with hair; in this case it is more like corn silk, long enough to reach the floor and thick enough to cover most of Ceres's body. It seems reasonable to think that the bald figures are priestesses enacting various dimensions of Demetrian power. Although I do not see them as androgynous, as Gloria Orenstein suggests[18] (the symbols of the feminine are too pervasive, and the lack of hair too easily understood as evidence of their dedication to the principle they represent), I do see them as embodiments of the ancient ideal of the virgin. That is, the female in this period of Fini's work is clearly "the woman who belongs to herself."[19] She is not entirely human, any more than her sphinx counterpart was. Her skin is too smooth, her face too expressionless, her breasts nippleless. She is distant and controlled, unrelated to any specific time or place, yet she performs the tasks we associate with nurturing. She is attached to nature, particularly when she appears in the form of a mermaid (in *The Veil, Le Voile,* 1956), but her frequent appearance with wings or winglike garments marks her as a spiritual figure. *The Thinker* (*La Pensierosa,* 1954) is an important painting in the series, partly because our cultural vision of a female thinker is so undeveloped, and partly because the darkly leotarded body seems more butterfly than human under the iridescent winglike cloak and train, which is surely the many-colored robe of Isis. Her face is wholly hidden from view; her hands form a cup that resembles the traditional headdress of Isis. Creator, mother, protectress, Isis was also knowledge or wisdom—in Mary Esther Harding's words, "the innate, inherent capacity to follow the nature of things both in their present form and in their inevitable development in relation to each other."[20] The image is important because it answers Yeats's famous question in "Leda and the Swan" ("Did she put on his knowledge with his power")[21] by reminding us of a figure who had both knowledge and power without being sexually violated to attain it. Fini's images of this great embodiment of manna are notable achievements, entirely consonant with the aims of modern feminism in that they reveal the feminine roots of our civilization; but they are not yet "savage," precisely because the civilization has managed to co-opt and confine the Great Goddess's power and knowledge.

In 1958, the last of Fini's priestesses appears in *The Friendship* (*L'Amitié*), in which she is shown sleeping with her head resting on the knee of a conventional skeletal figure of death. In *Love without Condition* (*L'Amour sans condition,* 1958), a vaguely similar female recedes into darkness as the skeleton fixes his gaze upon her. All the evidence of Fini's biography and paintings suggests that a momentous transformation occurred in her life at that time. Gauthier comments that after 1956, Fini began a series of drawings featuring sorceresses, each with her own devil and death's head, and that she was heard uttering raucous cries upon their completion.[22] In 1957, Fini discovered the pleasures of underwater diving at her home in Corsica. About the same time

her technique and style of painting underwent significant transformation, as she moved away from her highly polished surfaces
to rough granular surfaces representing the substances of her
themes: webs, vegetal pulp, animal cells, and membranes.[23]
From 1958 to 1963, Fini abandoned the stately priestess/goddess
and turned to the forms of earth itself, forms which mysteriously
contain humanoid faces and shapes. The central ritual that governed her pictorial world was no longer the tending of an altar
depicted in *The Ceremony* (1939); instead, it became her own
gathering together of animal, plant, and mineral forms, as in the
painting of the same name from 1960.

   This crucial third stage of Fini's development (Gaggi calls it a
watershed[24]) began auspiciously, in spite of the figures of death
that preceded it. In addition to *Place of Birth* (*Lieu de naissance*,
1958), which Gaggi interprets as an image of chthonian
metamorphosis rife with death and life,[25] Fini produced an image
of two partially human forms with expressive female faces and
hair, emerging from eggs or egg sacs, in a desert landscape (*The
Emerging Ones, Les Devenants*, 1958). Instead of emerging herself
from the marsh ground of the maternal sphere, Fini envisioned
other forms emerging.

   Her work then took an infernal turn. *Geological Memory* (*La
Mémoire géologique*, 1959), resembling stalagmites on the floor of
a cave, suggests a scene in hell through its fiery color and
humanoid shapes. *The Threat* (*La Menace*, 1960) takes place in a
lush green landscape but features two ugly bulbous forms, one
orange and decaying, the other pink-turning-purple; the reality
of metamorphosis is grim in this case. In *The Fermented Earth* (*La
Terre fermentée*, 1961) the fiery earth sends up shoots which may
result in the dense green vegetation at the very edge of the picture space, but the image suggests a lot of fire for a little warmth.
Another painting called *Chimera* (*Chimère*, 1961) shows a sooty
black face peering from a hole surrounded with brilliant red. The
image is decidedly vaginal, and the appearance of a tiny head at
the bottom of the hole encourages me to think of the painting as
an image of birth. A chimera can be either a daydream or a
monster, perhaps both; and during this period Fini may well
have wondered if her dreams would produce only monsters.
They did not.

   After 1961, the mood of her painting changes dramatically, becoming more beautiful without losing vitality. Daylight and lush new blue and green vegetation dominate her canvasses until 1964, and there can be no question about the activity taking place. The earth, its shadow, its water, its flowers are giving birth to human forms. Markedly different from the human woman who emerges from the water in *World's End* (*Le Bout du monde*, 1949) to assume conscious life, the beings in the later series of paintings are still partly unformed, partly vegetative, only one step from being flowers or dewdrops. The human head in *The Awakening of the Flowers* (*Le Reveil des fleurs*, 1962) is pushing a huge oriental poppy. We seem to be witnessing the birth of a new race of human beings. The process is profoundly irrational,[26] "savage" in the sense of being totally uncivilized. These paintings are not susceptible to symbolic decoding in the way that either of the previous stages of Fini's work are.

In *Fires and Ashes* (*Feux et cendres*, 1963), a distinctly female form becomes upright. In *The Sun Meal* (*Le Dejeuner de soleil*, 1964), a fattened version of this woman receives a diaphanous covering and a floral hat; versions of this will recur through the seventies, alternating with Fini's visions of nude women with brilliant red hair. One curious exception to this pattern is the image of a red-haired reclining woman so stiff she could be dead, whose dress, in fiery shades of red with animal shapes and textures, dominates her entire being. Called *The Useless Dress* (*La Toilette inutile*, 1964), it may be less related to Fini's love of costumes than to her need to explore the forms her "new" woman might take.

It becomes quite clear in *Héliodora* (1964) that a new goddess has emerged in Fini's life, and perhaps in human history. Fini's comment that the painting was "about" the disappearance and return of her cat may indicate that the red-headed vision was related to her previous images of Isis/Demeter.[27] The prominence of flower, fruit, and vessel imagery in her later work suggests a Demetrian presence. Fini had undergone a Persephone-like journey herself in the previous six years, and the appearance of a strawberry blonde called *Hécate* in 1965 (who recurs as a death angel and *la belle dame sans merci*) supports the notion that Fini was exploring new forms of the familiar goddess's energy. I am convinced, however, that Fini's experience was more momentous than a rediscovery of Demeter. The titles and images of her paintings in 1964 and 1965 indicate a significant "breakthrough." A room is unsealed. Beings from "the other side" are seen in silhouette. That which has been absent returns. A pair of floating female figures in blue appear through a window of a bygone summer. A secret feast is celebrated. Later in 1965, the redhead comes out of a life-sized keyhole, steps off a mysterious evening train, or "guards" the multicolored, floral-shaped stemmed glassware said to be the "source." The discovery of Heliodora marks another shift in Fini's style (and the fourth stage of her painting). She returns to the distinct rendering of figures but incorporates the rich texture and lush color of her third stage into her new work, which now features interior dream landscapes. We may infer that Heliodora is, likewise, a figure that incorporates earlier visions, yet transcends them.

While there is no precise mythological predecessor for Heliodora, we may surmise that Fini has in mind her own version of the sun-god, Helios. Without losing any of her feminine taste or demeanor, the goddess has taken on the masculine (sun-like) as well as the feminine (moon-like) power. Explicitly, she now assumes a war-like stance.[28] That she is a goddess becomes apparent in the early seventies, particularly in the three paintings (to which I called attention at the outset of my essay and to which I shall turn shortly) where she assumes power over the transitions between life and death.

Fini's paintings after 1964 have a ritual character somewhat like that of her first stage. Often a female appears out of an unlikely place to watch over either a prone male body or a symbol of female fertility. Still, the differences are crucial. The beautiful young male (called Phébus, another name for Apollo, a sun-god), whom the woman watches, now has a feminine face and demeanor and is clothed in a dancer's costume (leotards with a loose, diaphanous shirt). He may indeed represent the young man that Fini prefers,[29] but he is still the one who is visited by the death angel (*Without Doubt It Concerns the Death Angel, Il s'agit sans doute d'Azraël*, 1967). The attitude of Fini's women toward their "guardian" tasks has changed; they are capable of a coldness that did not appear in her first stage. In explaining *The Accomplished Fact (Le Fait accompli*, 1967), Fini said, "in a café full of girls, the outline of a man is drawn on the ground in chalk in the same way that police mark out the position of a dead body. It is in this outline that the witch rebels against the social opacity of men."[30] Indeed, in the *Anatomy Lesson* (*Leçon d'Anatomie*, 1966), a group of four young women look with total dispassion at a disgusting blue cadaver that is undoubtedly male. In *The Treatment* (*Le Traitement*, 1972), however, Hecate seems to be giving a manicure to a wretchedly deformed man whose head is enclosed in a glass box. Not only is Fini a feminist, as Gaggi claims, but in the late sixties she became the kind of feminist who tolerates only feminine males, or males under female power.

Fini's world in her later work (after 1963) *seems* more related to ordinary social reality, because she portrays explicit interior spaces; but it remains a visionary world nonetheless. It is a modern or future world where women and beauty predominate, instead of being a reference to a pre-historic world; Fini's vision is deeply psychological and startlingly new.

All the indications are that Fini's women have experienced "a separate reality"—that they are in touch with forces beyond themselves which cannot be shown in the "real" space of the paintings, but which lie beyond the windows, doors, and screens that figure so prominently in Fini's backgrounds. Perhaps their shared awareness accounts in part for their self-assured nudity or partial nudity; it is as common for them to be unclothed as elegantly clothed and hatted. They seem to exist in a realm where they set the rules, a reality that Victor Turner would call "liminal."[31] Despite the frequent elegance of their surroundings, the tasks they perform are not entirely pleasant. For example, *The Fitting* (*L'Essayage*, 1966) shows a tall armless blonde woman being wrapped and bound to an easel with string by another woman while a third looks on. *The Beautiful Lady without Mercy* (*La Belle Dame sans merci*, 1969) disdainfully carries her tray of potions past a woman whose blackened foot, in its soaking solution, is distorted out of shape. These women talk with each other (in *The Return of the Absent, Le Retour des absents*, 1965) and they may even be lovers (*The White Train, Le Train blanc*, 1966), but their attention is fixed on something besides human camaraderie. If they are involved in a ritual of rebirth, as the Demetrian imagery still suggests, it is not at all the sort imagined in *The Oval Woman* (*La Dame ovale*, 1959), in which rebirth is symbolized by human pregnancy.

In *Capital Punishment* (*La Peine capitale*, 1969), a dead goose is

Capital Punishment (La peine capitale), Léonor Fini, 1969, oil,
47-½'' × 47-½''.
Courtesy of Léonor Fini.

about to be beheaded by a kneeling woman in leotards and a
short dress who looks reverently at the red-haired goddess who
is naked apart from her blue stockings, and whose legs are spread
to reveal her brilliant pubic hair. A standing woman in an elaborate white dress and hat holds the knife. The setting is bare apart
from a tablecloth on the redhead's table/seat. This is the first
separation of woman from animals to occur in Fini's *oeuvre*, and
it is a sure mark of the difference between the Great Goddess of
her first two stages and the goddess who is apparently exacting
capital punishment of the symbolic goose. She is no longer the
protectress of the old natural order, which is already as dead as
the goose before the sacrificial knife touches its neck. In fact, the

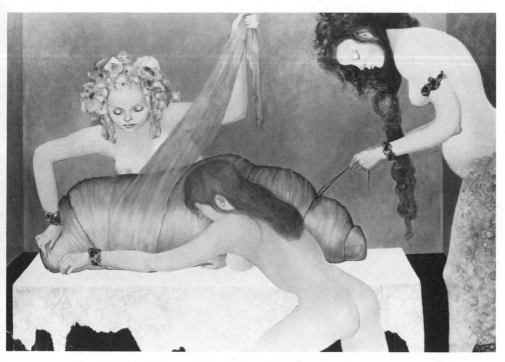

The Sending (L'envoi), Léonor Fini, 1970, oil, 35-¹/₁₆'' × 51-¾''.
Courtesy of Léonor Fini.

"sacrifice" seems cruel because the goddess's attention is focused elsewhere. The act is nearly meaningless.

In *The Sending* (*L'Envoi*, 1970), the goddess and her *guérillères*[32] are seen again in an interior space, whose only defined element is a table two-thirds the length of an adult human being. They wear matching wrist bracelets and the redhead wears an arm bracelet as well. Totally absorbed in their work, they are carefully wrapping a bulky child-sized object in a shiny translucent material. The redhead is tying the strange being, in the same way that the tall woman in *The Fitting* was tied. Fini offers us no other way to know the content of the bundle being sent, so we are thrown back on our memories of cultures that sent their unwanted children or aged citizens out to die, or we are encouraged to interpret the image visually. The strange object begins to resemble a phallus at the end where the goddess is tying it—not in color certainly, but in shape. As Fini's most compelling and energetic

The Strangers (Les étrangères), Léonor Fini, 1968, oil, 31-⅞″
× 46-¼″.
Courtesy of Léonor Fini.

image of women working together, *L'Envoi* is an important work. Both leader and warriors are ready for action, and no
viewer, however mystified, can escape the sense of purpose they
project. Fini does not criticize her protagonists in these paintings,
nor does she glorify them as she did the guardians. She merely
presents her dreams as if they were an accomplished fact.

The Strangers (Les Étrangères, 1968) is probably the most disturbing of Fini's paintings because its import is all too clear. In
this work, the braceleted goddess (with auburn hair now, but red
pubic hair) leans over a large glass bowl containing body parts
and prepares to stir them up. Another elegantly dressed attendant
stands ready with her spoon as well, though her facial expression

shows dismay. Another woman stands by, looking off into space, and two others are seen in the distance walking through a barren landscape with hats like overturned baskets on their heads. The painting is full of activity, but the gestures of the three main protagonists do not embody the same degree of confidence we find in *L'Envoi*. The new goddess seems somewhat less sure of this new process of creating life than she was of the process of "sending" the old on its way.

We will have to await the publication of new exhibition catalogues to see what happens to Heliodora in Fini's dreams of the late seventies. In the meantime, we cannot turn away from these images of a goddess who differs so significantly from the Great Goddess of Fini's early work and the visions of many a contemporary painter or poet. This figure is "savage" in a way that Genêt did not foresee. In his letter to Fini, he implied that she was holding back (clinging to fantastic images) from fear of being consumed by animal (sexual) instinct. The "wings and claws" he saw lurking behind the paintings were part of his sense of man's degradation—the knowledge of which would show through in Fini's portraits and make her a great existentialist painter at the end of the western tradition. He hoped she would abandon the appearance of civilization and steep herself in the "primitive" in order to revitalize the civilized perspective on the human being. But Fini's dreams took her well beyond any ordinary encounter with instinctual life. They took her first into the realm of the goddesses whose order preceded her own, out of whose partial destruction and partial transformation our civilization grew. Then they took her into the non-human vegetative and mineral realms, out of which human life evolved before there was any thought of civilization. And finally (remembering that Fini may dare to go further), her dreams brought her to a vision of life whose basic mythic principle is not love, but energy. As she has said, "All my painting is an incantatory autobiography of affirmation expressing the throbbing aspect of being; the true question is to transpose onto canvas the sense of play."[33]

Yves Florine's comment that her paintings of young girls in the early seventies involve the recreation of Eve, then, could not be further from the truth.[34] For Eve was bound, in a way that Fini is not, to the idea of love. The women and girls in Fini's

dream world of the late 1960s and early 1970s are not asexual by
any means (as her virgin goddess/priestess of the 1950s may have
been, apart from child-bearing), but they are not essentially loving, even toward other women, as Fini's comment on *The White
Train* makes clear:

> There are two girls, alone; one is like a beautiful cow, very white
> and sleepy, whereas the other, much more alive, much more alert,
> pulls the window-shade. She does not know what she will do
> next, if she will kill the other or make love to her.[35]

I am quite convinced by Fini's own repeated statements of her
tendency toward sorcery—her profoundly anti-social stance—
that her paintings are not so much a critique of present-day
Western society or an effort to establish models for a new society.
Instead they are visions of the profound change in human psychology required by the collective feminist dream of female
power. They are visions of a world where it is not the primary
obligation of beautiful women to be merciful and protecting. It is
a vision that makes us strangers to our old accommodating
selves. Indeed, the new human being over whom Heliodora
watches may be only a collection of parts awaiting the magic
formula that will allow her to come to life. Fini's "sauvagerie" is
nothing less than a revolutionary vision of woman. Her process
of seeing, and her incantatory affirmation of what she has seen,
offer us preparation we will surely need if we are to meet the
strangers of this new world.

Part Two
Collective

Visions

We do a lot of collective thinking, probably more than any other social species, although it goes on in something like secrecy.

—Lewis Thomas, *The Lives of a Cell*

CHAPTER 7

Mythic Patterns in Contemporary Visual Art by Women

My approach thus far has been to probe the lives and works of individual poets and visual artists who illuminate aspects of the process of "mythmaking" as it is taking place in contemporary culture. But I have left aside the question of the extent to which the process is collective rather than individual. Having completed all the above essays in draft form, and having wondered how these poets and visual artists related to others, I decided to spend a year in an open-ended search through poetry and visual art by women for any evidence of a collective project. My hunch was that any pervasive shift in cultural myths should show up in those bodies of images. I thought that poetry and visual art would offer fertile fields for such activity because of the persistent romantic notion that poets and artists see into and beyond their culture. Further, both forms were undergoing a renaissance that allowed expression of visionary thought in a variety of styles. Both arts were fueled by the women's movement of the 1960s; yet neither offered women easy entry into the establishment of culture (just as most of the prestigious museum shows still featured men, most of the anthologies of poetry ignored all but a handful of women). It seemed possible that many women in these two media would occupy the "boundary" position that Mary Daly recommended for the re-visioning of culture by women.

Since large slide collections of visual art by women seemed most likely to give me an overview of images created by women, I decided to begin with them. Unlike my previous studies, this one had to be confined to the United States for practical reasons;

within that constraint, I chose the collections to represent as many areas of the country as possible (the northeast, the south, the midwest, the southwest and the west) and to represent different methods of collection (juried and non-juried, individual, institutional, and collective).[1] I began by looking for known mythic images: goddesses or gods (*e.g.*, Isis); biblical or heroic narratives (the Adam and Eve story); or images that have been attached to specific myths (the veil, the snake). But I took notes on each work, or in large collections on each artist or type of work, to have a record that might show other patterns. I began by looking at painting, but found that it was fruitless to separate one medium from another in the traditional manner; painting spilled over into collage or printmaking, or even into three-dimensional "earthworks," with regularity. In order to guard against any tendency to impose a pattern on the material, I considered works by roughly a thousand artists.

Of course, I did not embark on the project with an "innocent eye." I was cognizant of Lucy Lippard's groundbreaking descriptions of recurrent tendencies in art by women: central imagery, layering, fragmentation, collage, autobiography, and so on.[2] I had also read Eleanor Munro's provocative suggestion that nature is to the female artist as the female body has been to the male artist.[3] Further, the powerful symbolic landscapes of Varo and Fini had sensitized me to images that I might otherwise have regarded as purely idiosyncratic—for example, the hybrid, the most surprising and intriguing image my study revealed.

The pattern I discovered is a network of related images or clusters of images—Lévi-Strauss would call them "bundles"[4]—concerning the transformation of one form into another, and amounting to a re-evaluation of "nature," both our own and the world's. On one level, the pattern involves explicit images of transformation: the mask, the seed pod, the veil, the shield, the magic box, the shadow, flight, metamorphosis. On another level, it involves the investigation of our relationship to animal life and the creation of hybrid forms, which are not restricted to the animal realm but spill over into the vegetable and mineral as well, as nature is remythologized in female forms. On a third level, it involves appearances of "The Goddess," by which is meant the vision of power and energy incarnate in female form, which seems to have preceded the Greek division of it into multiple goddesses and the Hebrew attempt to nullify it. The most expansive cluster concerns nature in its "cosmic" guises—the stars, the planets, the galaxies, the gases, the tides, the clouds, light itself.

The process of discovery was inductive. At first I was simply taken aback by the amount of work produced by women that showed a preoccupation with nature, either as landscape or as source of inspiration for abstraction or narrative. Although "the image" and "landscape" had become acceptable once again in the art world,[5] they did not appear in significant proportions in the gallery or museum shows I had seen. Only gradually, after reading the statements from dozens of artists, did it occur to me to link the images of nature with the images of transformation in the manner I propose here.

Whether the pattern I describe has or will have the significance of myth is a matter for history to decide (a myth is always a complex affair, operating in many spheres of life simultaneously); but it is not unlikely. Nature has always been a force that humankind needed to mythologize, and continues to be despite the efforts of modern science to remove it from myth's purview. The ecology movement of the sixties and seventies brought the subject to our attention again without resolving it to anyone's satisfaction. The image of ourselves as "masters" of the world gave way to the image of ourselves as part of an "ecosystem." But what part? Are we simply "motile tissue specialized for receiving information—perhaps . . . functioning as a nervous system for the whole being"?[6] Or are we masters, like it or not, because of our responsibility for its preservation? And what relevance do these images have to women?[7] The need for images that work to give our lives a sense of direction in these matters, as those of myth always do, could not be more apparent. I think that such images are beginning to occur in works by women.

Throughout this project I have struggled with our cultural tendency to assume that all members of a minority group are alike. Nothing could be further from the truth in regard to women artists, whose individuality is manifest in the multiplicity of styles, materials, and ideas in their work. By seeking to clarify our collective vision rather than simply proceeding individual by individual, however, I am hoping to make the point that in the process of addressing the issues of female experience, women are

creating work that reveals "the whole nature of the human condition."[8] In the light of current psychological and biological research, it seems possible that women's thought may differ from
men's. But even if this is so, it will not be taken seriously until a
body of such thought has emerged and proves complex enough
that it cannot be undermined by any one woman's mistake or
idiosyncrasy. For in spite of our individuality, we remain convinced that we share something more or less tangible called
"female experience." Of course, not all women paint or write out
of this experience all the time; yet we think of it alternatively as
our treasure and our cross. Certainly it is one resource for understanding the world. Perhaps the time has come for it to serve
as the basis for a coherent myth.

In a recent article subtitled "The Contribution of Feminism to
the Art of the 1970s," Lucy Lippard argues that the features she
described as common to women's art in her book *From the Center*
are "surface phenomena": "feminist and/or women's art is
neither a style nor a movement . . . . At its most provocative and
constructive, feminism questions all the precepts of art as we
know it."[9] Lippard calls this art "an ambitious art" because it
challenges the modernist tradition by offering "a socially concerned alternative to the increasingly mechanical 'evolution' of
art about art." The feminist values she finds expressed in it include "collaboration, dialogue, a constant questioning of aesthetic and social assumptions, and a new respect for audience."[10]
Thus the distinctive contributions of feminist art to the 1970s are
public rituals (such as those by Mary Beth Edelson); "public
consciousness-raising and interaction through visual images, environments, and performances" (such as *Womanhouse* by Judy
Chicago and Miriam Schapiro); and "cooperative/collaborative/
collective or anonymous artmaking" (such as Judy Chicago's infamous *Dinner Party*).[11] Lippard is interested primarily in what
distinguishes feminist art from other modern movements and
styles, and I find her characterizations just.

Although I share many of Lippard's interests (in the work of
Mary Beth Edelson, for example, or in the relationship between
art and fantasy or dream), my focus differs from hers. I am interested in the continuities of vision embodied in subject and
form, regardless of the status of the work in the art world. I
suspect that the body of work created by women in the 1970s

will turn out to be an ambitious act of rethinking cultural terms in addition to challenging the art world.

In this essay, I hope to lay out as clearly as possible the related sets of images I see in works by women, and to uncover the meaning of the larger pattern by interpreting the works of a few artists who may be said to be the anchors for a tradition—not of women's art or feminist art, but of women's vision of the place of the human in nature. Not that men are precluded from having such vision. That they are *not* will turn out to be part of its strength. It could therefore be a shared pattern. But my argument will be that the defining features of this vision emerge naturally from female experience of the human body in the world— that is, from the experience of the person as having permeable boundaries.

I. TRANSFORMATION

Ellen Lanyon's paintings offer a useful starting point because they deal with all the elements of the pattern I am describing here. In her paintings of animals (*i.e.*, a rabbit, a butterfly, a snake, a goose, a chipmunk, and a frog) spilling out of a teacup, she carries the idea of transformation to its logical extreme; and in her recent focus on exotic species of plant and animal life, she makes a case for ecological responsiveness. If she does not deal directly with hybrids, she does often create images in which one animal is packed in on top of another so tightly that they seem to be parts of one organism.[12] Lanyon is a Chicago artist, trained at the Art Institute and at the University of Iowa in the war years, whose work is just now receiving the national recognition it deserves. Since the early 1970s, Lanyon has been concerned explicitly with magical change. Envelopes go into the *Deceptive Change Bag* and come out as butterflies; or birds emerge from a cup into which tea has been poured.[13] Or birds and animals from the pictures on the walls of a fully-furnished doll's house come alive and escape through the windows; the remaining furnishings follow, and finally, in the last frame of the drawing called *Doll's House Illusion*, a life-sized woman emerges from the house with a smile.[14]

Boxes, cups, baskets, cottages, chairs, tubes, spheres, pouches, thimbles, mirrors, fans, kites, disembodied hands, flowers, thistles, flames, reptiles, animals, birds—Ellen Lanyon uses all these

Bewitched Teacup, Ellen Lanyon, 1970, acrylic on canvas, 48″ × 60″.
Collection of Mr. and Mrs. I. J. Markin, Chicago.
Courtesy of Ellen Lanyon.

and more to create a "visual poetry" whose images combine into narratives that extend beyond the artist's conception and "invite audience participation in transformations and unfoldings."[15] All the life processes are magical to Lanyon; the drama of stage magic is the drama of the world. In large part, it is a drama of animal instinct erupting from within well-ordered walls and asserting "squatter's rights" to civilization. Until the late seventies, animals appear in Lanyon's work to clarify the human condition. Recently, however, she has begun to document the appearance of birds and plants in their natural settings. As she has done so, her theme of transformation has taken a negative turn, as the live birds are presented beside porcelain ones portraying the threat of mass reproduction. No longer surrogates for the human, these beings are important in their own right, and as her concern for them grows, her belief in transformation seems to diminish.

Lanyon's favored images turn up so frequently in works by other women that one begins to wonder about lines of influence. But in my experience, the pursuit of influence turns out to be remarkably fruitless. To be sure, there are feminist networks in the art world. One can see, for example, the influence of Mary Beth Edelson's 1976–77 workshops at the University of Minnesota and The College of St. Catherine on the Minnesota artist Gail Jessop Diez. And each of the cooperative feminist galleries (A.R.C. and Artemesia in Chicago, A.I.R. and SOHO 20 in New York, W.A.R.M. in Minneapolis) seems to have an "identity" of its own that suggests considerable cross-fertilization among its members. This is as it should be. For the first time, women are experiencing some of the benefits of belonging to the art world. But the ideology of the art world in the sixties and seventies favored the "new," the distinctive, the idiosyncratic; and women did not escape its pressure. Many of these artists turned, as did Lanyon, to their own life experiences rather than to art for their inspiration.

Lanyon does not deny the links between her work and that of other women. She knows that her imagery comes from "a state of mind" that is related to "the way one is physically and chemically constructed, which creates a need to use a certain kind of image vocabulary." She also thinks that the "bank of registered details from one's life" may be different for a woman because, in our social life, a line has been drawn between male and female sensibilities, so that "different objects are used by men and women."[16] Yet she is uncomfortable with the notion that *only* a woman could have created her works. Her position seems well-chosen to me. That is, the evidence of my study does suggest that the experience of living in a female body at this point in history does often produce a certain set of images (many of which occur in Lanyon's work); yet nothing precludes the images being shared by men.

Many of the images of transformation I found most prevalent

have been identified by Lucy Lippard; it remains for me to interpret their meaning here. Take the mask, for example. Susan Dannenfelser, a San Francisco sculptor, thinks of it as "both a façade and a form of personal transformation."[17] What does this mean? In her mixed media piece called *Ascending, Descending*, a realistic porcelain hand cut off half-way to the elbow holds a fan which depicts a circus balancing act, while a smiling metal mask peers over the fan at the circus and at us. The performer in the center appears to be descending the struts of the fan, while on the left a large spider-like creature arches in mid-air from a line; another performer is using a similar line to gaily ascend a hoop, which is held by a fantasy figure similar to the good witch of story books. The tiny mask is a crucial element in the work, hiding the identity of the onlooker, yet making the fantasy of success and failure a subject for public inspection.

The piece perfectly expresses the meaning of art for Dannenfelser herself, who works primarily in clay and plaster to create art which simultaneously explores symbolic material in an autobiographical way and creates a "visual retreat" from the hard edges of the contemporary world (and of art). Art is both an exploration and a retreat. We have not moved far from Ellen Lanyon's preoccupation with magic.

What about the veil? The image occurs so often in so many media that it requires several examples. In Texas, Mary Fielding McCleary veils her *Heron*, a skyscape with the moon and an indistinct bird, with a grid-like design of tiny rectangles.[18] The effect is to create a sense of mystery. Jantje Visscher from Minnesota uses distorted surfaces as veils; behind them she makes abstract drawings related to landscape. She says that her work has to do with the way people respond to unexplored spaces and also with "the inevitability of change." Indeed, her titles, *Soaring, Gathering Speed, Rising, Dark Journey*, and so on, suggest the idea of the quest so prevalent now in work by women.[19] Abstractions by other artists, including Vivian Fishbone and Ruth Jacobsen, both from New York, present the idea of veiling in the context of life forces as different from each other as human generation and the black hole.[20] Visscher's colleague Barbara Benson uses the veil explicitly, along with the hat-helmet, the fish, the shell, and horns, in a medieval vision of spiritual growth.[21] Fiber sculptor Rosemary Mayer has a series of veils dating from 1971 that are intended to suggest her images of great women: Hypatia, Egyptian mathematician and inventor; the de Medici women of Italy; Galia Placidia, the last Roman Empress of the West. Mayer describes her majestic work as "color in space as transparent films, one over, under the next. Layers behind. Color on paper as lines of color, then fields of lines, overlaid. Unexpected colors juxtaposed and earthly."[22] Nancy Worthington's kitsch sculpture goes a step further in identifying the veil as belonging to Isis in one assemblage when she puts a piece of fogged textured plexiglass over the soft inner body of a cradle.[23] In some cases, then, the veil is a way of participating in the world's mystery, or even of attaining power; in others it is a device to protect an inner space.

The shield seems to function in a similar manner. In her *Sacred Shields/Healing Images*, Chicago artist Justine Mantor Wantz presents a series of works that are really invocations to the Goddess to protect the female spine. The images, in richly textured handmade paper with inlaid pulp and print collage, are by turns like the amoeba, the tree, the butterfly, the pussy-willow. *Moon Offering*, for example, suggests, in its four separate layers of paper, wood, and stone, the complex connections between the spine to be healed, the earth where it is "rooted," and the crescent moon which crowns the entire image.[24] The ritual healing power of the works is the result of several factors: they are made directly from the earth's substance and incorporate its forms which are sacred to the Goddess; the central image of the spine corresponds to the tree of life; and the works display the beauty of the goddess, at least as she is known through her symbols. In a work from an earlier series, Wantz shows an eye splitting open and "spilling out its glistening contents." She explains, "The underlying meaning is a positive one, indicating the opening of a woman's innermost self." The shields are for display and for protection; no matter how beautiful the precious "stones" of selfhood are, they cannot enter the world without safeguards.

The same doubleness persists in the image of the chair, another recurrent image of transformation; it is both a symbol of power (a throne) and a way of presenting the various stages or estates of life. In the work of Jackie Shott (d. 1980), the chair is a statement of female reclamation of power. Her sculptures are called *St. Jeanne, Demeter's Throne, Sappho's Stool, Aphrodite's Pillow*. Shott also hoped to reclaim the tree as a throne that belonged to the Goddess in her many manifestations. And in doing "chair portraits" of her friends, she sought to transform the Goddess's energy into human forms.[25]

Camille Billops's stunning chair called *The Mother* is an assertion of a power that is not altogether benign or controllable. The black and white figure is wounded in her womb, but still fierce in her mien.[26] Linda Kramer's chairs deal with decay rather than power, tracing the course of life "from birth, through youth and maturity, to death and dust."[27] One provocative series shows six porcelain chairs: a large chair evolves into smaller and smaller ones which finally collapse; in another series, the chairs grow until they too collapse from their excess weight. Kramer's interest in the ruins of previous cultures, shared by many of the women I studied, gives greater scope to her work; her references extend beyond their psychological bases to achieve cultural import. Thus her boxes (or caskets) for a young girl or an old lady or *Yellow Birds* suggest the demise of classes of life rather than of individuals—just as Lanyon's ceramic reproductions of birds next to the real ones send a chill of fear for whole species down one's spine.

Seed pods appear in Kramer's work, perhaps as signs of hope in an otherwise disintegrating environment. In Shirley Federow's sculpture, similar concerns with the pod, the chrysalis, clothing, and armor (or, more precisely, with "the borderline between clothing and habitation") evolve into handsome fiber sculptures in homage to the "weaving, seaming and caring that are so great a part of women's role."[28] She says that her image "remains mask-like, humanoid, but is a metaphor for renewal." *Muslin Queen III* is both cloak-like and vaginal, theatrical and spiritual. The artist works with castoffs and mundane materials and turns them into vestments, so that tokens of times past become symbols of metamorphosis.

All these images of metamorphosis have a special place in the work of women in the late twentieth century, not because they are new or exclusively female images (they are not), but because of their relationship to a belief in transformation that extends beyond the personal to the realm encompassed by the word "nature." Over and over again, the same connection occurs. After completing her exquisite metaphysical gold and silver drawings of seeds called *Genesis*, Minnesota artist Hazel Belvo turned to a series called *Transfusion Quartet*. Based on the experience of waiting while someone close to her had a blood transfusion, the images took on metaphysical significance until psychological and physical reality seemed inextricably connected. Belvo says, "I have wondered if the shape of our brain cells and nerve endings are those shapes we pull out of the darkest corners of ourselves and make visible."[29] How great is our power to change reality? This is the philosophical and religious question that informs many of the explorations by women in the art of the 1970s. I will argue that far from being "surface phenomena,"[30] the images and choices that recur in this body of art are meaningful parts of an emerging vision based on the experience of being female. Joanna Frueh once said of Ellen Lanyon that she creates "a form of humanism self-centered but turning outward to embrace universal as well as personal truths."[31] The same might be said of others treated here. It remains for us to articulate what humanism looks like when the defining self is female.

II. HYBRIDS

Animals abound in the body of work I am describing—animals of all kinds: birds, dogs, cats, fish, bears, wolves, horses, gorillas, even a sea turtle. Often they embody human qualities and serve to dramatize the human condition, as they do for a time in Ellen Lanyon's work. At other times they seem to replace the human, as in Wendy Eisenberg's drawing *Big Brother*, in which a parrot holds a tiny globe in its claw and seems to lick or peel it with its beak.[32] Still more often, the artist seems to acknowledge the animal as an ancestor. Linda Gammel does this in a series of striking photographs showing the shadows of exotic African animals in a Victorian attic. If our ancestry has been relegated to our attics along with other unwanted baggage, the artist will not let it rest there. A slide show on the self-image by one of Gammel's colleagues in W.A.R.M. suggests that she has gone even further; apparently the photographs are intended as self-portraits.[33]

The plethora of animals, in a decade whose most prominent style was color field painting, is less strange than the presence of countless images of the hybrid—by far the most unexpected and striking cluster or bundle of images I found. Hybrids appear in virtually all of their possible forms—as conjunctions between two animals or plants, between the human and the animal or the plant, and between animal, vegetative, and mineral forms of life—in traditional guises or in purely idiosyncratic forms of the artist's choice.

In Joan Danziger's sculpture, for example, the mixture is animal and human. Her well-known *Magic Sam* is a genial white plaster-of-paris being with a frog head and rubbery frog-like hands, seated in a tree-like chair, wearing a blue shirt with butterflies on it and one soft-toed shoe. *Sam* straddles two large sets of images in Danziger's work.[34] One presents life as full of circus-like tricks and deformations: *e.g.*, a zebra-like trapeze artist, birds on bicycles, a cow or an owl blowing a horn, a horse playing drums. The other set presents life as full of magical spirits and demi-gods or goddesses, as in *Philomela*, who stands near the entrance to the National Fine Arts Collection in Washington as if to make the point that mythological beings have not disappeared from modern art.

These impulses toward commentary and magic also serve to define the limits of work by other artists. Joan Brown, for example, presents a *Saga of the Greedy Cat* in seven paintings.[35] The cat, who rides a bicycle or paints or drinks like a human being, is foiled by two genii, one with a tail, the other with an elephant's trunk, and is finally devoured by a large purple snake. According to the title of the series, the cat is devoured by his own greed in a world "peopled" by hybrid genii who do not perform the saving functions of genii. Michelle Stone makes a similar comment in her fragile untitled sculptures of bird-people or double-headed horses. She thinks of human beings as beasts and asks us to confront our illusions or delusions of identity through her hybrid forms. "Mother evolution brings instinct," she says, "magically creating aggression and confusion, making arbitrary relationships." She presents us as "playing with time and extinction, matter and energy, trying to live with forces and limits, struggling for liberation."[36]

Stone's perspective is less harsh than Germaine Richier's in her post-war *Batman*, in which the human is but a deteriorated, emaciated shadow figure.[37] Other artists who seem to work in the genre of social commentary are June Leaf with her *Butterfly Lady*,[38] and Chicago artist Eleanor Speiss-Ferris, whose painting

Wild Horses, involving disembodied clothes chasing after horses' heads on sticks, leaves one wondering who is wild and what is alive.[39]

But Danziger's interest in magic and mythology is even more widely shared. In Hedda Saltz's work, the human form is left out altogether in a plethora of mixed animal forms. For example, in *Time Out*, a white animal with a single horn and a long mouse tail also has a frog face (not to mention green and blue hands).[40] Other paintings with titles that refer to the time of day or night, to birth or to dreams, are filled with partially familiar animal forms (not-quite alligators, lobsters, fish, cats, bulls, frogs, whales, and birds), often emerging from womblike spaces and depositing eggs everywhere and anywhere. The only signs of human civilization are occasional lighthouses, whose red and gold lights reiterate the colors in the circles of eggs. One cannot escape the image of fertility which, because of the fanciful quality of the images, refers both to the human imagination and to the animal world. Saltz's titles include references to the earth and to occasional pod and leaf forms; they embrace the fecundity of plant life as well. The paintings work by the curious logic of dreams wherein logical systems are reversed or scrambled: *Flower Dreams* is full of cat forms; *Earth Music* features the white whale.

These works could easily be the unconscious acknowledgements of the extent to which our bodies are "assemblages" rather than the separate and totally evolved specimens we had imagined. Lewis Thomas, in discussing the relevance and perhaps the imaginative necessity of the animal myths and bestiaries that contain so many hybrids, says this in their defense:

> The new phenomenon of cell fusion . . . . denies the importance of specificity, integrity, and separateness in living things. Any cell—man, animal, fish, fowl, or insect—given the chance and under the right conditions, brought into contact with any other cell, however foreign, will fuse with it. Cytoplasm will flow easily from one to the other, the nuclei will combine, and it will become, for a time anyway, a single cell with two complete, alien genomes, ready to dance, ready to multiply. It is a Chimera, a Griffon, a Sphinx, a Ganesha, a Peruvian god, a Ch'i-lin, an omen of good fortune, a wish for the world.[41]

The magic in these paintings may be wiser than these artists know.

Many women seem to share a preoccupation with the bird and

the bird woman. This phenomenon deserves more attention because of Ellen Moers' hypothesis, based on fiction, that the more
feminist the artist (writer), the more fierce the bird.[42] That
would not seem to be the case in visual art, in which the bird and
its hybrid forms are nearly always benign, no matter how
feminist the artist. In Suzanne Jackson's paintings, the bird takes
the form of a hen-woman in a large acrylic wash called *It Is Our
Woods*; casts a huge shadow in *Clouds*; rises out of a black person's
head-tree in *American Sampler*; sits on a branch (which is also the
arm of the mother figure) in *When I Wake Up*. In her paintings
the bird is nearly always present in a symbolic and magical, if not
always mythological, form. For her, as for many other women,
it is symbolic of transformation—part of her process of "freeing" herself in "a continuous cycle of rediscovering who, in fact,
I really might be."[43] Betty LaDuke's ritual mask of a bird woman
called *Cry the Inner Bird* reinforces Jackson's meaning.[44]

LaDuke's concern with ritual is shared by Houston sculptor
Roberta Harris, who makes five-foot totems of fish and human
forms, sometimes combined with images of the heart, the star,
and the crescent moon. These images recurred frequently in the
work I saw, most notably in the assemblages of Betye Saar.[45]
The element of magic is clear, totems being the well-known
means of honoring one's ancestors. Countless other images, such
as Lee Bontecou's untitled three-dimensional animal with the legs
of a mammal, a head with a trunk that also forms a beak, and a
textured surface made to look like feathers, partake of the same
impulse.

Not all the hybrid forms involve animal life. Other common
occurrences are images of trees growing out of the human
female's hair,[46] or, conversely, of earth giving birth to humanoid
or even human forms.[47] Sylvia Sleigh's *The Water Lily*, for
example, shows a realistic image of a woman emerging from a
life-sized plant.[48]

Perhaps the most powerful of these images is the series in clay
by Mary Frank, in which the female being emerges only partially
from the folds of earth presented in thin sheets of clay. As the
curator of the exhibit called *The Painterly Print* has said of her
monotypes: "They are Daphne: woman turned to tree; or they
are waterlily, poppy, laurel, and amaryllis; leaf turned into
flower."[49] It would be just as accurate—and more true to our

River Figure, Mary Frank, 1976, clay, 19″ × 12″ × 14″.
Courtesy Zabriskie Gallery, New York.

experience of Frank's works in clay—to speculate that the earth turns into woman.[50] In *River Figure* (1976), for example, the strong diagonal lines of the woman's earth-skirt, formed in ridges by waves on sand, encourage us to think of this as a figure in motion. The feet supporting that motion, however, are primitive, only a step away from being webbed structures. And the arms are more like fins or wings. The skull opens at the back, suggesting in still another way the figure's connection with previous stages of evolution. All these details are in striking contrast to the woman's thoroughly human mid-section and beautifully formed, thoughtfully expressive face. In the presence of this sentient, active form, we witness the recapitulation of a momentous process of transformation.

In the body of work I have been discussing, the direction of the process of transformation does not seem to matter—from the human to nature or the reverse; one form spawns another which retains traces of the first, in a cycle where distinctions between levels in the "great chain of being" are unimportant. What is important is the process of metamorphosis, with all its magic or mystery. Even when the images seem to comment on human foibles, they do so gently, without demeaning the animal, plant, or earth forms they use. Whether they are made for the purpose of instructing human beings about their origins or for the purpose of courting change by magical means, the images of hybrids seem to be good omens for the future.

III. WOMAN AND NATURE

Several pages ago, I said that I found in Ellen Lanyon's paintings a sense of respect for animal and plant life as sacred—in her case, a desire to describe the endangered species so enchantingly as to move the viewer to bring them back to life before it is too late. This sense of the sacred in nature permeates works by women at this moment in time, taking several different forms of expression. Sari Dienes's transitory paintings in snow, for example, are an "attempt to reveal the inherent intelligence in things." She says, "Everything has mind, spirit, intelligence; I honor these in everything and do not separate myself as a human being from them." She prides herself on taking a stand "that will permit nature to be revealed." Her position that "nothing is so humble it cannot be made into art" has allowed her to make art from animal bones, from xeroxed images, from sound, from archeological rubbings, and from all manner of found objects, long before these ideas came into vogue. Her resolve not to "imitate" nature is part of her philosophy that "all the forces working in nature are alive"; none is to be frozen in art. Her effort is to participate in a process of transformation that is inherently and productively mysterious.[51]

The idea is stated differently across the country, according to the background and focus of the artist. Halina Rusak bases her organic abstract paintings drawn from the land on a belief that "positive human values come from things that are wild and free," and adds, "This is not a sentimental statement about flowers, but rather a symbolic interpretation of life forms."[52] Joyce Lyon, whose paintings of shadows cast by plants on her studio floor explore the subtleties of form dissolving and distorting in light, says,

> My work always connects to the organic, to the land, to the cycle of growth and decay, and through that metaphor, to a vision of our lives in their small, proper, cyclical position. An iris in full bloom carries with it its own death. Which does not minimize its exaltation.[53]

Yvonne Pickering Carter's abstract expressionist paintings, based on a recollection of waves pounding over rocks in Dakar, come from her feelings of tenderness and thankfulness toward nature. As she said in her M.F.A. thesis for Howard University,

> Man is not above nature, but a part of nature. Earth, water, sun and man are parts of the world; the white pigment [of paint] supplies that supernatural force upon which life rests. The rocks are only particles of a vast bed covered by the liquid blanket of a natural force.[54]

Nature, not mankind, is the measure of all things.

This idea is perfectly expressed in the architectural drawings and sculptures of Patricia Johanson. Her works are literally models of how to use forms from nature—even the structures of organisms seen only under a microscope—in order to live unobtrusively on earth. She describes one womb-like design, called *Foliose Lichen (Peltigera Collina)/Plan for a Park with Pools and Fountains*, in the following way:

Lichens are dual organisms, composed of two kinds of plants: a fungus, which provides the structure and determines the form of the plant body; and green algae, which provide the fungus with food. Foliose (leaf-like) lichens attach themselves to the substratum, and expand outward from the center as they grow. The park should become the poetic equivalent of the plant.[55]

In designing any of her organic structures, she faces "the same sort of challenge that nature does." And if her designs seem difficult to grasp, yet strangely familiar, it is because they are "pieces of an infinitely complex puzzle, . . . the embodiment of an underlying order immediately recognizable, but not necessarily understood."[56] In contrast to Sari Dienes, Johanson does try to imitate nature, but in such a way that the mimesis is only visible from the air once the object is built or made.

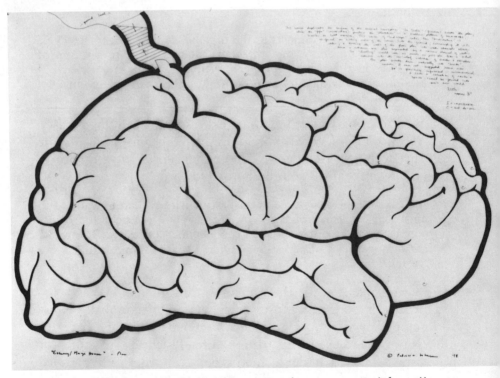

Estuary/Maze House-Plan, Patricia Johanson, 1978, ink, 30" × 42".
Courtesy of Rosa Esman Gallery, New York.

Her sense of the place of the human in nature is indicated by her willingness to use the cerebral hemisphere as a plan for a structure called *Estuary/ Maze House*. The brain's "gyri" or convolutions create "a shallow pattern of hummocks, similar to salt marshes." That is, the brain is the pattern for the image; yet the

> "dwelling" should look as much as possible like a tidal estuary with its low-relief network of creeks and marshes. The plan breaks down naturally into "suites," however I have not suggested room uses. It is gloriously unfocused—and such a collection of routes and spaces should be formed into one's own world.[57]

Brain, house, marsh—the three are one.

Johanson shows no particular consciousness of the way her forms often suggest the sexual organs of the female body. In this she is somewhat atypical. Often the symbolic exploration of life forms takes place in explicitly female terms. Certainly this is the case in Ana Mendieta's works. Her color photographs of earthworks called *Silueta*, (*Silhouette*), for example, show outlines of the female body rendered in paint in an ancient ruin, or on snow, in succulent plants on sand, in leaves and vines on rocky soil, in lightbulbs against dry grass, with fire in a stump, and so on. There are several recurrent figures: one is a goddess symbol with elbows raised and forearms up; another is the many-breasted Diana of Ephesus; another is the mummy. Lucy Lippard has said that the silhouettes "leap vertically from the earth like growing organisms or merge with earth to confuse human and other roots."[58] But there is no disorder here—no embarrassing mistaken identity. Instead we have a range of images, some bright, some dark, about the various relationships, some exuberant, some depressed, the female body has with various landscapes. And all of them, even those rendered in ashes or burned images, hold the promise of renewal in them because of their setting. Nor is William Zimmer's reduction of the works to vaginas just; they are not uniform in their meaning—not mindless identifications with nature that obliterate conscious life.[59]

Michelle Stuart's earthworks are less obviously concerned with the female body, although not less intentionally so. As Lucy Lippard said in her essay on "A New Landscape Art," there is in Stuart's paper pieces "a clear relationship between the female body and Mother Earth. . . . not only in the physicality, the

rhythmic rubbing of the working process, but in the tactile surface that results."[60] Stuart's work now deals increasingly with the
interwoven strata of earth and civilization apparent in archaeolog-
ical digs. A huge piece in the 1981 Hirshhorn exhibit called *Stone/
Tool Morphology* uses color photographs of sites, with soil from
each site rubbed on paper images of tools found there. In viewing
it, however, one is less concerned with the scientific correlation
of images than with the rhythm of relationships established by
color and texture; indeed, one is primarily aware of the artist's
respect for the earth. As Stuart said in her *Return to the Silent
Garden*, "The earth lives as we do, elastic, plastic, vulnerable.
. . . [Rock is] bone under flesh of soil in the body of earth. . . .
Stone is self. Return stone to land."[61] Instead of imagining a
Garden of Eden where a god from outside of nature breathes life
into a chosen species, she returns to a garden of stone.

Often, as in Judy Chicago's well-publicized case, images from
nature that are related to the female body, such as the orchid or
the butterfly, are used by women to describe the "blooming" of
the self or to re-evaluate the beauty of women. But in just as
many other cases the artist uses her sensitivity to nature, perhaps
the result of centuries of identification of the female body with
nature, in order to reach beyond the realm of the human.

There can be no doubt now that Georgia O'Keeffe is the latter
kind of artist, much as she has staunchly resisted symbolic
readings of her paintings. When she spoke of bones, for example,
as equivalents for the quality of *life* in the desert, she became the
visual and philosophic precursor of many artists treated here:
"The bones seem to cut sharply to the center of something that is
keenly alive on the desert even tho' it is vast and empty and
untouchable—and knows no kindness in its beauty."[62] She
stands in awe of nature, recognizing its power; yet she continues
to stand.

O'Keeffe's works, whether abstract or representational (and
sometimes they are both), have always been "objective correla-
tives" for states of feeling, perception, or insight; but their focus
has been on the world. In the earliest phase of her maturity as an
artist, roughly 1915 to 1919, in South Carolina and Texas, she
did abstractions based upon images in her head or in the sky over
the plains. If *From the Plains I*, an oil actually completed in 1919
after she had gone to New York to live with Alfred Stieglitz, is a

representative example of her vision at that time, she did see the
world in terms of the female body, combining breasts and eggs
and jagged shots of energy within a womb–like space.[63] Given
the infamous preoccupation with sexuality in the twenties, it is
no wonder that her paintings were reduced to erotic ciphers with
no thought of their general significance as visions of nature.
Thus, Paul Rosenfeld wrote in *The Dial*:

> Her art is gloriously female. Her great painful and ecstatic climaxes
> make us at last know something the man has always wanted to
> know. . . . All is ecstasy here, ecstasy of pain as well as ecstasy of
> fulfillment. . . . Her masses are . . . like great concentric waves
> that spread outward and outward until they seem to embrace some
> sea. . . . The entire body is seen as noble and divine through
> love.[64]

O'Keeffe's fury over this and similar interpretations of her intent
led her to reject all psychological interpretations of art. For of
course she was not painting a defense of the female body. She
was painting a vision of the world seen through her own eyes.

Though we may abhor the excesses of the critics then, we
must not forget that the paintings were immediately and uni-
versally received as statements of a female sensibility. Stieglitz
himself was at the head of the pack proclaiming that O'Keeffe
was "like Eve—the first woman who could genuinely paint what
it was to be 'Woman.'"[65] Nor can we forget how O'Keeffe herself influenced others like Meridel LeSueur to "have confidence in
'the woman experience,'" or how she told Michael Gold, then
editor of *The New Masses*, that she was trying with all her skill
"to do a painting that is all of women, as well as all of me."[66]
When Lewis Mumford said that she was

> the poet of womanhood in all its phases: the search for the lover,
> the reception of the lover, the longing for the child, the shrinkage
> and blackness of the emotions when the erotic thread has been lost,
> the sudden effulgence of feeling, as if the stars had begun to
> flower, which comes through sexual fulfillment in love. . . . [67]

he may have been right about the energy behind the paintings,
but not about their "subject." Instead of inventing a visual vocabulary for the expression (or veneration) of heterosexual love,
she was inventing a vocabulary for envisioning nature.

We will never know the direction her experiments with abstraction might have taken without the critics' interference, because in the mid-twenties she turned away from her sweeping organic landscape images to the so-called "realistic" portraits of flowers.[68] Instead of making the expanses of light and space intelligible by reference to images of gestation, she sought to make the all-too-familiar and therefore unnoticed flower visible through enlargement. Instead of noticing the flowers, of course, the critics noticed the vaginal forms. Rather than ask why the vaginal form was significant, they assumed that the flower was a "cover" for what she really wanted to paint. But there is no evidence of repression in O'Keeffe's adult life. If she had wanted to paint vulvas, no doubt she would have done so, just as Stieglitz photographed her genitals. She wanted to paint flowers, but through her female mind's eye, which was particularly sensitive to the folds, the softness and the recesses of their forms. As she consciously revalued the flower, she subconsciously revalued the female; neither was to be seen as an object for human use. Both were to be appreciated as valid forms of life.

Her third great period, from the late thirties to the mid-forties shows a similar development as she struggled to come to terms with the desert. She succeeded in doing so when she used the vaginal pelvis bone as a window to the sky, or when she juxtaposed the skeletal rib cage to the hills seen in labial or clitoral colors and folds.[69] Not until the late fifties or sixties, when she turned to painting rivers seen from the air and vast expanses of clouds from the ground, did the feminine forms become recessive visual elements in the paintings. When Zelda Fitzgerald saw a retrospective of O'Keeffe's work in 1934, she commented on the "cosmic oysters."[70] She was probably referring to the shells O'Keeffe did in the twenties, but her adjective was remarkably perceptive. In a sense, from the beginning, all of O'Keeffe's major works were cosmic.

The initial focus on the "erotic" quality of O'Keeffe's painting was due in part to the assumption that her relationship with Stieglitz was the dominant concern of her life. Feminist attention to her vaginal forms in the seventies marked the recovery of female imagery from the realms of pornography and advertising. One can understand O'Keeffe's rejection of both kinds of interpretation. Indeed, if we look closely at the correlations between her life and her work, it seems likely that her awakening sexuality, important as it was to her development as an artist in the teens and twenties, was not the most important force in her career. Her great breakthroughs ("peaks") came during periods when her drive for independence was strongest. By her own admission, the charcoal drawings of 1915 that brought her to Stieglitz's attention came from a desperate feeling that if she could not do, say, or be what she wanted without hurting someone, she would have to paint what she wanted to paint in order for her life to amount to anything. Her flowers, which took Stieglitz completely by surprise, emerged from her effort to define an artistic identity in a milieu where her work had been pigeonholed by critics or discounted by her fellow artists because of her liaison with Stieglitz. Her third distinctive development in vocabulary came in reaction to the near disintegration of her relationship with Stieglitz, and the necessity of gathering the strength to survive alone. The breach began in the late twenties and was exacerbated both by her discovery of New Mexico and by the developing intimacy between Stieglitz and Dorothy Norman. The tangible result was a nervous breakdown that kept O'Keeffe in the hospital for several weeks and sapped her artistic energy for months. After barely resisting a liaison with the black writer Jean Toomer, she once again made a commitment to her art that saw her through the last years of Stieglitz's life. After his death when she was fifty-nine, and after the inevitable stress of doing honor to his work, there was the challenge of establishing a permanent home in New Mexico. Each phase of painting for which O'Keeffe is known corresponds with a struggle for survival.

In her book *Literary Women*, Ellen Moers found that a number of otherwise dissimilar novelists (George Eliot, Georges Sand, Willa Cather, and Isak Dinesen) had created remarkably similar landscapes in their novels, representing a "complicated topography" of female genitalia; further, she found that the writers used them "for the purpose of solitary feminine assertion."[71] Certain lands, she says, have apparently "been good for women . . . open lands, harsh and upswelling, high-lying and undulating, vegetated with crimped heather or wind-swept grasses, cut with ravines and declivities and twisting lanes."[72] And "whatever component of sexuality enters into these literary landscapes, its inspirational residue is of the highest, not the lowest order."[73] I am intrigued by the way O'Keeffe's life and work seem to fit the fictional model presented by these writers—by the way her images express her fiercely independent nature, and by the way her vision reaches beyond the personal and the human feminine to encompass the vegetative, mineral, and cosmic realms.

I will have more to say about the cosmic images of nature in works by women shortly, but first I want to probe another cluster of images explicitly concerned with women and nature.

IV. THE GODDESS

Despite the press that the revival of interest in pre-Christian goddess-oriented religions has received, relatively few *representations* of the goddess occur in visual works produced by women in the 1970s. Still, one feels the effects of this current of thought in a great number of works. The specific images that do occur are frequently related to the constellation of images I am sketching here, particularly to the images of transformation and to those of nature in its cosmic aspects.

Nancy Spero, for example, does multi-partite works dealing with Artemis-Hecate, whom she understands as mistress of fate—birth, conception, and the crossroads of life—and of the world of the dead.[74] Julia Barkley does enamel-on-canvas paintings based on the energy of the Christian miracles of healing, raising from the dead, casting out of demons, and ascension to heaven, which she traces to the fertility goddesses.[75] Her colleague Elizabeth Erickson does assemblages based on the Alaskan goddess Sedna.[76] Erickson's works are black and white boxes (to stand for the search for voice) and cloth-wrapped packages (to stand for the elusiveness of the unconscious). Her accompanying poems concern death, suggesting that Sedna, like Hecate, is primarily a goddess of passages.

Judith Williams seeks to transform the image of the Virgin Mary by painting *The Madonna with Horses*; the traditional madonna figure is shown with a ring of galloping horses around her head in place of a halo, and a rearing horse on her hand. Flames come out of a pot in the place of her heart which is encircled by white flowers and floating rose petals.[77] Clearly, this is an act of restoring another passion than that of grief to the madonna. Mary Fuller performs a similar service for Eve. Her sculpture *Eve and Friend* shows the mother of us all with a snake wrapped around her as if she were an ancient goddess. She looks meditative and supported, perhaps reflecting the fact that snakes were used in early religious practice to induce vision.[78] Terry Schutte's abstract expressionist oils titled *Madonna* and *Goddess* seem to her to stem from "something created years [centuries?] ago on the other side of the globe. . . . something as elusive as a shadow: pre-awareness, the stage before words, the scream of a baby—that universal sound which signifies fear, touches below and beyond language, culture, time, and space."[79]

Sometimes the goddess is not named in the work itself but is part of its inspiration. This is true in the case of Donna Byars who seeks to create legends of lost civilizations in her sculpture and earthworks. Her *Oracle Stone's Grove* was based upon a dream

> that a friend and I drove in my red truck over a hill and came upon a stone woman who sat in a grove of trees in beautiful filtered light. She spoke in vapors—not words—but, as it is in a dream, it seemed only natural that we understood. The vapors made us able to comprehend the meaning of life. It was a moment of unbelievable beauty.
>
> Suddenly, she slipped from her chair into a hole in the ground. We caught her just in time and put her back on her chair. She was no longer able to speak.
>
> I woke with a terrible feeling of sadness.[80]

It is not hard to see how a work like the one Byars did on Wave Hill in the Bronx, with a nude woman encoiled by a snake, a winged crescent moon and a pair of ladders (or shutters), expresses the sense of being in contact with an ancient mystery.

In keeping with Byars's sensitivity to the light in her dream, several striking images by different artists connect light directly with the female body. Dorothy Heller's *Womb of Light* was the first image of this kind that I had seen, and it has remained in my mind for several years, despite the fact that I have not uncovered any other works by this artist. Shown in the famous "Women Choose Women" show at the Brooklyn Museum in 1972, it is an acrylic painting of modest size ($35'' \times 33''$) that is utterly black except for brilliant lines of light radiating outward in the shape of a womb.[81] The image is sculptural; that is, it so convinces one of its reality that I expected to be able to touch the womb and walk around it.

Just as it is not uncommon to see a tree or plant growing from a woman's head in art by contemporary women, so it is not un-common to see light emanating from her head. Dedree Drees's pen-and-ink watercolor drawing, *Self-Portrait of Down Step Trans-former*, is a case in point;[82] the artist identifies herself as the light source. Diane Nudo Mostek has a series of untitled multimedia works that show the female amidst a burst of light. In one case, the female emerges with upraised arms from a yellow and blue background; in another she steps from a blue-green space into yellow-red. Mostek's themes are sexual power and the visualiza-tion of energy.[83] Perhaps the most ambitious of these light-filled images is *Light Weaver* by Houston artist Lynn M. Randolph. In it, a naked woman is shown on a mountain top surrounded by other peaks. She is touching the sunbeams. In another painting, *Transform*, the woman holds an unidentified organic form in both hands, in an otherwise barren landscape.[84] Randolph's colleague Tralene Vassilopoulos has a portrait of a gold woman, suspended in the sky on a red shape, with a white figure in her womb; each of the forms is repeated in the distance to create a sense of multi-ple sources of power.[85]

These works and others recover a special place for the idea of "woman" in the universe. Rachel Rolon de Clet, for example, draws on science for her paintings of *Cosmic Landscapes* and *Cos-mic Woman*, and especially on this statement from Carl Sagan:

> In the cosmic perspective there is no reason to think that we are the first or the last or the best. . . . We realize our deep connected-ness with other life forms, both simple and complex. We know that the atoms that make us up were synthesized in the interiors of previous generations of dying stars. . . . The cosmos revealed to us by the new advances in astronomy and biology is far grander and more awesome than the tidy world of our ancestors. And we are becoming part of it, the cosmos as it is, not the cosmos of our desires.[86]

Rolon de Clet's images are nonetheless decidedly female in their symbolic import; she contends that this is as it should be, since she "can't imagine a male artist approaching his art and ignoring his maleness." Her *Cosmic Woman as an Abstraction of Incidental Gravity*, for example, places an adult human form in a uterine shape suspended in the sky in surreal relationship to a range of mountain peaks. Beneath the figure, in the foreground, resting in a substance that looks like liquid rock, is a dark sphere that could be a planet or an eye. Clearly the womb is the most powerful symbol in her work. In her *Cosmic Woman* series, Rolon de Clet uses real models, both male and female, presenting them without body hair and skin pigmentation in order to penetrate beneath the conventions that camouflage their essential similarities. Her concern with the interconnections of inner and outer space is appropriately subsumed under the title "Cosmic *Wo*man" because the female offers her a symbol of rebirth in a world otherwise filled with grotesqueries—or so it seems in viewing the paintings. The woman, then, has a special affinity with the creative force that keeps us all alive, and perhaps a special responsibility to exercise that force. If Rolon de Clet's works do not refer to the goddess directly, they recapitulate the essence of her meaning as creatrix.

The rituals that accompany such realizations of what might be called "goddess energy" are nowhere more imaginative and coherent than in the performance pieces by Mary Beth Edelson. In her first influential piece, *Woman Rising* (1973–74), she sought to invoke the goddess by embodying her herself. She developed a series of photographic images of her own nude and decorated body in nature (in the Outer Banks, North Carolina) in order to define "not who I am but who we are." She says, "I was summoning Goddess to make house calls, talking to Goddess with the body. . . . These rituals were photographic evidence of the manifestations and recognition of a powerful feminine force: Everywoman."[87] Her alternative way of presenting the goddess, in the second part of the same work done in the same years, was in thirteen stylized plywood figures, eight feet high, called *Goddess Tribe*. These were icons of wisdom and nurture, embracing supposedly opposite images—Sophia and Venus, light and dark, sun and moon, bird and vessel—as related parts of female ancestral heritage.

Edelson's works also include two manuscript-like mural-sized drawings which she structured in three sections to divide past, present, and future time and "microcosmic, mesocosmic, and macrocosmic space."[88] The drawings include written comments presenting Edelson's world-view: she was "searching for essences, primary matter, mysteries—to make some sense and order out of it all."[89]

One especially complex performance piece involved a group of women who caused one of their number to "fly" by lifting her above them; the event, called *The Nature of Balancing* (1979), took place in an environment that included a cave-like sculpture in the form of a woman, called *Toothless*, and a flat mound-like sculpture aglow with pink light from its interior. An accompanying exhibit of books included images of winged rocks and Celtic energy. In the first movement of the performance, the group flying the "birdwoman" above them crashes into a wall. Regathering their energy for a second movement, the performers put their arms on each other's shoulders for balance and, each performer on one leg sways in another simulation of flight. Thus, the piece creates two models of collaboration: the first is unsuccessful because it imitates the idea of the battering ram; the second is successful because each woman gives and takes support to sustain her balance.

Other rituals incorporate into them the experience of fire, as in burning braided rows of cornstalks. Another, billed as a contemporary creation myth, uses green and orange lights on the backs of three performers who are either wise women or tricksters, depends on the effect of the light on the symbols painted on their backs. One of the performers said of this ritual:

> Slowing we merge into one undulating sea of energy, waves swaying us, vocal and tidal sounds enveloping us. Connecting, we calm our movements ebbing in the shape of a half circle, a harbor, a crescent moon. I am woman/artmaker/art simultaneously, all alienation from my body or my artwork fades as idea and instinct unwittingly express themselves in the movement.[90]

Since the three wise women are covered with a cloth at the end of the ritual to simulate a moving mountain, the implication is that creation may extend outward from woman to nature.

V.   NATURE IN ITS COSMIC ASPECTS

Nancy Graves's sculptures, paintings, and prints from 1969 to 1981 suggest a direction taken by many artists who have been sensitive to the idea of the goddess and to the claims of the earth. The goddess with whom Graves identifies is Cerridwen, the Celtic goddess whose name means cauldron or fortress of wisdom, and whom Graves understands as a keeper of death and immortality.⁹¹ Described in a sixteenth-century Welsh treatise as a witch, Cerridwen was nonetheless credited with prophetic foresight and magical shapeshifting abilities. Carefully observing the movement of the sun, moon, and stars in order to add each herb or root at the proper astrological moment, Cerridwen brewed a potion designed to pass on her magical powers to her son Gwion. When the potion was stolen by Gwion, she chased him, changing from greyhound to otter to hawk to hen in order to capture him as he used her shapeshifting power. But he grew again in her womb, and instead of destroying him, she put him into a leather sack and threw him into the water—whence emerged Taliesen or Merlin, prophet or wizard.⁹²

Graves, unlike Edelson, is very guarded in talking about the meaning of her work; thus she does little more than acknowledge sources such as Cerridwen. She prefers to discuss technique, saying that she is concerned with making and viewing, not with philosophy. Still, she is the most "intellectual" of all the artists I have treated so far, preferring to mine books, photographs, maps, museum exhibits, and now her own completed work for forms susceptible to metaphoric construction, rather than seeking to "represent" nature. Yet her twenty-minute film *Izy Boukir*, devoted to the sight and sound of a herd of camels (done after her famous camel sculptures), begins with a prologue from the naturalist Henry Beston:

> We need another and a wiser and perhaps a more mystical concept of animals. Remote from universal nature, and living by complicated artifice, man in civilization surveys the creatures through the glass of his knowledge and sees thereby a feather magnified and the whole image in distortion. We patronize them for their incompleteness, for their tragic fate of having taken form so far below ourselves. And therein we err. . . . For the animal shall not be measured by man. In a world older and more complete than ours, they move finished and complete, living by voices we shall never hear.⁹³

Graves's concerns, whether they are motivated by Cerridwen or simply by her childhood association with the natural history museum where her father worked, are with the world that cannot be measured by man, hard though he (*sic*) and the artist may try to use scientific technology as extensions of human sense and sensibility. Graves's fascination with science, as stated in the catalogue of her La Jolla show, lies in the connections she finds in it between "local pinpoints and cosmic points."[94] She is interested, as are others I will mention shortly, in the contemplation of "infinite time and space, whether it be evolutionary, ethnographic or geophysical."[95]

Graves is also concerned, as are others treated here, with the relationship between inside and outside. Having dealt with the outer form of the camel in her sculptures from 1967 to 1969, she turned to the fabrication of camels' bones, and even hung them from the ceiling in order not to be trapped into one way of seeing them.[96] Emily Wasserman explains Graves's process as a phase of the shaman's initiation, "in which the psychic death and rebirth cycle is seen in terms of physical dissection and reconstitution. He [sic] must pass through the spiritual phase to return to conscious life."[97] The interpretation is not unlikely, given the fact of Graves's sculpture *Shaman* (in which one image resembles the circle atop the pyramid used by Edelson to symbolize Sophia, the Hebrew goddess of Wisdom) and her *Totem with Shadows*, both based on the religious tradition of American northwest coast Indians. The totem was made from animal skins, hung from the ceiling in such a way as to cast shadows—her notion being that the idea of the totem incorporates its own shadow.[98]

In 1972, Graves turned abruptly from sculpture to a series of paintings based on sea animals whose pigmentation and shape serve as natural camouflage in their environments. As Linda Cathcart comments, her intent was to "re-evaluate the way one sees and how one can accomplish a mental completeness of complex images."[99] From these, she turned to bathymetric (undersea) and topographic maps of the ocean floors, once again thinking of the earth as a prehistoric form. About her further development, Graves says:

> Then I moved into the moon, which was not only poetically but scientifically considered to be a fossil of the earth . . . and then began to consider anything that had been made by man which was a system in two dimensions as a possible point of departure for my concerns, which would continue to fall into the category of mapping.[100]

Mapping the earth's prehistory. Mapping forms that are no longer visible to the naked eye. Why the preoccupation with learning to see remote or defunct realities? Surely it is to awaken us to their beauty and to similar beauty in ourselves.

What no one has said about this intellectual artist is that the aesthetic ploys she uses to awaken us are precisely the ones described by Lippard as typical of the female sensibility in art.[101] That is, after the phase of "dissection" in her sculpture during 1969–70 and the expression of totemic and shamanistic concerns in 1970–71, she turned to curvilinear two-dimensional works that achieve her objective of "mapping" by means of layering, which draws the viewer further into the spaces beneath the surface. Her preoccupation with female shapes evolved quite naturally from two gouaches in 1971 based on a frieze of women and

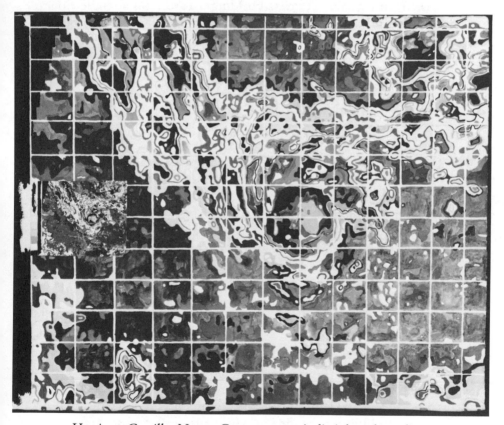

Hurricane Camille, Nancy Graves, 1973, india ink and acrylic on paper, 22-½″ × 30-½″.
Courtesy of Nancy Graves.

bison and paleolithic carvings. It continued in her 1972 acrylic renderings of *Antarctica, The Montes Apenninus Region of the Moon*, and *Part of Sabine D. Region of the Moon*. Perhaps her most striking contribution to a female aesthetic tradition is *Hurricane Camille*. In it, two light blue centers, one the microcosm of the other, suggest infinite space. They are surrounded by grey and black, then by turbulent beige, and finally by sensuous reds and purples. A grid is then superimposed on the larger of the two images. The contrast between the irregular shapes and the grid could not be more moving, nor the insufficiency of the grid more clear.

As in O'Keeffe's case, Graves was struggling in this period for independence—from a deeply embedded set of family expectations, from the Yale style of building a career on a single image or technique, and from the effects of a bad marriage to the up-and-coming artist, Richard Serra.[102] What Graves achieved in this period was unprecedented. Exploring the most distant and formidable aspects of our universe by reference to the internal structures most familiar to her,[103] she gave us a way to recognize them, even in their threatening guises.

My research uncovered a surprising number of such cosmic images—that is, works concerned with nature's vastness in sea, sky, mountains, planets; with its grandiose qualities of brilliant color, massive size, imposing shape; and with its grand and minute kinds of orderliness, its smallest detail reflecting its largest aspect. Some of these features have already become apparent as aspects of works in the other clusters of images I have discussed. Perhaps evidence of a similar preoccupation with the universe would turn up in a study of male artists in the 1970s.(In the same breath I want to say I hope so and, because of my recent experiences in galleries and museums, I doubt it.)

What is remarkable about the images, however, is their female bias. Not only are they often based on female body forms, but they are also related to the female experience of the human body as a permeable form whose boundaries expand and contract to take in or to deliver other bodies or beings. This fact is regarded as a psychological liability for adult women who have to function in a society built on the idea of competition among separate egos, striving to define themselves in terms of their differences from others of their kind and other kinds of life. But it may turn out to be the source of an alternative vision of human life that is more in keeping with the science of our times—the science now being popularized by Carl Sagan and Lewis Thomas. Certainly the images in the body of work reported here could, if they were treated seriously, offer ways to make the new science visually intelligible, psychologically acceptable and aesthetically attractive—no mean achievements.

The variety of images in this cluster is striking, despite their similar origins. In a 1970 exhibit of her recent paintings, for example, Texas artist Dorothy Hood showed several large (120″ × 96″ or 80″ × 70″) oils dealing with the vastness of the sky and the architecture of space: *Space Bolts, Space Pillars, Extensions of the Sky, Sky Span*, and so on, all completed within a few months before the exhibit. Her accompanying statement says:

> Almost everything in life can be imagined as receptacles, vessels, and with reverence, even chalices. Trees, had they consciousness, might well be seen to receive—as willing receptacles, light and gravity. . . . Light is the measure and the return of the gift of magnetic fields; space extends itself over and is the breath of every essence. The eye is our own earthly right of possession of the cosmic orbs.[104]

From the vessel, the ancient symbol of female spiritual power, to the magnetic fields of space, we journey through the artist's eye. The artist is receiver of light from the cosmic orbs.

Several artists are similarly concerned with light as a unifying force. Light is the subject of nearly all of Irene Rice Pereira's mature work. She became something of a fanatic about light, claiming that an understanding of it would overturn the western concept of perspective and place the human being in an entirely different position in the universe. "Man is the center of a right angle of vision between inner and outer reality," she said.

> The functioning of the mind is identical with the manner in which light propagates itself. . . . Light propagates itself rectilinearly and polarizes itself geometrically as a spherical form. . . . ; the nuclear core of the matter of mind is identical . . . so there's a homogeneous correspondence between man and the entire cosmos.[105]

Not mind over matter, but mind in matter or matter in mind, and light in both. Pereira's insight stemmed from an experience in the Sahara desert early in her life; as the light of the sun disappeared from the horizon at sea level, she experienced both the smallness of the earth and the sense of being surrounded, even protected, by the dome or sphere of stars when she looked up into the night sky. Her paintings, among the most purely geometrical and multidimensional in my study, concern the infinite layers of reality that are unified by light. Light becomes the only absolute for Pereira—an unchanging, yet ever-changing, reference for the rest of her life—the primary force in the universe.

For Alice Baber, light is also the central actor in space. Art critic Ann McCoy comments that one feature distinguishes Baber's paintings from those of her (male) contemporaries who also explore light: for Baber, it "exists in a realm of its own, with no apparent source"—as if it comes from infinite directions of outer space.[106] Yet, paradoxically, she thinks of this sourceless light as a place (the middle of Jacob's ladder). And, alternatively, she says that it exists in her mind's eye. Whether she paints ladders to the sun, paths through the mountains to the hermit's cave, or dreams of the Peruvian jaguar, her works dissolve the usually solid forms of reality into the materials of color infused by a kind of light that casts no shadows. Reality as we know it is dissolved, yet remains material.

If Pereira and Baber seem to revise Platonic theory in some inexplicable way, Barbara Foster chooses a more practical and earthly approach in her surreal series *By the Speed of Light*.[107] In it, plants are shown growing under the floor of a building; above this scene is a constellation against a black sky. Or we might say that the floor sprouts constellations as well as flowers. Or rootless ferns arise out of different spatial layers while constellations lurk behind their fronds. By the speed of light, all these separate realms would be bridged.

Much of the work I saw was holistic, concerned with bridging gaps or seeing things whole. Stephanie Pogue, for example, prefers the circle over all other shapes. She says, "It is the most perfect of forms. The undulating line is synonymous with life and can be symbolic of the rhythms of the heartbeat, the sea and the land before the wind. It is a line that would be straight were it not for the ebbing and pulling of external forces."[108] In her print *Memories*, a black woman's head is haloed by the moon; if we remember completely enough, we arrive at one of the primary circles informing human life. Betye Saar's assemblages *Sky Window* and *Mystic Window of the Universe* are even more explicit in their revelation of a cosmic order underlying human life.[109] Likewise, Donna Billick's *Night Gallery* stems from her sense of space as a "vitalizing force from the innermost womb to the universe beyond."[110]

Not all the connective images concerned with the cosmos are positive ones. Vivian Berman's intaglio prints show cross-sections of waves breaking, giant spheres in motion, the majestic grandeur of the universe; but they also convey a sense of unravelling or foreboding. *Ariel*, presumably named after the air spirit in Shakespeare's *The Tempest*, suggests a tornado over the plains. Another image of a tiny earth with the planets enveloped in blackness is called *Doomsday*.[111]

While some artists concentrate on the predicament of the earth, others are more preoccupied with our effect on elements of the universe beyond the earth. Faye Watts-Maxwell includes among her acrylics of the earth's strata and the sky's thunderheads an image based on quiltmaking called *Patched Cosmos*, implying that our universe is coming apart and that it is created to some extent by human hands.[112] Far more devastating is Helen Lundeberg's post-surrealist oil called *Cosmicide* (1935), which seems to foretell the death of the cosmos.[113] In it the water has become solid and turned red; flowers and seed pods are dislocated from the earth.

June Wayne's prints reflecting the cosmic aspects of nature provide a useful capstone for many of the ideas I have considered here because of the complexity of the artist's vision and the longevity of her concern. After World War II, for example, she chose the mushroom as her insignia, partly to express the delights and dangers of the plant and of sexuality, but also to refer to the atomic mushroom; and this "doubleness," or richness of perspective, characterizes much of her work. As she says, "Even my most pessimistic works include the ambiguity of pleasure or wit or satire."[114] Her satirical edge is most apparent in a series of prints called *The Lemmings*. Rodents with an insidious tendency to band together and march willingly toward mass suicide, the lemmings appeared as early as 1955 in Wayne's prints as a metaphor for human folly. The most powerful of these lithographs, important enough to Wayne and others to be recreated in 1971 as a large (7′ × 9′) tapestry, was *At Last a Thousand*. The title has both a literal meaning, as a reference to the number of prints produced at the Tamarind Lithography Workshop, and a catastrophic sound that is appropriate to the visual impression the work creates. The image involves two imperfect circles, the smaller one nested on top of the other, giving the appearance of a volcano or a cyclone. A salt wash causes a granular texture that adds to the disturbed quality of the image. The tiny human figures familiar from the series appear to fall off the rims of the circles. Whether printed in various gradations of black and white to emphasize the darkness, or in orange to suggest fire, it is an ominous image.[115] It is far more disturbing, perhaps because of its satirical bite, than is *Nature Morte*, Wayne's direct description of an atomic explosion.

Wayne's concern for nature involves a curiosity about the human condition which informs the series she began in 1970 on the genetic code. The series includes a tribute to Rosalind Franklin, the scientist whose research into the x-ray crystallography of the DNA molecule first identified its structure. Her male colleagues (in Britain) ignored her findings, however, thus delaying the breaking of the genetic code until a later time. The series also includes a rare self-portrait, titled *Base Pair*, showing the artist with the shadow of her mother in a field of double helix referents. Both of these prints signal Wayne's commitment to feminist concerns. Subsequent titles in the series (*Diktat, Blueprint, Transcript*) show her interest in the anatomy of the helix, transformed as metaphor. At one point, the molecule becomes a choker of lights which Wayne uses symbolically, printing them in different colors (white, red, black) to suggest relational processes (*Weighed Wanting, Hung Jury, Thou Shalt Not, Standoff*). These experiments place the helix on a solid black or white rectangle above a grey cliff of irregular layered or folded forms which could suggest flesh, hills, rock, or paper, depending on the texture of the print. In one particularly striking example, the oddly shaped eight is turned up on end to resemble a constellation in the night sky over a range of mountains. The title, *Not a Star after All*, suggests a close relationship between the genetic code and the cosmos. *Night Swim* (1971), an unfinished oil marouflaged to canvas, plays with the dramatic possibilities of such relationships—transforming the idea of the helix into a chain of mushrooms in one horizontal frame, or into the air hose of a diving outfit in the next underwater frame, and thereby suggesting a generating civilization in the next two. A brilliant orange sky with a fiery sun in the top frame leaves the state of the world in question.

Wayne's series on the wave, also begun in 1970, freezes waves in motion, making their enormous power evident to us visually by stopping the image at its peak. In her images of tidal waves, begun in 1972, the waves become solid walls of water rising into arches that disintegrate more or less violently. In case we wonder about the scale of the image, Wayne provides a solid red sun on the horizon which is smaller than the wave. *Demented Tidal Wave* loses its shape earlier than the others, spreading out into a chaotic spray that obliterates the horizon. These works explore the overwhelming force of nature. And yet, Wayne understands these waves as expressions of an energy that is also shared by humans.

In the *Visa* series, begun in 1973, this perspective on the relationship between the human and the cosmos becomes clear. In *Tidal Visa*, for example, the large tilted fingerprint that dominates the dark blue expanse of the top of the picture space is cut away at the bottom to form a negative image of a wave. All of the "Visas," made from Wayne's fingerprint against various soft backgrounds, are positioned in a suggestive way: *Visa* is darkly shaded on one side so that the white print seems egg-shaped like a planet. *White Visa* is laid on its side to suggest a sea animal or skeleton. The most powerful of all, *Time Visa*, in brilliant red, luminous blue, and several shades of purple, with white specks on the fingerprint and smaller specks emanating from its surface and drifting away, suggests both a human imprint and an elongated view of our universe from the outside, wherever that might be. The fingerprint, the most individual mark of human identity, becomes an image of a non-human world.

There is, in Wayne's work, a union of perception, in the close observation of actual forms; fantasy, in the juxtaposition of disparate elements of existence; and science, in her preoccupations with optics, genetics, or the tides. At some point in this continuum of vision, the wave and the fingerprint are one.

In the presence of Wayne's images, I am reminded of Lewis Thomas's alternative to the myth of human mastery over nature:

> We have become, in a painful, unwished-for way, nature itself. We have grown into everywhere, spreading like a new growth over

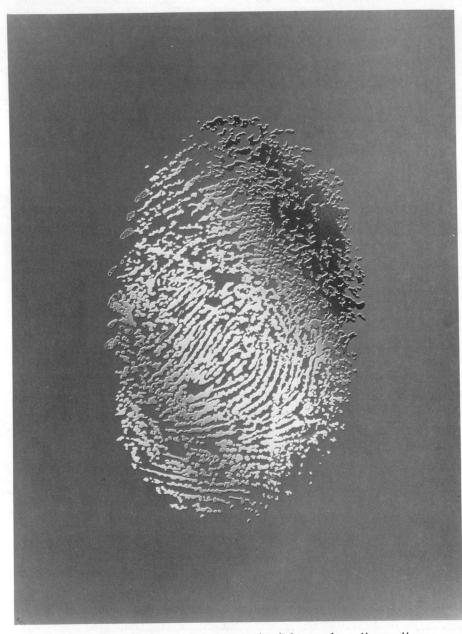

Visa, June Wayne, 1978, three-color lithograph, 35″ × 25″.
Courtesy of June Wayne.

the entire surface, touching and affecting every other kind of life, *incorporating* ourselves. The earth risks being eutrophied by us. We are now the dominant feature of our own environment. Humans, large terrestrial metazoans, fired by energy from microbial symbionts lodged in their cells, instructed by tapes of nucleic acid stretching back to the earliest live membranes, informed by neurons essentially the same as all the other neurons on earth, sharing structures with mastodons and lichens, living off the sun, are now in charge, running the place, for better or worse.

Or is it really this way? It could be, you know, just the other way around.[116]

It is the spirit of openness, curiosity, exploration, embodied in Thomas' last sentence, that Wayne seeks to affirm rather than any doctrine about our relationship to the cosmos. But it is her great achievement, along with others presented here, to have given us a way of *envisioning* ourselves as the "incorporated being" that Thomas describes—as part of the universe, yet with a creative or at least a regenerative role to play within it.

VI. CONCLUSION

Most of the artists considered here are relatively unaware of participating in a mythmaking process. They see themselves as working out their own images; indeed, given the emphasis of the art world on "newness," they probably hope that no one else in the country is doing the same thing. Yet many of the works come from the depth of psychological and spiritual exploration where the "universal" concerns of myth seem to have originated. Nothing so specific as a religion or a single mythic story has emerged, but it is possible to see the impulse toward myth taking shape. We can only guess now at its final form (or perhaps myths never have a final form). What we can say is that there is at present a widespread concern, among women in the visual arts, for processes of metamorphosis that touch on all forms of life— animal, vegetable, and mineral, as well as spiritual. This concern moves beyond the impulse toward personal growth, which is natural in a culture devoted to the idea of individualism, to the universe itself in its least favorable guises. The concern seems less oriented toward human survival than one might expect, given the current thrust of our ecological philosophy (of saving resources for future generations of human beings), and more toward the preservation of and reverence for the basic elements of life. In some cases, the reverence is specifically linked to a goddess figure or sacred female, but more often it is unattached to any religion. In their exploration of cosmic aspects of nature, these artists have drawn attention away from the familiar political squabbles over geographical boundaries and oil rights, away from the concept that makes earth a human domain to be used by mankind, and toward a concept of nature as inextricably bound to the human—our source and our homologue and our trust.

Some who believe that ritual always precedes myth will be relieved to know that the images I have traced here have already been expressed in ritual form. Mary Beth Edelson's explicitly feminist rituals, are a case in point. But the earthworks of Mendieta, Byars, and Stuart, with their varying degrees of acknowledgment to the goddess, are also contributions to the rituals of an alternative mythology—one in which "man's monuments" are less important than humankind's willingness to see itself in nature. These latter rituals are at the moment more open to participation by men; indeed, men are creating similar earthworks, whereas they are not, so far as I know, creating rituals to the goddess. As I have said, this accessibility of the ideas and images to men is a strength. No cultural myth could survive for long or develop into greatness without being open to participation by diverse groups.

But perhaps this myth had to receive its impetus for development from women, for it is essentially rooted in female psychology in a way that the Greek and Christian traditions of human dominance over nature are not. That is, it depends upon a different conception of appropriate boundaries between things—human, animal, plant, earth, and sky (not to mention fire and water, which I have not traced); a looser conception, one that does not erase the boundaries altogether, but allows the easements which cannot seem entirely rational to our culture in its present form. The female's actual or potential experience of menstruation, penetration, pregnancy, birth, lactation, and menopause may leave her more open to a "story" of human relationship with nature which is non-hierarchical and less compartmentalized than the one to which we have become accustomed. Again, we are discussing differences in degree, not in kind, so some men would tend more toward the female model (because of either nature or nurture) and some females more toward the habits of categorization in a culture built by men. The emerging mythology I am examining here, with its particular symbols of transformation and its reverence for the natural order even to the point of sacrificing the purity of human form—these are attributable to female genius.

The fact that common images emerge in the works of women from so many different parts of the country, in different media and styles, different phases of life, with different models and aesthetic aims, in a society that prides itself on competition, and in the midst of a movement that emphasizes female achievement on the terms of the dominant masculine culture is remarkable in its own right. The fact that most of these women arrived at their images through introspection rather than through direct contact with one another, and that most remain unknown to one another even now, makes the case for an emergent mythology even stronger.

It is possible that such a myth has been taking shape for centuries, its roots in pre-Christian religions covered for centuries except in brief periods when women gained the wherewithal to express their visions. The medieval period (the last to take stock in bestiaries) was such a time, and the twelfth-century abbess Hildegarde von Bingen may have been a percursor of the women treated here. Certainly her work called *Cosmos*, from her illuminated manuscript *Scivias*, is a potential antecedent.[117] For her the cosmos, presented in the vibrant colors of earth and light, fire and water, was both egg and womb—indeed, perhaps it was a cell.

At the very least, after taking stock of so rich and interesting a body of work, we can no longer claim that women in the visual arts have failed to use their experience to reveal the whole nature of the human condition.

CHAPTER 8

"Woman and Nature"
Revisited in Poetry by Women

As we have seen in previous chapters, key elements of Western mythology are currently under revision by women. These elements concern the powers and responsibilities of women to envision, to create, to change society, to transcend the claims of erotic love, to protect human life, and to preserve nature. Thus far, I have explored the mythmaking processes employed with respect to these elements by individual creators, and I have traced related patterns of images in visual art by many women. In order to be accepted as living myth, however, images must cohere into a story that seems "true" to significant numbers of people. It is not possible for a single individual in a complex modern culture to *create* a myth. It probably never was. Homer's *Odyssey* was the product of many generations of storytelling, and the *Bible* was compiled by many hands. To my knowledge, no single text has emerged in the post war period to equal even *The Waste Land* in its capacity to express an age, but a collective *situation* does exist in the art world as a crucible for myth. Had it not been for the proliferation of the arts in the 1960s and 1970s, many of the insights recorded here might have remained individual and private. With these considerations in mind, I have searched the large (and growing) corpus of poetry by women for the signs of myth: the repeated images, narratives, ritual gestures, attitudes, or tones that might belong to a coherent story. Among the patterns I found, one in particular concerning women's relationship to nature seems sufficiently extensive and resonant to be identified as part of a mythic story—more incipient than formed. In this chapter, I trace some of its contours.

172

Again, I want to clarify that in turning attention to a myth about women in poetry by women, I do not mean to imply a necessary contrast with works by men. If the same materials are present in poems by men, the myth will simply be that much stronger. Nor do I mean to imply that all women poets or readers share the same ideas. Quite the contrary; I am profoundly interested in the differences of vision in women's works. But I do want to give women's poems the same knd of scrutiny accorded to men's works in graduate schools all over the country when scholars ask, for example, "What was the Renaissance view of nature?" I am interested in women's views, whether or not they are different from men's, out of a commitment to understanding women's thought—and a belief that women's thought will not be reckoned as a force until its patterns have been amassed.

I think it is fair to say that Susan Griffin's *Woman and Nature: The Roaring inside Her* already serves the functions of myth for many feminists, particularly those associated with the influential feminist journals, *Chrysalis* and *Heresies*.[1] But I want to investigate here the possibility that Griffin's book serves a summative function for mythic expressions in works by many women, regardless of their degree of allegiance to feminism. Specifically, I propose that Griffin's book contains many elements of the emerging myth I have identified in other volumes of poetry by women.

These elements occur in their most concentrated form in the prose poem called "This Earth: What She Is to Me" near the end of *Woman and Nature*:

> One should identify oneself with the universe itself. Everything that is less than the universe is subjected to suffering . . .
> —Simone Weil, *Notebooks*

As I go into her, she pierces my heart. As I penetrate further, she unveils me. When I have reached her center, I am weeping openly. I have known her all my life, yet she reveals stories to me, and these stories are revelations and I am transformed. Each time I go to her I am born like this. Her renewal washes over me endlessly, her wounds caress me; I become aware of all that has come between us, of the noise between us, the blindness, of something sleeping between us. Now my body reaches out to her. They speak effortlessly, and I learn at no instant does she fail me in her presence. She is as delicate as I am; I know her sentience; I feel her pain and my own pain comes into me, and my own pain grows large and I grasp this pain with my hands, and I open my mouth to this pain, I taste, I know, and I know why she goes on, under great weight, with this great thirst, in drought, in starvation, with intelligence in every act does she survive disaster. This earth is my sister; I love her daily grace, her silent daring, and how loved I am *how we admire this strength in each other, all that we have lost, all that we have suffered, all that we know: we are stunned by this beauty*, and I do not forget: what she is to me, what I am to her.[2]

Without loss of sexual energy, Griffin transforms the act of "penetrating" the earth into an act of communion. Instead of being a repository of natural substances to be mined, the earth is a source of transformative stories. "She" is not dead matter to be plundered, but wounded matter, from which renewal flows. The two bodies, woman's and earth's, are sympathetic. Consciousness of the earth's pain allows the woman to feel and accept her own pain. Earth's intelligent survival of disaster is a model for woman's survival. Instead of being mother, whore, or crone, *"this earth is my sister"* (emphasis mine). In a simple brilliant stroke, Griffin subtly alters centuries of images of nature.

The combination of sexual attraction, religious solace, grief, empathy, and, finally, respectful love expressed here must raise anxieties for many. The Marxist-feminist critics Rozsika Parker and Griselda Pollock reject any association of women with nature as the product of stereotypical thinking.[3] Others might join them in thinking it dangerous to be beguiled by another image of nature as female—and a sexual one as well. Besides, isn't the image incestuous? Might it not be open to fantasies of sibling rivalry? Isn't Griffin simply returning to a "primitive" vision that renounces human evolution? Of these concerns, only the last is easy to address. Griffin does so herself in a later poem. "Matter: How We Know." "We know ourselves to be made from this earth. We know this earth is made from our bodies. For we see ourselves, and we are nature. We are nature seeing nature. We are nature with a concept of nature. Nature weeping. Nature speaking of nature to nature."[4] Griffin does not have in mind the abandonment of human consciousness. On the other hand, she does not imagine that our consciousness separates us from nature by placing us above it (*sic*; the neutral pronoun is wrong from her perspective).

Griffin's "new" image of nature as our sister has tremendous power, however, despite our initial anxieties, because we find in it familiar elements. Our sense of familiarity comes, in part, from the other poems that have prepared the way for this subtle, crucial revaluation of woman and nature. Here is May Sarton, for example, in "The Godhead as Lynx":

> I feel a longing for the lynx's bed,
> To submerge self in that essential fur,
> And sleep close to this ancient world of grace,
> As if there could be healing next to her,
> The mother-lynx in her pre-human place.[5]

Nature here is animate and motherly. But the balance of human consciousness with "natural" sentience is remarkably similar to Griffin's. Despite Sarton's longing for the animal's grace and her admiration for the lynx's guiltless self-possession, she remains allied to the god at work inside her to produce "this laboring self who groans and thinks." Sarton wanted to give her ultimate allegiance to a force beyond the human which does not negate human consciousness. In "The Waves," as she walks in a forest of firs on a rocky coastal island, listening to the booming, churning ocean, she says,

> Oh love, let us be true then to this will—
> Not to each other, human and defeated,
> But to great power, our Heaven and our Hell,
> That thunders out its triumph unabated,
> And is never still.[6]

The poem is related to Wallace Stevens's desire for a less human god than any of our anthropomorphic religions allow—a god who moves "as sunlight moves."[7] But Sarton's vision of nature differs radically from Stevens's in that she understands it as the source of love. So it is "love's thundering rumor" that she hears in the waves, and that rumor is present "in the blood." Love, in her view, is in the "earth, the wave, the air" ("Invocation," p. 72). Human consciousness, then, calls love forth from the world.

Each of the poets I discuss here has a slightly different way of handling this problem of the relationship between human consciousness and the natural order. Marge Piercy is constantly aware of the human power and responsibility to choose; yet the wheel to which she is bound is "the wheel of the seasons,"

> moving
> some part of the way toward
> a new and better place, some part
> of the way toward dying.[8]

Over and over again, Piercy chooses to be a participant in the process of preserving or even creating the earth, with the sense that she is part of it, belongs to it, will return to it. As she says in a characteristic passage,

> I am kneeling and planting.
> I am making fertile.
> I am putting
> some of myself
> back into the soil.
> Soon enough
> sweet black mother of our food
> you will have the rest.[9]

These lines resolve a short poem which reviews other positions one might take toward nature: that its sand is the product of the action of the wind on quartz; or that the earth is "Compost . . . / sediment of our pleasures"; or that nature is a set of mysterious processes we must control by marriage in order to avoid starvation. But even in the stanza where Piercy seems to adopt the Enlightenment position that the earth is inert matter, the sand is "crystalline children/ of dead mountains." Most often, even in her most scientific frame of mind, Piercy chooses to see nature as a mother.

   Piercy's vision is cyclical. At various points on the wheel, the relationship between the human and the earth changes so that one has more power than the other; but always we are reciprocally involved in creation and destruction. We enrich "the frail dirt" through our "human castings"; wipe out "galaxies" with each oil spill; watch the tide undulate and percolate through the marsh "slithering/ with its smell of life feeding and renewing"; are blasted open by lightning. Even in describing her relationship to culture, Piercy has the cycle of human choice and nature's necessity in mind. "I belong to battle as the heron to the reeds/ till I give my body back."[10]

   No element of nature is foreign to her, and none is ultimately terrifying, not even fire:

> Our cells are burning
> each a little furnace powered by the sun
> and the moon pulls the sea of our blood.
> This night the sun and moon dance
> and you and I dance in the fire of which
> we are the logs, the matches and the flames.[11]

In this poem, written to commemorate the longest day of the year, we are at one and the same time that which is burned, that which starts the fire, and the heat and light resulting from the ignition.

Another wonderful poem from the same series on the lunar calendar recounts a dream that clarifies Piercy's acceptance of nature's fiercer aspects, those the pioneers found most disturbing. In the dream, "two hundred times the same":

> The waves leap
> at the shore like flames out of control.
> The sea gnashes snow capped mountains
> that hurl themselves end over end, blocking
> the sky. A tidal wave eats the land. Rearing
> and galloping, tumbling and with tangled
> mane the horses of the surf with mad eyes,
> with snorting nostrils and rattling hooves
> stampede at the land. I am in danger
> yet I do not run. I am rooted watching
> knowing that what I watch
> is also me.[12]

The poet feels both small in comparison with the power of this "cold fierce mother," and at the same time strengthened by the knowledge that this power exists in her—not only as dream but as part of her "nature." She writes her poems, as it were, from the eye of this hurricane, part of it, yet apart from it. "What I watch is also me."

This degree of identification with nature, without fear and without loss of consciousness, occurs in the works of surprising numbers of women.[13] But why surprising? Perhaps I internalized Robert Bly's perspective, stated several years ago at a C. G. Jung conference, that poetry by women only rarely concerns the non-human world. Or perhaps I internalized Bly's respect for what he now calls the "object poem," based on "spontaneous, sober observation of the external world."[14] Certainly many women writing poetry do enter into the consciousness of things. But it is not, I believe, a consciousness of the world as totally separate from the human. It is one thing for Robert Bly to ground his energy in nature as an aspect of the external world. It is quite another for the female poet to do so, recognizing, as she must after centuries of reminders, the similarity of nature's body to her own. Perhaps Helen Vendler's criticism of Sylvia Plath, that in her work "all nature exists only as a limit of her sensibility; nothing exists that is not herself,"[15] is unfair, at least in the present state of our cultural mythology. At any rate, the poets I treat here offer another way of conceptualizing the relationship between "man" and nature. Neither the objectivity recommended by Bly nor the loss of self modelled by Plath, perhaps it is most like the state of homologous being proposed (but never realized) by William Carlos Williams in *Paterson*.[16]

The difficulty, of course, with a homologous relationship between woman and earth is that both have been subject to rape. Surely part of our uneasiness with Griffin's highly sexual encounter between woman and earth has to do with our fear that all such relationships may finally work on the model of rape. Griffin's emphasis on the sensual aspects of the encounter (caressing, speaking the body's language), does little to assuage our fear since what we discover in this instance, as in so many others, is our mutual pain and suffering. It is useful, then, for the purpose of remythologizing woman and nature, to know that the sexual aspect of our identification with nature could be imaged in other ways. May Swenson's poem "The Little Rapids" is a case in point.

Nature is not always female for this intellectually sophisticated poet. The whale-shaped ocean carving its cradle is clearly female, but the inarticulate sea, whose argument (like that of Demosthenes) is never finished, is male. The sun is female as it hatches from a crack in the cloud-shell, but male when it strides across the sky and rips the clouds apart.[17] When Swenson identifies with nature, however, its form is female. In "The Little Rapids,"[18] her most explicit poem of identification, she begins with direct observation of the rayed water splashing over a cliff, then moves to her own body, to the clitoris ("precipice of bone") and vagina ("snake-mouth muscle") which she understands as analogous to her heart—"knot and nubbin/ of the jutting flood."

In the course of the poem, her body becomes the ravine or gorge into which she will be hurled to her death. But throughout, she maintains the image of the rushing stream, its leaps and drops, swirlings, padded roar, springhead, primal pool, and so on, so that her body and the rapids are completely interwined. The poem presents both "bodies" as sexual beings in their own right, neither penetrated by the other, whose "queer sweet thrills" are a product of the zest of living and whose death will be a final orgasm. The poem offers a celebratory model of relationship that is hard to fault.

Not all of the acts of identification with nature in poetry by women are sexual acts. Audre Lorde, for example, identifies with coal as a way of valuing blackness—and as a way of revaluing words, which are open to coloration by the person who speaks them. The "I" spoken by the black person is potentially a diamond, carbon (like coal) that has crystallized. Here a substance which has been devalued by culture is understood positively. Nature is re-established as the ultimate source of the human "I." Instead of coming from a voice abstracted from nature (as in the Y H W H, I-am-that-I-am, assertion of identity on which Hebraic-Christian culture rests), that "I" emerges in Lorde's poem from "the earth's inside."[19]

In fact, it is fair to say that nature is re-spiritualized in poetry by women—that is, it is understood as co-equal with the human self, with layers as mysterious as our own. Linda Pastan's poem "Secrets" is explicit in this regard:

> The secrets I keep
> from myself
> are the same secrets
> the leaves keep
> from the old trunk
> of the tree
> even as they turn
> color.[20]

As it happens, these secrets are comparable not only to nature's slow and predictable changes, but also to its force (the waterfall stunned on rock), its absence (the sound of the stream "after weeks of drought"), its transformation by fire, and its silent flower songs. The poet's secrets are also comparable to the infant's howl and the whippoorwill's song, which is explicated here by virtue of the poet's empathy: "never tell/ never tell/ never tell." Instead of wanting to uncover those mysteries, to get to the bottom of them, to possess them for her own, the poet is content to respect them—and her own mysterious self.

This quality of respect is repeated over and over in works by contemporary women, but rarely more effectively than in Judith McCombs's "Loving a Mountain." As if in direct response to René Dubos's book *The Wooing of Earth*[21] (the dates of publication show that this is not the case), McCombs gives instructions for a different kind of loving than our culture has been willing to articulate. McCombs begins with the warning that

> Loving a mountain is not
> easy. You will have to take it, stone
> by stone, into your hands & your skin
> & into the space in your head that is prepared
> for mountains.[22]

Loving a mountain will require radical changes in our "habits of eating, of reason," for which we cannot expect help from the wind, trees, or birds; in fact, we might expect the opposite. It is decidedly not a mutual activity, and, the poet adds, it may not even be a useful one. So much for René Dubos's idea of a long-term marriage that benefits both partners.

But the poem continues with specific instructions about how to love the mountain properly:

>   Learn where the mountain
> is tired, where it's unwilling to hold any more,
> underfoot or over your head. Learn
> the days when the ledges are happy & the great folds smile,
> basking like pigs in the light. Stop being jealous
> of the dust & the fauna: they got here first
> & besides have adapted
> better than you will: of course the mountain prefers
> them. Learn when it wants you
> to get off its back: stop staring, stop grabbing,
> stop thinking of it. [p. 8]

Here we have a model of behavior based upon empathy for the mountain's physical condition, respect for her preferences, and celebration of her good qualities without excessive (obsessive) concentration on her. I use the feminine pronoun even though the poet does not because McCombs is so obviously revising stereotypic behavior toward the female.

The poet goes even further later in the poem, challenging the Kantian notion that human consciousness constitutes reality, by insisting

> The mountain is there, a mountain. It is not
> inside you. It has all it can do
> being a mountain. It does not want
> to be loved.   [p. 9]

Thus the problem of the relationship between human beings and nature is redesigned as that of loving a being who does not desire our love, whose focus is on being itself (herself) and not on being something for man. The kind of love the poet has in mind for such a being occurs spontaneously, "in the back of your head," when the mountain is so well-known, so respected, that it seems to move "lumpishly" of its own accord to become "your mountain." McCombs's image is far less ecstatic and romantic than Griffin's, but it does still involve some measure of reciprocity— not, to be sure, the concern for the human that Griffin and Sarton attribute to nature, but the possibility that we will "begin to belong."[23]

The desire to love or to belong in nature becomes a desire to preserve it or to watch over it, in some cases, and this motive is linked to the figure of the woman poet as seer. Two examples are striking because of their unusual form of address. Nancy Willard's "When There Were Trees" is written from the point of view (stated in the last two lines of the poem) of "the oldest woman on earth," and it is an elegy for a time already legendary when there were spruce, beech, birch, sassafras, maple, cherry sycamore, chestnut and lime trees. In addition to being a partial catalogue of trees, however, the poem is an act of mythic preservation, recording an ancient ritual of climbing the tree of life to bring back "the souls of the newly slain," and quoting Christopher Columbus's ecstatic reaction to the trees of America. The poet remembers being blessed by the trees, making peace with her own shadow through them, and receiving their absolution for her sins. She admits,

> I never thought men were stronger than trees.
> I never thought those tribes would join their brothers,

the buffalo and the whale, the leopard, the seal, the wolf,
and the men of this country who knew how to sing them.[24]

But, the poem implies, she was wrong. "Already the trees are a
myth,/ half gods, half giants in whom nobody believes." The
strategy of writing an elegy from the future for elements of earth
that are not yet dead should have the effect of raising the reader's
ecological consciousness, yet nothing in the poem is didactic or
hortatory. The moral weight falls on the figure of the seer or
"wise old woman" who has known the trees.

Susan Fromberg Schaeffer's fantasy, "The Witch and the
Weather Report," gives the role of caretaker (and savior) to the
witch from "Hansel and Gretel." The poem begins with the last
night's weather report: "FORECAST FOR TOMORROW:
BLEAK," to which the poet adds in italics, as if from a dream
*"A metal-making wind or rain will surely fall/ From the night-time sky.
Dress up green."*[25] The speaker and her silver cat set out into a
woods, which has turned to metal, where a motherly witch with
tears running down her silver cheeks wants to assist them in getting something to eat by using the sun as an incinerator to melt
down the metal. She insists that she too be thrown into the con-
traption; when the speaker refuses to comply, she "walks into the
red round sun herself," emerging with a blade of grass:

> "Follow this, follow this," she says, beginning to melt:
> "Oh my little children,
> Dress up green." [p. 47]

With all the whimsy of the fairy tale that it revises, the poem
articulates what has become the central problem of our age: that
we may use our technology to destroy ourselves. And here the
agent of survival, not merely the observer of earth's demise, is a
witch. Perhaps we could call her a cross between woman and
nature. Privy to the transformative processes of the sun, she is
nonetheless capable of human tears.

Over and above the general melancholia Bly claims that nature
induces in poets,[26] the emotion that distinguishes many poems
by women is grief. It appears in the witch's tears in Schaeffer's
poem and in the elegiac form of Willard's. Griffin shows that our
suffering cannot be transcended, as Simone Weil hoped, by turning our attention to the universe; it must be gone through.

In Susan Astor's poem, "The Farmer Lost a Child," the woman's grief causes her to disturb nature's pattern even as she completes her cycle of chores. "She milks the cow at midnight,/ Resting her head against the warm brown flank." And the noise of the other creatures in the barn steadies her as she feeds them at this odd hour of the night. "Then, numb and purposeful,/ She plows the field for hours," combing the land as she might have tended her child under more favorable circumstances. Finally, she collapses into sleep:

> Day breaks on schedule;
> The wheels of waking turn evenly.
> Only she, off kilter with a bubble of pain,
> Breaks rhythm,
> Halts to a lopsided sleep.[27]

Her relationship with nature is such that she can draw solace from it even when she breaks its rhythm.

Besmilr Brigham's grief is for the men who have been destroyed by war and for the mountains they have stripped to the bone in the process. The mountain ridges are like weeping dinosaurs, or old men, or the snake head without its body, or, in the central image of the poem, like abandoned women:

> warped bones
> struck up white in cold and filled with
> skeletons of women
> a woman flung her hair out weeping
> the great still female from the shoulders
> haunched down
> moves us—[28]

The speaker is offering a lament; she weeps in grief. But the mountains themselves, in the poem's final image, are "weeping in anger."

The powerful combination of grief and anger is realized perhaps most poignantly in Griffin's poem "Our Nature: What Is Still Wild in Us," written from the point of view of the elephant young whose mother has just been killed by a hunter. It is part of the second group of poems in Part IV ("Her Vision") of *Woman and Nature,* the group called "Matter Revisited." Coming after a long poem that seeks systematically to restore dignity to the human female body, and just before the declaration of what earth means to Griffin, it is a burial chant that creates an essential link between woman and matter. It is uttered by the young elephants as they cover their mother's wounds with mud and her body with leaves and branches:

> though all traces of her vanish, we will not forget. . . . Her wounds will fester in us. We will not be the same. The scent of her killer is known to us now. We cannot turn our backs at the wrong moment. We must know when to trumpet and charge, when to recede into denser forest, when to turn and track the hunter. . . . We will pass this feeling to our young. . . . They will learn fear. . . . From us, they will become fierce. And so a death like this death of our mother will not come easily to them. This is what we will do with our grieving.[29]

Our wildness, the poem's title implies, is parallel to that of the young elephants. Our human mothers have been similarly violated (as Griffin shows in earlier sections of her book). Only if our grandchildren "never know this odor" of violence can we afford to let our grief and anger subside. As Meridel LeSueur has said, "What strikes you, my sisters, strikes us all. The global earth/ is resonant, communicative."[30]

Throughout this body of poetry, nature has, for the most part, a female form; the relationship between human life and nature, however, is not exploitative. The radical proposal underlying the images is that the claims of the human and nature are *equal*. "This earth is my sister." Such a position means something different from any of the alternatives proposed by Lewis Thomas in *The Lives of a Cell*. We've gone from believing, Thomas says, that the earth is "man's personal property" to the painful state of being "nature itself" by virtue of our *invasion* of all forms of life. Thomas takes solace in the possibility that we are being used by nature in the same way that the giant clam is used by the algae—as a "Handyman":

> This might turn out to be a special phase in the morphogenesis of the earth when it is necessary to have something like us, for a time anyway, to fetch and carry energy, look after new symbiotic arrangements, store up information for some future season, do a certain amount of ornamenting, maybe even carry seeds around the solar system.[31]

Thomas speculates that if we were to think of ourselves thus, as "indispensable elements of nature," we might discover in ourselves the sources of delight we have found in all other aspects of nature and even begin to see ourselves as a "valuable, endangered species."[32] How quickly man's subservience is turned into a special status! The concept of relationship women poets express involves neither subservience nor special status.

Perhaps the implications of our collective idea that we are co-equals with the earth will become more apparent when we consider the images of our relationship with animals. If one reads through the separate volumes of poetry by contemporary women, the profusion of images from animal life is striking. Not only have several poets (Margaret Atwood, Anne Sexton, and May Sarton among them) produced bestiaries, but one (Susan Fromberg Schaeffer) has written a "Bible" of the beasts, and another (Diane di Prima) has written a full-scale epic in praise of the mythical wolf-woman called "Loba." Worms and butterflies, unicorns and phoenixes, all manner of birds, pets, farm and forest animals, snakes and rodents, fish and other creatures of the sea abound. Although later in this chapter I will claim that animals are often the vehicle for releasing the darker aspects of vision in this body of poetry, their primacy is rarely questioned. As Susan Astor says in "Sea People,"

> We pile our cities up like blocks
> And climb them, chattering,
> While underneath
> The vowel-voiced animals
> Just swim
> And arch their bodies into smiles.[33]

The porpoises and whales Astor has in mind as the undercurrent of human civilization are mammals who "meet and rub," love and nurse as we do, but without the consonants that turn our language into chatter.

The women whose work I have examined are often concerned to hear the speech of animals and to penetrate beneath the names and identities assigned to them for human purposes. One of the most ambitious of these efforts is Schaeffer's "The Bible of the Beasts of the Little Field," written in the style of the Psalms. The "savior" of this poem, however, is a cat named "Nameless,"

whose back was broken in a trap set by a man, and whose recovery, tantamount to a resurrection, restores the speaker's faith
in life:

> he has caused me to green into life,
> As a dry root in water, as a wire into its current,
> As each green leaf to the sun,
> To turn from my winter, to come forth green and golden,
>
> My earth full of petals
> My branches heavy with leaves.[34]

"Nameless" is part of a kingdom of animals who "feel no fear"
and "call to each other," resenting their place beneath us and
denying that they know us. Yet the cat lets the speaker touch his
head when he returns from his deathbed. He makes it possible
for her to dig up a worm without fear or disgust, to see its body
as a "living wave," and to appreciate its commitment to darkness. She hears the "timbrels and psalteries and little bells" of the
flowers who live only "one short season" and dream ten months
of the year. She puts sugared milk on the lips of a dead baby
squirrel in case he wakes in the box. In the last stanzas, the voices
of the weather, the sun, the children gathered round the squirrel,
the Lord (who threatens to destroy Ninevah), and the speaker
(who asks if her Nameless must be destroyed) accompany the
burial of the squirrel. The implication is that the Lord will destroy everything, despite the care she has learned to take, and
despite the regenerative powers of Nameless.

The same sense of doom informs another of Schaeffer's poems,
but on the smaller scale of seasonal destruction. "Hunting Season" captures the sense of dislocation experienced by all forms of
life during this annual ritual: human beings dislodged from their
houses, birds from their nests, animals from the open fields.
Even the air turns thick with fog so that the compass rusts, and
the "pines walk back/ Into the clouds" as if to avoid the spectacle
of death. But the focal point of the poem is the animals:

> They will be hunted down
>
> And they touch each other's faces
> For the last time
> Like braille.[35]

As capable of affection as any human being, the animals bid one another goodbye. The poem challenges our assumption that animals do not have human prescience, and it anticipates their sense of loss with sympathy.

Another of Schaeffer's poems, "Mistress," embodies the voice of a magical winged creature who has "long, gauzy wings/ The shape of stained glass windows" and a "long green tail/ Like a magnificent lizard." She promises to change the color of the sun and moon, having already changed the roles of cats and birds. She adds,

> And this is just the beginning
> Of what I will become for you
>
> If you stay.[36]

The animal world is not without its powers of regeneration, then, but its effectiveness is dependent on human attention. The insect here is another kind of mistress—not one who offers sexual favors, but one who offers change, even reversal of the polarities we have come to accept as unchangeable. If we remain intent on stumbling over the cliff into death one at a time, Schaeffer says, we will miss this communal possibility of change.

Denise Levertov shares Schaeffer's respect for animal life. What makes the animal's presence "holy," in her famous poem "Come into Animal Presence," is its clarity of purpose and lack of guile—in a word, its integrity:

> Those who were sacred have remained so,
> holiness does not dissolve, it is a presence
> of bronze, only the sight that saw it
> faltered and turned from it.[37]

The point is not to degrade the human but to recognize the animal as a source of joy.

Like many other women whose poems I read, Levertov is capable of identifying with the most devalued forms of animal life. In "The Earth Worm," for example, she understands the worm as an artist, the artist as a worm:

> He throws off
> artifacts as he
> contracts and expands the

> muscle of his being,
> ringed in himself,
> tilling. He
> is homage to
> earth, aereates
> the ground of his living.[38]

The poet constructs "castles of metaphor" by means of his passage through the earth. In so doing, "he" expresses fealty or deference and, at the same time, prepares the ground for the fruitful continuation of his own life. (The use of the generic pronoun is jarring in the present context; it would have been understood quite differently in the 1960s when this poem was published.)

Another more original and striking example of this tendency to identify with the devalued animal is Levertov's "Song of Ishtar," in which she imagines herself as a pig and the moon as a sow in her throat, the two of them devouring each other in desire, the poet becoming the vehicle for the moon's shining.[39]

In a darker or at least less ecstatic mood, Levertov identifies human life with that of a burrowing animal. "Life Is Not a Walk across a Field," her title proclaims;

> rather a crawling out of one's deep hole
> . . . .
>   To be
> an animal dodging
> pursuers it smells but can't
> see clear, through labyrinths
>
> of new walls. To be mangled or
> grow wise in escape.
> To bite, and destroy the net.
>   To make it maybe
> into the last of day, . . .
>   To go down
> back into the known hole.[40]

Along the way, the benefits of life are mainly aesthetic ("gazing, listening, picking up/ the voices of wheat," witnessing the "crimson wings" of the bird coming home at sunset) and communal (finding the "trail of other/ animals telling the nose the night's news"). The building of civilization is not understood as a threat to nature; the "labyrinths" of new walls begin to crumble as soon as the multitude of workers goes home. But the threat to individuals is intense, and the only solace from it is to return to one's hole in the earth.

Human life is frequently vulnerable in these poems, at the same time that it is the source of destruction. May Sarton understands this condition of weakness as the source of our pity for "The Frog, that Naked Creature," whose "every mood/ Glows through his cold red blood":

> We feel his being more, now
> We have grown so vulnerable,
> Have become so wholly exposed with the years
> To primeval powers;
> These stones are often terrible,
> Followed by sudden snow.
> It is alarming to feel the soul
> Leap to the surface and find no sheltering wall.[41]

Sarton is referring to her own growth as a poet, struggling with "the godhead as lynx" or with the goddess Kali. But other poets I treat here have had encounters with similar "primeval powers," and the results have been to increase their sensitivity to the animal world. In this case, Sarton is forced by her own honesty to admit a similarity between herself and the frog: her increasing tendency "to show the very pulse/ of thought alive." Human and animal lives are bound together, forever it would seem, in guilt and mercy, beyond the limits of our pride.[42] Finding herself in a "clean anodyne/ Hotel room in Athens," the poet longs for the white lizard, the "articulate frog" and "wandering shrew" that visited her dark room in India—misses "the chittering,/ The cry of despair,/ The silent, lunatic trot."[43] Instead of leading her into self-pity, Sarton's recognition of her connection with animal life leads her beyond the human into a wholly different set of concerns.

Perhaps this vision is most beautifully and delicately presented in Sarton's poem "Beyond the Question," in which she abandons the usual restrictions of her form. She wonders first if she can weave a nest "of listening" for the phoebe's silence as she waits day after day for her eggs to hatch, and concludes,

> But one must first become small,
> Nothing but a presence,

> Attentive as a nesting bird,
> Proferring no slightest wish,
> No tendril of a wish
> Toward anything that might happen.[44]

Only when "all is in order" and "silence flows in" does illumination occur, perhaps in the disintegration of the peony blossom
torn apart by "Creation itself." Voices of spiritual illumination
"do not speak/ From a cloud./ They breathe through the blood./
They are there in the stem/ (Plant or human flesh)."[45] The same
force that breaks down the seed pod and pushes out the new leaf
also inhabits us. But Sarton does not have in mind the orgiastic
vision of Dylan Thomas. Sarton's illumination is merely the beginning of a "dialogue" that requires intense listening on the part
of the poet:

> I lay my cheek on the hard earth
> and listen, listen.
>
> No, it is not the endless conversations
> Of the grasses and their shallow roots;
> No it is not the beetles,
> The good worms, I hear,
> But tremor much deeper down.[46]

That tremor, as I said at the outset of this essay, is what Sarton
calls love.

Perhaps it would be useful to compare Sarton's act of attention
with Sylvia Plath's mode of response to nature. Plath differs
markedly from most of the others quoted here, perhaps because,
as Joyce Carol Oates contends, she was caught in "the death
throes of Romanticism"—afflicted with the loneliness of having
"lost the Cosmos."[47] In "Black Rook in Rainy Weather," for
example, the rare miracle of illumination that could bring "brief
respite from fear/ of total neutrality" will occur or not according
to some plan the poet cannot affect by any means.[48] Likewise in
"The Colossus," she crawls like an ant over a portion of earth
("weedy acres"), which she imagines as a gigantic ruined image
of her father, and which she must (but cannot) laboriously piece
together.[49] Even in the moment of her closest identification with
nature, when she lay on the "altar" of a flat warm rock at
Swampscott, Massachusetts, in 1951, she felt that she was being
raped by the sun.

> With the sun burning into rock and flesh, and the wind riffling grass and hair, there is an awareness that the blind immense unconscious impersonal and neutral forces will endure, and that the fragile, miraculously knit organism which interprets them, endows them with meaning, will move about for a little, then falter, fall, and decompose at last into the anonymous soil, voiceless, faceless, without identity.[50]

The dichotomy between the human intellect and the insentient world could not be more strongly stated, nor has the frailty of the human been more strongly felt. She was overwhelmed by nature.

Plath would not adopt the stance of the nesting phoebe in order to listen to the sounds of the earth. The mother bird would be symbolic of an unattainable degree of selflessness, and the "words" of earth would require laborious translation. The attitude of respect for an other who is essentially one's equal (rather than one's inferior or superior), adopted so often in the body of poetry I am presenting here, would be foreign to her. Nor would she feel the "sweet/ sensation of joy" Elizabeth Bishop records in response to the sudden appearance of a female moose — towering, homely, otherworldly all at the same time — in front of her bus on the way home from the shore.[51]

There is, in this body of poetry by women, a refreshing sense of kinship with animal life without the romantic sense of separation. There is Bishop's poem about the experience of catching "a tremendous fish" with "five big hooks/ grown firmly in his mouth," trailing the lines he had broken in his previous struggles.[52] After feeling a momentary sense of victory, she lets the fish go — presumably out of respect for his heroic character. This sense of kinship allows for the revival of an anthropomorphic attitude that results in human understanding of the animal's predicament, as in Maxine Kumin's poem on the death of her barren brood mare who had previously borne eighteen foals. Kumin sympathetically observes the signs of her false pregnancy and wonders if her death was caused by false pride.[53] Just as Levertov's identification with the sow caused no degradation of the poet, so Kumin's perspective involves no degradation of the animal, no obliteration of the animal's identity by subsuming it under human psychology.

There is both a loss and a gain in our evolutionary differentiation from animals. As Margaret Atwood says, we are the ones who forgot them, relegated them to our dreams, leaving only "their masks behind."[54] We are the ones who have made them "relics" and put them on the "square glass altars" in museums of natural history, where the "brittle gods" are also kept.[55] But perhaps we were unwise in assuming that they lacked intelligence; perhaps they had and still have a kind of intelligence we need. Atwood ponders this possibility in "Notes from various pasts," as she imagines ocean creatures "swimming/ far under even the memory/ of sun and tidal moon";

> some of them fragile, some
> vicious as needles; all
> sheathed in an armoured skin
> that is a language; camouflage
> of cold lights, potent signals
> that allure prey or flash
> networks of warning
> transmitted through the deep core
> of the sea to each other only.[56]

She wonders if she has gained lungs and freedom only to lose an "electric wisdom" contained in their language. The idea is not so far-fetched. Carl Sagan describes the language of the dolphin, for example, as a "sort of aural onomatopoeia, a drawing of audio frequency pictures."[57] With no illusions about their moral superiority, Atwood contemplates the value of the animals' system of communication.

Atwood's clearest insistence that human beings are *not* superior to animals comes in her "Songs of the Transformed," where she demonstrates what reincarnation might mean in our present state of development. It is not a pleasant prospect. In the manner of the medieval bestiary, she writes the "songs" of several animals (the pig, bull, rat, crow, worm, owl, Siren, fox, hen, *and* human corpse) to set the human record straight. These animals are real, however, rather than allegorical as they would have been in Atwood's medieval models. They have access to human consciousness because they have been human at some point in the life cycle. The pig was formerly one of the men whom Circe bewitched; the owl is the heart of a murdered woman; the fox reminds his fallen human god that "this tongue/ licks through your body also."[58] The cycle includes the inanimate as well; the bull, for example, was once grass. The Siren is a human disguised as a bird whose fatal cry is an appeal to the heart of Western civilization's belief in the individual human being: "Help me!/ Only you, only you can,/ you are unique."[59]

The assorted beasts presented here, domesticated and wild, are a sorry sight. The bull, in the throes of death after a fight, could not be less enchanted with the "gods" who arranged it, for whom his death is a game disguised and justified by the religious category of grace. The rat sees through the human plan to kill her as an ugly parasite; she desires only love from her mate, who she claims is stuck in the human throat. The crow cannot raise the banner of *"Hope"* above the field of rotten corn because hope has been worn thin by "too many theories/ too many stray bullets" (p. 33). The worms are planning their revenge against the boots that crush them when they come into the open air to love. The hen's head contemplates the word "no" (the last she uttered) from the chopping block while her inarticulate body "still runs/ at random through the grass" (p. 41). Finally, the corpse brings the live body news of its future:

> soon you will have no voice
> . . . .
> Therefore sing now
> . . . .
> or you will drift as I do
> from head to head
>
> swollen with words you never said,
> swollen with hoarded love.[60]

The irony of the human being swollen with hoarded *love* in the midst of all this evidence of his *hostility* is nearly unbearable. The sequence is a biting criticism of the assumption of human superiority which leads us to kill bulls for sport, trap foxes, feel contempt for pigs, rats, and worms, and live our lives politically, without hope, murdering and being murdered despite our protestations and calls for help.

The sense of kinship with animals leads at other times not to outrage at their abuse but to fascination with them as mirrors. The reason that animals continue to serve as symbols for us, anthropologists say, even though they are rarely present in our lives now except as pets, is that "the animal" is the only aspect of life

that is both *in* us and *not* us at the same time.[61] Anne Sexton's
bestiary focuses on the animal in us. As she says in her epigraph:
"I look at the strangeness in them and the naturalness they cannot
help, in order to find some virtue in the beast in me."[62] Again,
the modern poet's strategy differs from that of her medieval
predecessors in her desire to *value* the beast in herself rather than
to moralize about how to overcome it. This sequence of Sexton's
poems is longer than Atwood's and is perhaps less aesthetically
certain of itself, since it was written near the end of her life when
she took less time to polish her poems. In some cases, she may
have even strayed from her original purpose, tempted by the rich
associations of her subject.

It is easiest to see the difference between Sexton's attitude and
Atwood's if we compare their poems on the pig and the
worm—the only animals their bestiaries have in common. In
Atwood's sequence, the pig comes first and attributes his present
transformed state not to his lust but to his greed. He is as ugly as
possible ("a stinking wart/ of flesh, a large tuber/ of blood") and
sings a "song of dung" (p. 30), presumably representing Atwood's contempt for the greed of men. The worms, who come
out from underground to "invade like weeds/ everywhere but
slowly" (p. 35), are presented positively because their revenge
against the human boots that crush them is just. Sexton's "Hog"
also comes at the beginning of her bestiary (it is second), but she
focuses on the animal's fate in the stockyard. Just as the hog lies
"sweetly" in its pen, being fattened for the slaughter, so the poet
lies in her bed putting her mind to rest for her own death by
counting the hogs going to theirs. Sexton's "Earthworm" is concerned with the "resurrection" of the worm when it is cut in
half. The poet asks: "Have you no beginning and end? Which
heart is/ the real one? Which eye the seer?"[63] She sees the worm
as a "slim inquirer" who reworks the soil filled with the debris of
civilization "while the old fathers sleep." A mysterious line also
has worms fondling the "dark stars" as they would fondle the
beaks of the birds that eat them—as if they welcomed not only
the darkness of night, but of death as well, in spite of their mi-
raculous power to regenerate themselves. Whereas Atwood's intent is the moral indictment of the human, Sexton's intent, in
these two and some other poems, is to learn from the animals
how to die.

Sexton's explicit identifications with animals tend toward this theme of death. The sequence begins with a poem on the "Bat" that allows her to identify her own witch-like aspect—the flying part of herself that makes her "something to be caught." The quills in "Porcupine" are reminders of all the non-human medical devices that have held her in place, and she removes them, "spine by spine," in order to push them into earth to bring out diamonds. These poems, like "Hog" which comes between them, are relatively "realistic." But the next poem of explicit identification, "Seal," which comes late in the sequence, is nearly pure projection. It is a portrait of a discontented seal who is "sick and tired of the rock off Frisco" and wants wings so that she can fly to "the prairie, the city, the mountain." The seal's complaint ends with the poet's characteristic desire to see Jesus, "crawling up some mountain, reckless and outrageous,/ calling out poems/ as he lets out his blood."[64]

Other animals in the bestiary appear, however, because they have the power to help her. The field horse, whose energy, plenitude, and earthiness make her feel like a "pale shadow," is nonetheless capable of nuzzling her fear out of her body. The gull, who comes last, can with its cry take her back to her childhood when she could turn away death with a Coke. These animals could not, of course, offer permanent help, and the sequence ends with Sexton's condemnation, actually more global than Atwood's: "all that flies today/ is crooked and vain and has been cut from a book."[65]

Still other animals seem to be included to enable Sexton to make her own points about American culture, since she entitled the poem "Bestiary U.S.A." The "Lobster," for example, another animal that is capable of resurrection from her point of view, is defiled by being trapped "as the U.S.A. sleeps" and then by being painted red for his consumers. The beached "Whale" affords her the opportunity to comment on the American character: "We want the double to be big,/ and ominous and we want to remember when you were/ money in Massachusetts and yet were wild and rude/ and killers."[66] But not all her commentary is critical of Americans. She calls the "Moose" the "American Archangel" because of its size, and she participates freely in the American desire to preserve this animal as symbol rather than as presence. Nor is she above hurling a curse at the Australian and

African markets which are ruining the world wool trade in which her husband made their living.

The bestiary is in fact far richer than Sexton's epigraph implies. She expresses sympathy for the drowned mole who lies at the edge of the pond "like the Pietà." She shares her bafflement regarding her relationship to the snake who is clever while she is "halting"; her only way of relating to it is through the story of Eve's fall. She is playfully indignant at the masked bandit "Raccoon" who dances over the lawn clanging the garbage pail. She pictures herself "bouncing" like "shoes after a wedding car," presumably in irritation at the "June Bug" who

> wants us to know how expensive it is
> to keep the stars in their grainy places,
> . . . .
> and so he pulses at each window, a presence,
> a huge hairy question who sees our light.[67]

Still, it would be consonant with the self-searching honesty of Sexton's later poems to say that all the poems are in some sense portraits of Sexton. "Hornet," for example, is managed entirely in the masculine third person, and yet it speaks of a desire to disturb us and to get under our skin that is characteristic of Sexton's poetry. The "Snail," who desires to lie in his mother/shell/house all day undisturbed, is ultimately eaten as Sexton fantasized she herself would be eaten by God. The "Cockroach" is presented here as the "foulest of creatures," presumably that which is furthest removed from God and the poet. Yet in Sexton's poem, a girl holds it cupped in her hands for an hour "like a diamond ring," providing the poet the protection she yearned for against the dark forces in her life. Sexton does not, however, include in the bestiary the dog who was her public *persona* in her last years, or the rat who appears in the palindrome she requested as her epitaph—perhaps as a symbol of new life.

Finally, the bestiary is more than a mirror of the beast in Sexton. It is more nearly a mirror of the various relationships we have to animals. Significantly, none of the relationships portrayed by either Sexton or Atwood involves rejection of the animal as inferior.

In Sexton's case, and in others as well, the "beast" is often a dark force within the poet which is the primary source of her power. May Sarton makes this predicament vivid in "The Invocation to Kali." The "voracious animal" whose violence is her "perpetual shame" is a lion pacing and roaring in the cage of her body, but it is also "poetry" and the "terrible god." The goddess Kali is the symbol of this force. The poet cannot overthrow her, cast her out, forget her, jail or kill her, for "until she, the destroyer, has been blest,/ There will be no child, no flower, and no wine."[68] The poem insists that we confront our potential for violence—even the violence of the Nazi concentration camps—full face, praying openly at Kali's altar. Sarton's invocation, then, is a request to the goddess of violence to

> Help us to bring darkness into the light,
> To lift out the pain, the anger,
> . . . .
> Put the wild hunger where it belongs,
> Within the act of creation,
> Crude power that forges a balance
> Between hate and love.[69]

The goddess symbol is well-chosen, since Kali is quintessentially the divinity of evil *and* good, darkness *and* light.

Sarton's poem and the two bestiaries I have just presented afford the appropriate background for what is otherwise the most difficult and baffling poem of our time: Diane di Prima's *Loba*. Epic in its proportions (190 pages), the poem is composed mainly of lyrics loosely arranged in eight parts, susceptible to rearrangement by the poet at any point; it would be truer to say it is an epic in process. The only certain thing about it is that it is a reconstruction of history in terms of myth—an attempt to subsume all the goddesses and several mythic mortals as well under the name "Loba."

The term comes (though di Prima never says so) from a folktale about a child who is raised by a wolf and grows to adulthood with both wolf and human characteristics. Thus the figure affords a readymade symbol for the close association between the animal and human life I have been tracing in poems by other women.[70] The poem works back and forth unsystematically between the past and the present, myth and reality, animal and human life, to create an image of wolf/woman that will not easily be disentangled:

Sometimes she slips sinuous thru green
transparent waters, flicking her tail
she dries on white rocks watching dolphins
her small breasts rise, point skyward, while she
brushes her dripping, tangled hair. . . . [71]

But the poem also traces a vague chronology from prehistory
through the rise of civilization and the development of Hebrew,
Greek, Christian, and medieval thought—from the one nature
goddess to her later separation into many names, to her reduction
to mortal status in Eve and Mary, Helen and Guinevere, her
survival in Lilith and her recovery in the minds of sister human
beings like di Prima. The epic is not more straightforward because it cannot be; at every turn the poet must imagine what our
history does not tell us. The structure also reflects the nature of
the Loba.

The Loba is a shapeshifter. She can never be fully described. In
the poem, she assumes the forms of wolf (p. 17), witch (p. 20),
goat (p.22), woman (p. 40), mother (p.45), savior (p. 49), white
crow, white dog, mistress owl (pp. 53–54), wind, fragrance,
incubus, face at the window, harpy, cornucopia, deathgrip,
madness,

Black grain in green jade, sound
from the silent koto, she is
tapestry burned
          in your brain, the fiery cloak
of feathers carries you
               off hills
when you run flaming
          down
               to the black sea.[72]

The poet prays to her as if she were synonymous with the universe as we know it, from the willow tree to the milky way; but
when the Loba reveals herself in a dream,

she-who-was-to-have-devoured me
stood, strong patient
               recognizably
goddess.
     Protectress
great mystic beast of European forest.
green warrior woman, towering.

> kind watchdog I cd
> leave the children with.
> Mother & sister.
> Myself.[73]

Once again, the paradoxical beneficent destroyer turns out to be the poet's self.

In di Prima's poem as in Susan Griffin's, both nature and the so-called supernatural are envisioned as our sisters. Di Prima begins her poem with an "Ave" (salutation) to her wandering "lost moon sisters," who are both the human and the non-human stuff of life she moves within. She says:

> I dip my hand in you and eat your flesh
> you are my mirror image and my sister
> . . . .
> I am you
> and I must become you.[74]

Near the end of the poem (at least in its present version), the Loba becomes a whirling dervish "to undo/ the winding sheet," the "remembering skin," of "pain which is claim/ to womanhood." She does this in order to be "born/ in uniqueness."[75] She is speaking to Apollo at his healing fountain, but her healing consists in rejecting his bondage. Apollo is a god of light because of his association with the sun, but in the next poem the white wolves glide through their own grove of light; and in the next, the Loba (or the poet) prepares to drink "black water" from a well more ancient than, and abhorrent to, Apollo. She then promises to get her sister's ancient jug home unbroken and to tell her story. Finally, like Piercy and Atwood, di Prima embraces the metaphor of cyclical being: "when we have won clear/ we must return to the circle," and, conversely, "when we return to the circle/ we have won clear."[76] Only by recovering our "early fierceness" do we regain the possibility of becoming unique selves. In becoming authentic selves, we tap the wolf and the goddess within us. The present (1978) version of *Loba* ends with a warning that "there is another Lilith, not made for earth" who lures human beings away from home "to wander, forever, between quasars."[77] The Loba may fly like a witch and write *noli me tangere* with the stars; the hem of her garment may be the sky; but her power is *of the earth*:

> Her power is in spittle
> & in the lentil,
>   it rises like smoke
> from the reopened furrow.[78]

Di Prima's poem badly needs the kind of cutting and shaping that Pound gave to Eliot's *The Waste Land*, and even then it would take longer to work its way into the culture than Eliot's poem did. Yet at moments it is as moving as anything Eliot wrote.[79] It simply requires a willingness to step outside the myth we have adopted about the linear progression of intelligent life, category by category. Di Prima's great triumph is to have created images that transcend categories of both wolf and woman. They are perhaps as close as we can come, in poetry, to the images of the hybrid in visual art. But her vision requires us to re-examine the stories we have accepted along with the scientific data about our evolution.

The poems I have presented here are not anti-scientific so much as they are against the hierarchy that thinkers have established on the basis of their interpretation of the data science has amassed—a hierarchy that has in turn been used to justify all manner of atrocities against women and the earth. We know now through anthropology that many of the cultures of the world do not accept the anthropocentric perspective we have come to regard as the Truth itself. Judging from the reports of men like Lewis Thomas and Carl Sagan, who are the sole link between most of us and the highly specialized enterprise of science, some scientists are beginning to question the degree of our separateness from certain animals, and to value some aspects of animal intelligence far more highly than was possible a century ago when our mythology took its present shape. Likewise, the poets I interpret here look at the story of evolution and see in it the evidence of our similarity to other species. Perhaps they are predisposed to do so by the venerable habit of identifying woman with nature. Perhaps it is merely a strategy of survival, to *re*value the *dis*valued world to which one is said to be similar. Whatever the reason for its development, we have here the makings of another myth quite different from the one we learned in school.

It is a perspective that allows us to see, as Robin Morgan does, a relationship different from the ones hypothesized between the Lady and the Unicorn portrayed in the famous fifteenth-century tapestries at the Musée de Cluny in Paris. In Morgan's version of the story, the Unicorn is neither a Christian symbol of divine innocence nor the symbol of male sexuality, but an animal who has somehow escaped bondage to human civilization. The Lady sees how the mythmakers will disbelieve the story of their love and "brand" her "human." But, she says,

> I see beyond all this as well,
> to a time when we will not be hunted or adored,
> because their fear exhausts itself, even as our progress
> inexorably strips us of attendants.
> And there, like a leap of thought or matter
> toward the other's grace, we are transformed,
> merged across species—
> female and male, myth and human,
> beast, bird, leaf, fruit, flower,
> music and blood and visions
> all facets of one jewel, faultless.[80]

Neither worship of Christ nor worship of sexuality is at the core of the relationship between the Lady and the Beast, but something far more disturbing to the anthropocentric mind: love across species. Is our century the time the Lady in Morgan's poem foresees when woman and beast will be neither hunted nor adored? As Morgan points out in her introduction, the tapestries that carry this vision of nature's wholeness were created during the Inquisition when the Wiccean religion that espoused such a vision was driven underground for centuries. Will there be another Inquisition to equal the first? Or has the fear of nature exhausted itself?

When I return with these works in mind to Susan Griffin's prose poems in the final section of *Woman and Nature*, I find there a moving articulation of a shared story about the relationship between women and nature—a story that emphasizes not subservience or fear, not husbandry or dominance, but equality.

In the book's final poem, "Matter: How We Know,"[81] Griffin literally weaves descriptions of human consciousness into her descriptions of earth, so that the passage I quoted near the beginning of this essay ("We are nature seeing nature") is embedded in a rich texture that illuminates its meaning. The pattern of Griffin's association is autobiographical, yet it is not difficult to share. Patches of silver and brown grass are *"Like the patches of silver in our hair. Worn by time."* We are *"shaped like the earth, by what has gone before. The lives of our mothers"* (p. 223). The song of the bird is like the flute or the cello, part of a symphony we imagine as we also imagine the lives of our grandmothers, or *"what lay under the surface."* Griffin imagines for us the space under the surface of a marsh, *"our voices calling for help and no one listening."* She envisions our emergence from the marsh, since the daughter *"always comes back."* And she imagines a reunion of mother and daughter, despite all *"those who had tried to keep us apart"* (p. 224). The mother and daughter emerge holding the stars and their light *"in our hands, this light telling the birds where they are, the same light which guides these birds to this place, and the light through which we imagine ourselves in the bodies of these birds, flying with them."* Griffin returns to the marsh, this time to observe and to listen, but from a distance, *"because though we can advance upon the blackbird, though we may cage her, though we may torture her with our will . . . this bird will never be ours"* (p. 225). Dissect her to train her as we will, we cannot control her; for the tamed bird *"we must make a new word,"* as we invented a name for the wild bird and are naming ourselves. But we must not think that we invented either the blackbird or ourselves. The blackbird *"flies in us, in our inner sight. . . . We are moved. We fly. We watch her wings negotiate the wind. . . . And yet the blackbird does not fly in us but is somewhere else free of our minds, . . . flying in the path of her own will."* We belong to a natural cycle: the sunlight in the grass "enters the body of the bird, *enters us"* (p. 226), pours from one body to another in lovemaking, filling us with light, movement, and sound, and dispersing again into the earth in an endless process. This is the essence of our "knowledge." The light that infuses our being is natural light. As Griffin says, in her wonderful style that elaborates in a feminine way by connecting elements without subordinating them,[82] "and all that I know, I know in this earth, the body of the bird, this pen, this paper, these hands, this tongue speaking, all that I know speaks to me through this earth and I long to tell you, you who are the earth too, and listen *as we speak to each other of what we know: the light is in us"* (p. 227)

The implications of this vision are awesome if we take it seriously. It requires a different societal structure, a different use of energy, a different religion, and much more for its fulfillment. Perhaps if it is not realized, the reason will not be fear of woman or nature, but fear of change. Yet the myth itself is firmly grounded in traditional mythology of woman's relationship to nature. All we need do is to recognize woman as fully human.

CONCLUSION

The Light
Is in Us

> . . . because I know I am made from this
> earth, as my mother's hands were made
> from this earth, as her dreams came from
> this earth and all that I know, I know in
> this earth, the body of the bird, this pen,
> this paper, these hands, this tongue speak-
> ing, all that I know speaks to me through
> this earth and I long to tell you, you who
> are earth too, and listen *as we speak to each
> other of what we know: the light is in us*.
>
> —Susan Griffin,
> *Woman and Nature*.

In my introduction, I said that my work here is analogous to the
art of the action photographer. If so, the display you have seen is
analogous to the grid format which is so central in contemporary
photography and in visual art in general. The format marks a
shift in epistemology from the cubist approach to the interpretation of reality, in which the task was to show how multiple perspectives converging on the same object altered our sense of the
object's nature. It also marks a shift from the surrealist her-
meneutics which assumed that our task was to explore the relationship (usually the gap) between aspects of reality shown to us
by different layers of our consciousness. The grid marks our
recognition that reality itself is a more complex phenomenon
than either group of artists supposed, and that in our present state
of knowledge, the most honest thing we can do is to set down in
the same large frame multiple images that seem to belong together, allowing their elements to reflect upon each other in the
richest ways possible.

Thus, the works I have treated here belong together because

they are by women and because they illuminate the process of mythmaking; but these are not their only appropriate framing principles. As reader-response critics of literature have taught us, each new grid will change the perceiver's interpretation of the works. But luckily, as action photographers have taught us, no grid will determine the future of the action it records. Mythmaking is likely to continue in works by women no matter what we say of it. Our job as interpreters is to be aware of its would-be imperatives so that we may see more clearly how they interact with our own. It remains for me to say what I think this grid shows about women as mythmakers and about the results of women's mythmaking enterprise.

I.   WOMEN AS MYTHMAKERS

This study highlights a number of "trouble spots" for women in western mythology: the emphasis on the masculine in our images of God; the confinement of the mother to the realm of intimate relationships; the emphasis on the seductress in every woman; the definition of creativity in terms of a heroic (masculine) quest; the identification of woman with nature to the detriment of both; the assumption that woman is the guardian of love; the hierarchical arrangement of the species, as if the ladder were the most "natural" principle of relationship; and the dichotomizing tendencies of our language and thought, as if it were really true that "without contraries there is no progression," or as if "progression" were the only viable option in our lives.

The mythmaking strategies that have been tried in response to these troubles are sufficiently varied to give us pause in our efforts to describe the process of mythmaking in general. As I said earlier, sometimes in this body of work a myth takes shape in collision with other myths; thus, Griffin's "simple" phrase, "the earth is my sister," emerges from her battle with the patriarchal mode of identifying women with nature. Thus also, Atwood's sense of the possibility of a qualitatively different relationship between males and females, human beings and the earth, emerges from her vision of Circe's conflict with Odysseus; and the result of her strategy could be a radical change in our understanding of the quest.

Sometimes a myth takes shape within another myth, as when

Varo uses the skeleton of the quest to explore female creativity and spiritual power; or when Wakoski transforms her relationship with the moon, starting from an identification with the moon goddesses, Isis and Artemis/Diana; or when Griffin discovers in her empathy with Persephone on her return to her mother that "the light is in us."

Sometimes, also, a myth takes shape with no conscious reference (or only the most tangential reference) to mythology, as in the case of Kollwitz's image of the powerful mother, or in her image of death as a woman. Certainly we, as interpreters, can find general antecedents for her figure of the mother in the goddess religions, but I have been unable to locate a specific precedent for the icon she creates in the *Tower of Mothers*. Kollwitz seems to have created this image, and *Death with Woman in Lap*, out of a pressing internal need whose mythological roots were not apparent to her at all.

When we create mythic images without awareness of their possible precursors, as Sexton's work shows, we may endanger ourselves. Without a tradition to serve as a reference point or, alternatively, a community to affirm our direction, we risk an unbearable degree of isolation.

Diane Wakoski and Léonor Fini model another possibility that deserves our attention: that one person may go through different phases in the process of mythmaking. Wakoski's process apparently began with her acknowledgment of an affinity with the moon, and proceeded through a series of rejections and affirmations toward a radically different self-concept and sense of her role as a woman and a poet. Fini's process is even more striking. It began with a set of paintings (1942–50) about her own emergence into consciousness: selfconsciousness, awareness of responsibility for others or power over others, and identity. I have in mind a painting which shows her separating herself from other women who are still sphinxes; another in which, as the dark chthonian guardian of a beautiful young man, she is benign; another in which hers is the only human form emerging from a swampy lake;[1] and another in which the artist surrounds herself with the symbols of the goddess and seems to assume her powers and responsibilities. This was a phase of identification with the paleolithic stage of our prehistory.

In the next phase of her mythmaking (1952–58), Fini focussed on a set of bald priestesses who belong to a later stage of the mythology of the goddess (specifically, the "Lady of the Beasts"), but do not correspond precisely to any specific myth, and who apparently do not represent the artist's struggle for self (they are not self-portraits) so much as the ancient idea of the virgin, she-who-is-one-in-herself.[2] Fini insists that these figures came from her dreams and not from literary or mythological sources, but they were the dreams of a woman who spent her childhood climbing on statues of mythological figures. These beings are not entirely human, any more than their sphinx counterparts were. They are distant, controlled, unrelated to any time and place—yet nurturing, at least symbolically. In them, Fini links fertility with order, perhaps for the first time since the medieval revival of the goddess Natura (as in Chaucer's *Parliament of Fowls*).[3]

The third phase of Fini's mythmaking (1958–63) involved a turning away from the human form and from specific mythologies to the elements themselves, and to a mystical frame of mind that challenged all the boundaries we know among things. A self-portrait during this period shows her as a sorceress with certain witch-like attributes, indicating that her imagination had been stirred by the mythological figure of the witch. But the results of that stirring—the bizarre images of mineral and vegetal growth, and later the beautiful images of human forms emerging from flowers—were not prescribed by any witch's story known to me. I have said that Fini undertook a journey like Persephone's in these years; but Fini herself does not acknowledge this source, and in fact her journey may have been more like Inanna's descent into death in Ereshkigal's realm.[4] Or maybe it is futile to look for specific mythological precedents in the work of an artist whose one consistent hallmark has been her independence.

Fini's fourth phase of mythmaking (1963–74 and beyond) involves a sense of "breakthrough": a room is unsealed; beings from "the other side" are seen in silhouette; that which has been absent returns; a secret feast is celebrated; and so on.[5] The human figure returns—almost exclusively in its female form—sometimes even with a recognizable name: Hecate, Heliodora, Narcissus, *La Belle Dame sans Merci*. In this phase of her painting, Fini represents a world more nearly like the one we inhabit (with cafés, trains, painting studios, fashionable hats, and so on), but which is also decidedly imaginary, so that no one-to-one correspondence with our lives is possible. In some ways, it is even more strange than the three prehistoric realms she had previously created. And although there are traces of Fini's features in the faces of her characters, there are no more self-portraits. Indeed, the mythic issue is no longer the nature of the self or the relationship of self to nature, but the female's responsibility to culture. Death is just under the surface in several paintings: the "death angel" appears as a unisex figure with long flowing hair. An outline of a man is drawn in chalk in the same way that police mark out the position of a dead body.[6] The redheaded Heliodora presides with boredom over the sacrifice of the goose (pl. 8). But death is the underside of life. Three women wrap a humanoid package for "Sending," or stir dismembered or forming body parts in a glass cauldron (pl. 9, 10). The paintings have an eerie power to awaken the belief that human life can and will be transformed.

These analyses suggest that women mythmakers may be moving through stages from greater to lesser dependency on traditional myths. And they suggest that our relationship to the history of mythmaking is even more complex that it has seemed. Clearly, the women I have treated here are not in the position Julia Kristeva described as refusing the symbolic.[7] Nor are they bent on taking it over. The symbolic code is present as history in the myths that serve alongside those of prehistory as materials to transform. As Alicia Ostriker observes, "H. D.'s concept of the 'palimpsest' seems to be the norm, along with a treatment of time that effectively flattens it so that the past is not then but now."[8] Neither history nor prehistory is regarded as *binding*. The artist is free to go on into imaginative realms of her own making—and does. Kollwitz's mother and Fini's world of women guérillères are the most powerful examples of such freedom treated here.

We *could* say that Kollwitz and Fini returned to matriarchal prehistory for their female figures; the interpretation would be justified in Fini's case by her use of the sphinx and the goddess in her early work. But where in that early mythology do we actually see the birth of the woman from the sphinx? Or where do we see the thinking aspect of the lady of the beasts?[9] Likewise, where do we find the "history" of the amazons' daily activities? Fini's vision goes well beyond earlier "texts."

The argument that these artists returned to a specific stratum of myth that predates our present symbolic code is doubtful. The more likely interpretation, I think, is that the artists' images arose out of a sense of collective female experience which women have missed during much of their patriarchal experience. Kollwitz was a feminist with a deeply felt political allegiance to women; Fini found her mature identity as a "sorcière."

The phenomenon of the "return" of the goddess in contemporary arts is fascinating. It has suggested to some that there must be an "essential" female or feminine experience which has persisted through the ages even in the face of patriarchal oppression. But if we see the archetype as a tendency to form images in relation to repeated experiences, would it not be more accurate to say that for the second time in history (the first ended with the witch trials), women are experiencing the kind of female collectivity that spawned those early images. Once again, female creativity is much in evidence. Perhaps we find much that is familiar in our prehistory, then, because we are repeating an experience of collectivity that underlies the formation of the culture's symbolic code. We are repeating the imaginative state that produced myth in the first place.

If archetypal images mark the places (intersections) where the gap between "inner" and "outer" becomes visible—that is, if they represent persistent problems of human experience—then the images of the goddess mark recurrent questions about female experiences rather than essential characteristics of Woman. They mark generative experiences—of problems that occur without being completely solved—that can lead to new resolutions as well as to the repetition of old ones.

Now if we re-examine women's relationship to patriarchal myth, we can see that women participate in the male tradition of mythic revision that Albert Cook describes, and also in mythic processes that both predate *and* supercede it. Whatever our desire for purity, we are unlikely to be able to disentangle our roots in prehistory from our roots in history. In fact, there seems little point in doing so, since by means of female collectivity we have discovered our ability to generate images and stories of the sort that should lead to changes in the symbolic code itself. It may be more fruitful to begin to look for new branches in our mythological tree.

In the two mythic statements ("There is no other" and "The

light is in us"), Atwood and Griffin recognize that other positions are more familiar within the established code, but they
brush these aside to articulate the truth of their experience.
Whether that experience is *purely* female is less important than
the fact that it marks a boundary of the dominant culture and
therefore belongs to one of the "muted" cultures.[10] And because
both statements express the same reluctance to dichotomize, we
may ask what leads these two very different women to the same
position.

This line of inquiry leads directly to the larger question about
women and myth that I raised in my introduction: what is the
raison d'être of myth for contemporary women? What leads
women poets or artists to engage in mythmaking? As I reported,
Eric Gould argues that mythicity arises in the gap between event
and meaning, and registers the inadequacy of language to bridge
that gap. For him, the central problem of experience always addressed by myth is "nothingness." He starts with Heidegger's
notion that "all Being is available only as a phenomenological
crisis, a coming-into-consciousness":

> Furthermore, "What-is" is nothing more than itself, so what is
> Nothing? The problem lies in defining—as I want to show myth
> itself always tries to do—why that Nothing-more always seems
> like something-more. Nothing is not an object, yet we live with
> the experience of nihilation. It has a presence in our consciousness.
> Even in the midst of our cultural contexts, we are beings projected
> into Nothing. We have always been beings projected into Noth-
> ing, and for that reason there has always been myth. For it is first
> myth, and then, I would suggest, modern interpretation theory,
> that reminds us strongly today that without a sense of Nothing,
> there is no self or freedom. In Heidegger's annoying paradox,
> Nothing is the ground of Being. And flirting with that proposition
> is like flirting with the stuff of myth. For myth . . . is, if nothing
> else, the history of our inability to authenticate our knowledge of
> Being, and yet it is at the same time a history of our attempts to
> understand that inability.[11]

Even in the midst of our cultural contexts, nothingness is present
in our consciousness as the experience of nihilation. Myth is the
history of our inability to authenticate our knowledge of being
against this experience in order to attain a sense of self or freedom. Myth is also the history of our attempts to understand this
inability. Gould applies his theory convincingly to James Joyce,

D. H. Lawrence, and T. S. Eliot. But can it be applied successfully to the poets and artists I have treated here? The question takes on additional significance, since Carol Christ has pos-
ited that women's spiritual quest begins with an experience of
nothingness.[12]

Curiously, such an experience at the metaphysical level Gould
has in mind seems to have occurred in only one of the lives I
have treated here—in Käthe Kollwitz's cumulative response to
the war and its aftermath, as described in her *Diary*. But several
aspects of her experience deserve attention here as we think about
what leads women to make myths. Her experience occurred in
the spring of 1921, less as a crisis than as a state of gradual collapse of faith in herself, her relationships, her work, and her
society. It occurred near the beginning of a new stage of high
productivity rather than during a period of "silence" or non-
productivity; since her mythic themes were well established and
her shift to the media of the woodcut and sculpture were already
accomplished, it was not really so much a beginning as a transi-
tion. And the experience of nothingness was not so much one of
nihilism as of something like censorship. She wrote:

> One horrid symptom is this: not only do you not think a single
> matter through to the end, but you don't even feel a feeling to the
> end. As soon as one arises, it is as though you throw a handful of
> ashes on it and it promptly goes out. Feelings which once touched
> you closely seem to be behind thick, opaque window panes;
> the weary soul does not even try to feel because feeling is too
> strenuous.[13]

Thoughts and feelings, then, continued to occur but were not
brought to fruition; they could not *matter* (become realized in
consciousness) because Kollwitz remained *out of touch* with them.
A few months later, she described her ability to work as a "tide"
that rose and ebbed of its own accord within her, regardless of
her external environment.[14]

In fact, Kollwitz's account of her experience corresponds more
nearly to my description of Anne Sexton's situation in the last
four years of her life than it does to the experience of nihilation.
In both cases, the pressure came not from nothingness in the
sense of emptiness, but from the presence of thought and feeling
that exceeded the woman's capacity to deal with it. In my in-

terpretation, the pressures on Sexton came from the flood of unknown images into her consciousness, and from her inability to name them to her own satisfaction.

To be sure, there are painful confrontations in this body of work with the problems of being unrecognized by one's society. Such confrontations are poignantly imaged in Diane Wakoski's *The Motorcycle Betrayal Poems*; but they are problems of social authentication, not metaphysical nihilation. These seem to be the issues Carol Christ has in mind when she describes women's experience of nothingness in terms of self-hatred, self-abnegation, and being a victim.[15] Important as they are, they are by no means the primary motivating force of all the mythic works I have treated here.

It does seem reasonable to say that the mythic explorations I have detailed may have occurred in response to existential crises, although their exact nature remains a matter of conjecture. For Sexton, the gap between the pleasurable reality of her body and the guilt she inherited from the Christian tradition may have achieved crisis proportions. For Kollwitz, perhaps the gap was between her love for her son (who came to symbolize all youth) and the ideology of war that destroyed his life, or between her belief in socialist ideals and the realities of German life between the wars. Varo's commitment to wholeness may have developed out of the series of displacements she endured as a young European woman in a war-torn era. The harmony she desired among the various orders of being required the kind of spiritual quest that would resurrect the fruits of the earth itself. Wakoski's quest may have stemmed from the loss of her father in childhood, so that she had to provide for herself the approval and support she deserved from him; in the process, she too transcended the concern for self. Fini also experienced an early family trauma, which may have brought her and her mother even closer together than would normally be the case in a nuclear family; perhaps her vision stems from her witch's sense of her own sufficiency in defiance of societal expectations that she would depend on men. But these are only conjectures. In Atwood's case, we have too little biographical information to speculate at all along these lines.

Whatever their differences, and they are substantial, these women share at least one characteristic: they are only partly concerned with authenticating the self and establishing its freedom.

For the self, in many of these works, shades often and easily into the not-self. The works often operate on a principle that Gloria Bonder calls "transitionality":

> Transitionality . . . is a permanent process in life (not merely, as [D. W.] Winnicott observed, a developmental stage in the infant), and it is a process more characteristic of women than of men. [It is] that type of subject-object relationship which is neither total fusion (confusion of boundaries) nor total separation, but a relationship that is paradoxical, intermediate and dynamic. In ideological discourse the certainty of this distinction is challenged. Thus, one need not, indeed cannot, differentiate subjectivity and objectivity so sharply. All objects are subjectively experienced as part of the subject, yet not *as* the subject; that is, object and subject are not coterminous but *are* and *are not*, simultaneously.[16]

While I am not claiming transitional discourse as a female preserve or saying that it informs all mythmaking by women, I think its presence in works by women may necessitate some revision in our theories of myth.

If the central issue of myth for men has been to truimph over the threat of nothingness, then the central issue for the women I treat here is significantly different. Tentatively, I would describe it as a tension between the multiplicity of being (experienced often as an overflow of images, feelings or thoughts) and the man-made structures that are supposed to order being and giving it meaning. Instead of a wasteland, we have here a landscape teeming with interwoven forms of life, whose affinity with our own form we need only recognize to enjoy. Perhaps there is no metaphysical gap between event and meaning once we give up the desire to *possess* the event in language. The job of myth under such circumstances would not be to fill the void of nothingness but to overcome the restrictions on being we have built into our symbolic code.

Having traced the various processes of mythmaking in these works, and having proposed answers to the questions concerning women's role in the history of mythmaking and reasons for involvement in it, I must return now to the question that initiated my study. What changes are women making in our cultural mythology?

II. SOME RESULTS OF WOMEN'S MYTHMAKING

Joseph Campbell's speculation that there are no "mythogenetic zones" today save the individual heart—no geographical areas or communities in which a "language of mythic symbols and related rites" can develop in sufficient depth to become myth[17]—is contradicted by the works of countless women who share Griffin's conviction that "the light is in us." The conviction shows up most powerfully in memorable paintings such as Remedios Varo's *Emerging Light*, in which the lamp the woman carries through the vaginal opening in the wall is filled with fluid distilled from a spiritual quest conducted in relationship to the cosmos. It shows up also in less well-known works such as Léonor Fini's *Heliodora*, in which Fini's female version of the sun god first emerges from the keyhole of the underworld the artist had explored for several years in her paintings. The conviction seems to come from the process Wakoski calls "slipping down/ soft silver stairways" of ourselves—that is, a process of re-envisioning the categories of woman and nature.[18]

Such a conviction involves an acceptance of our material being, so that Marge Piercy can celebrate dancing "in the fire of which/ we are the logs, the matches, and the flames." It involves a willingness to assume and transform the powers of Apollo, as in Diane di Prima's imagery. It may also require (as in Susan Fromberg Schaeffer's horrifying fantasy of the witch's self-immolation) our sacrifice on behalf of nature. This conviction about our affinity with light, so different from the Western tendency to consider the mind a penetrating searchlight,[19] has its symbolic counterpart in the belief in female strength, creativity, and wisdom, shown in such diverse sources as Kollwitz's mother who assumes responsibility for preserving civilization and Atwood's Circe who refuses to let Odysseus rest in the "clutch" of his story. Even Anne Sexton, who could not finally believe in her own powers, could briefly envision a female creatrix of a new dawn.

Throughout the works treated in these essays, certain images, themes, and attitudes recur with sufficient intensity to suggest the presence of a myth that is not the product of community life in a particular geographic region so much as the product of women's common "ground" of experience in patriarchal societies. It may also be the product of our newly-found sense that we form an audience for each other, so that we can speak directly to each other across great distances. Thus, we are sharing more broadly than ever our rich inner worlds[20] known only to intimates for so long. And, as it turns out, these inner lives resonate with common chords, such as the one I just touched concerning the light we share with nature.

If the proverbial visitor from another planet were to analyze this cross-section of words and images, as if it were an orchestral score,[21] what vision would emerge? Thus far, I have interpreted the "melodies" played by several individuals, and I have suggested in my essays on contemporary poetry and visual art that these melodies are not idiosyncratic developments. They are themes that belong to a growing mythic tradition. Now it remains for me to analyze the score vertically, exploring whether these lines of images harmonize with each other to create a meaningful whole.

First, it may be useful to repeat the stories we have heard so far. They concern our relationships with God, man, and nature, with particular attention to our roles as mothers, lovers, and caretakers of the world. The actual stories are more specific, if not entirely finished. Sexton's is a "complaint" (in the venerable literary sense of the word) about the need for a god who is more responsive to the realities of the body. Kollwitz's is heroic in its praise of the power of the mother. Atwood's voice provides ironic commentary on the traditional mode of achieving heroism by domination, and rejects the female's complicity in this masculine enterprise. Varo's is an ecstatic, perhaps tragic, testimony to the possibility of an authentic female quest. Wakoski's is a lyric/ epic of triumph over the negative evaluation of herself and nature. Fini's is a playful but radical drama of the construction of a new social order defined in female terms. These stories are supplemented and enriched by others in poetry and visual art by women where the themes of metamorphosis and empathy are dominant.

A vertical analysis of the same material across the line of individual *oeuvres* and media shows many more patterns than I can hope to treat here and suggests that feminist archetypal critics have a lifetime of work ahead of them. The "chords" (or harmonies) I want to examine now in relationship to the mythic idea that "the light is in us" are those having to do with what I have repeatedly called the "permeable boundaries" between the female self and other phenomena.

These permeable boundaries manifest themselves in many ways in the poetry and visual art I have discussed thus far. In Kollwitz's art , for example, the woman often extends herself to include two or more children, forming a shelter (*Seed Corn Shall Not Be Ground*) or a barricade (*Tower of Mothers*) for them. And, in a few powerful works, Kollwitz lets the woman slide into the comforting arms of a maternal figure of death. These are "down-to-earth" versions of a process which includes acts of shapeshifting that are not so familiar in our daily lives.

Varo has her female protagonist become owl-like in order to create the birds (*The Creation of the Birds*), or butterfly-like in order to catch the moon (*Star-Huntress*). Sexton has Eve come out of Adam's ribs "like an angry bird," clothed in the sun. Or Anne flies in the face of God in her "fire clothes." Wakoski navigates magical beasts (a porpoise, a black camel) into mythical spaces where she assumes either the guise or the responsibilities of the goddess. Atwood's Circe is also a medium between the world of nature and spirit and the world of men. Fini portrays the most radical form of shapeshifting in her exploration of the reality behind her visions when she makes the elements themselves give birth to human forms.

These are not merely the delusions of a few crazy women, as my thematic essays on poetry and visual art show. Poets such as Marge Piercy, Denise Levertov, May Sarton, Susan Fromberg Schaeffer, Susan Griffin, and many others are no less involved in an exploration of the boundaries among the categories of "kind" (the medieval word for nature) that have made our experience "manageable." Visual artists as diverse as Ellen Lanyon, Patricia Johanson, Mary Beth Edelson, Georgia O'Keeffe, Nancy Graves, and June Wayne are engaged in similar explorations.

In the poems, I have traced the contours of a story about our relationship with nature that emphasizes not subservience or fear, not husbandry or dominance, but equality arising from acceptance of our similarities to other forms of nature without obliterating our differences from them. I have written at length about how Susan Griffin's "Matter: How We Know" embodies this delicate balance, but it appears explicitly elsewhere as well. It could not be more effectively rendered than in the 13th section of Margaret Atwood's "Daybooks II," where the female protagonist speaks to the male about the battering, imploding, crushing effect of the noise of modern technological life (here figured as radio impulses) on his body—which has led to the thickening of his skin for protection. She continues:

> But there is one rift, one flaw:
> that vulnerable bud, knot,
> hole in the belly where you were nailed
> to the earth forever.
>
> I do not mean *the earth*, I mean the
> earth that is here and browns your
> feet, thickens your fingers,
> unfurls in your brain and in
> these onion seedlings
> I set in flats lovingly under
> a spare window.[22]

This is the poem that ends, "there is *no other*." We are *of* the earth, made of the same stuff; there is no *other*, no division between us and "lower" or "higher" forms of being. We return to earth (or to "dust" as the Bible puts it), not to be "saved" and become immortal spirits, but to give back to nature what was, and is, and always will be, her own.

Likewise, in visual art by women, the widespread concern with processes of metamorphosis in animal, vegetable, mineral, and spiritual forms moves beyond the impulse toward personal growth to encompass cosmic aspects of nature. This ecological concern is oriented less toward human survival and more toward the preservation of and reverence for the elements. In some cases, such reverence is specifically linked to a goddess figure, but more often it is linked to the human female. The universe is an extension of ourselves—our source, our homologue, our trust—rather than a force to be propitiated or a domain to be used for our convenience. The images and forms presented in this body of work depend upon a different conception of appropriate boundaries between things—a conception that does not erase the boundaries altogether but allows for easements.

These "chords" of permeability are often "played" in a style that underscores their theme. Julia Stanley and Susan Wolfe describe a female style of writing in terms that will seem appropriate to many of the poets I have quoted in these pages:

As women strain to break through the limits of English, certain patterns begin to emerge, recurrences of similar syntactic ways of ordering perception that is always moving and often contradictory. One observation may negate another. The natural imagery of growth, proliferation, and evolution replaces nature as object and product. Flux, not stasis, characterizes experience. Labels and abstract nouns as viable perceptive categories give way to active, process verbs and concrete nouns, the language of touch; verbs of specific action replace the abstract, more general verbs. On the discourse level, we find a discursive, conjunctive style instead of the complex, subordinating, linear style of classification and distinction. It is not that there is no classification taking place, but rather that the syntactic structure must accommodate itself to the shifting perspectives of the writer's observing mind.[23]

This is the style that allows the earth to brown feet, thicken fingers and unfurl in both brains and onions as Atwood sets seedlings under her window in "Daybooks II." It is the style that allows Griffin to interweave the blackbird, the light, perception, inner sight, mother and daughter, the bird's flight and our own, pen, paper, hands, tongue and knowledge into her ecstatic affirmation: "The light is in us."

Likewise, in 1973 Lucy Lippard found in women's art certain stylistic tendencies which she described as

a uniform density, or overall texture, often sensuously tactile and repetitive or detailed to the point of obsession; the preponderance of circular forms, central focus, inner space (sometimes contradicting the first aspect); a ubiquitous linear "bag" . . . that turns in on itself; layers or strata, or veils; an indefinable looseness or flexibility of handling; windows; autobiographical content; animals; flowers; a certain kind of fragmentation.[24]

Later, Lippard said that there is "no technique, form or approach that is used exclusively by women,"[25] and surely this is correct. Yet surely she had also correctly reported what she had seen. Her descriptive terms would apply to many of the visual works I have treated here. Still later, Lippard revised her hypothesis to say that the distinctive feature of much women's art is its "inclusiveness" in structure, style, form, medium, subject, situation, and audience. Such works of art are sometimes more like webs or networks than artifacts. Like the collage, they offer ways of "knitting the fragments of our lives together."[26]

My study suggests that such stylistic features, when they occur (and they do not always occur in women's work), may be related to an emerging world-view or myth of relationship between self and world which does not accept the categories that have enclosed our lives. Although I believe this myth arises naturally out of the female person's actual or potential bodily experience of menstruation, penetration, pregnancy, birth, lactation, and menopause, which may leave her open to a less hierarchical story of human relationships than the accustomed one, I do not think that the myth excludes men. At least, it does not exclude those men who are like the curly-haired boy in Adrienne Rich's "Mother-Right," who runs in a field with a short-haired woman, their hands clasped, under the "hawk-winged cloud." It may exclude the man the pair seems to be running from. That man is the kind who walks the boundaries of his land to measure it:

> He believes in what is his
>   the grass   the waters underneath   the air
>
>   the air   through which child and mother
>   are running   the boy singing
>   the woman   eyes sharpened in the light
>   heart stumbling   making for the open[27]

The belief in the permeability of boundaries embodied in the works I have examined here seems to be also an attempt to extend the sphere of the woman without overriding the integrity of others. The female envisioned (or hoped-for) is one with vastly increased responsibility. I have described Kollwitz's model as a fully-conscious adult woman who exercises her agency (her capacity for self-protection, self-assertion, and self-expansion) to move society toward a less repressive condition. She is the ancient "virgin" who may be either a matriarch or an unattached woman and who may extend her concern well beyond the human realm. As creator, she may be (as in Varo's model) in tune with powerful non-human forces, capable of transforming herself and of collaborating with others to "save" both herself and the world. Or, as in Léonor Fini's work, the female may preside over the creation and maintenance of a new order of being.

Many of the women whom I treat here would share Sexton's desire for a world in which nursing and copulation, child and adult, love and power, life and death, soul and body were parts of a continuum and not irreconcilable opposites. Traditionally such desires are satisfied by images of gods or goddesses, and indeed, Demeter and associated figures such as Isis, Hecate, Ceres, Persephone and Mary do appear in these works. At least two of the artists, Fini and di Prima, envisioned a sister to Apollo, whom Fini names Heliodora (a name the poet H. D. used for herself in an early poem). Varo seems to have had Athena in mind in her *Creation of the Birds*. But none of the traditional stories of the goddesses seems completely adequate to the modern woman's needs. Instead, we have the makings of a "new" story whose roots may be in the ur-Goddess that Paul Friedrich describes as a combination of Aphrodite and Demeter—whose double powers of generous sexuality and maternity may have posed a threat to civilization, which needed to emphasize the maternal in order to evolve.[28]

The "new" story might develop from Sexton's revisioning sympathy with Mary's sexual nature, or Atwood's insight into Circe/Aphrodite's creative aspect, or Varo's belief in Athena's procreative potential. If the goddess were to be presented in her motherly phase, presumably both her power over nature and her vulnerability would be stressed as in the myth of Demeter, but she would also be presented as a woman with interests of her own—some of them having nothing to do with procreation and caretaking. If she were presented in her sexual aspect, her passion would be stressed as in the myth of Aphrodite, but it would not negate her wisdom. A Lady of the Beasts combining the interests of body, mind, and spirit, she would be in tune with the ancient cycles of nature, familiar with the worlds revealed by modern science, and capable of the mystic's vision of wholeness. Fully conscious, she would be a reflective being as well as a sexual, procreative one. Perhaps di Prima's Loba is the most powerful and original image of her to have emerged so far: both protectress of the forest and towering warrior-woman, she stands patiently by—mother and sister and self.

This developing model or story, pieces of which emerge with great clarity, has implications for our myths about love and death. As I said in my chapter on Sexton, no language has been invented to separate the kinds of love a woman feels for her children, her lovers, her mother, and her deity. Until it is invented, the problem of maintaining life-supporting boundaries among these various figures will remain; or perhaps, when such a language is formed, those boundaries will be transformed.

Likewise, until now, there has been no language for the love we feel for nature.

Such languages are emerging, particularly in regard to nature, although the results are far from complete. The love for nature that is imaged here so frequently is based on respect for something that is other but equal—different, mysterious, a source of knowledge and joy—not *other* in the sense of overwhelming, all-important, all-consuming. This model extends to love between the sexes as well. Wakoski's recognition that no one can penetrate the darkness that is the source of her "light" is crucial here; it is related to Linda Pastan's insight that both she and nature have secrets that must be kept. This sense of respect extends to the deity, where she appears, so that the goddess is not expected to be a final judge or constant companion but is rather a presence within the woman that sets limits of creation and destruction.

Likewise, death is not so much a force that is alien to the body as it is a tendency within: Sexton's ambition bird or her icy baby; Kollwitz's desire for maternal comfort or her overwhelming maternal grief. It is not something one battles, then, warrior to warrior, but something one uncovers, transforms, or comes to understand.

Over and over again this "chordal" analysis of common images and themes leads us back to a view of relationships with the world in which the customary boundaries are not preserved. Inside is barely distinguishable from outside, and the distinction matters only momentarily. What matters is the flow of energy from one realm to another, so that life is sustained. Although I have used Lévi-Strauss's recommendation for uncovering the meaning of myths, my results are radically different from those he would predict.[29] The images (or bundles including images, stories, themes, ideas) that are repeated in the separate lines of myth I treat here *include* antinomies rather than mediating them. Mediation implies the maintenance of opposition and the uneasy, probably incomplete, resolution of the otherwise irreconcilable claims. But when Susan Griffin says "the light is in us," she knows that the light is also outside us. There *is no opposition* between these statements. We share with nature the cells that provide illuminative energy. We collaborate to produce the phenomenon we understand as light. The whole point of her work is to eradicate the opposition between the knower and the known.

Griffin's image and the works of many women correspond

with and serve to illustrate certain claims by the contemporary philosopher Hilde Hein concerning a female epistemology. Hein asks if there are distinctive aspects of women's experience that are "sufficiently widespread and germinal" to play a determinative role in shaping women's mode of cognition or way of knowing. She thinks, as I do, that our "biological adaptation to reproduction" renders us "more amenable to the notion of integration and less threatened by intermingling and spatial interpenetration." Sexual intercourse, for example, is experienced by many women as an "active and *mutual* engulfment" wherein there is neither a loss nor a triumph of self, but a commingling and redistribution of self and reality. Similarly, "mother and child mutually shape each other not merely through the period of their direct physical attachment, but . . . throughout their lives."[30]

These facts do *not* predispose all women toward a concern for "inner space," as Erik Erikson hypothesized rather prematurely.[31] But Hein argues that they do "generate a new model for the understanding of knowledge"—a model she calls "interpenetrative." And although there is nothing exclusively feminine about such a model of mind, Hein argues that "the conditioned absence of ego-boundaries, the lifelong preparation for a reproductive role, the denial of individuality and the plurality of relational tasks women perform" make it more familiar to women. Hein sees this way of knowing as analogous to love:

> Imagine knowing as an act of love . . . a giving of self to the subject matter, rather than an "objective" standing at a distance. As one allows the known to suffuse one's being, one takes it in, envelopes and is enveloped by it. The knower, as Aristotle said, becomes the known; but it too becomes transformed, though not fixated, by the act of being known. As on the traditional model, the distance between subject and object is closed, but it is not by an act of mastery or conquest, and far from being affirmed in subjectivity, the knower becomes literally absorbed by that which is known.[32]

To use Margaret Atwood's words, "there is no *other*" in this model. Likewise, the "self" becomes an "active receptor"—a being who is purposefully passive, who goes forth to greet the other as a guest.[33]

As I summarize this model, images from previous chapters pass before me in review: Sexton's desire to enter the mother sea "skin to skin"; Kollwitz's ability in her later work to greet death in a friendly manner; Atwood's capacity to see through the story of Odysseus; Varo's defiance of the taboos against women playing with the cosmos; Wakoski's identification with the moon; Fini's preparations for the strangers of the new world; Graves's absorption in the beauty that lies beneath or beyond what we can ordinarily see; Johanson's analogies between microorganisms and houses; O'Keeffe's insistence that bones are living; Wayne's ability to see the world in a fingerprint; Piercy's knowledge that "what I watch is also me"; and countless others that embody the possibilities of interpenetration in form, content, or perspective.

Hilde Hein offers her model in the spirit of initiating a philosophy of mind that is more universal than traditional models in that it is based upon the experiences of females as well as males,[34] but she expects her work to be received only by a community of women— precisely because the myth of male supremacy governs even the disciplines presumed to be most free of myth.

In ending her book *Woman and Nature* with a section entitled "Matter: How We Know" Susan Griffin engages that myth of supremacy at its roots, where humanness is defined as the triumph of mind over matter. As the anthropologist Mary Douglas explains:

> Whenever we consider the nature of things, there is this tendency to exempt ourselves. Thus appears a boundary between us and animal creation, a boundary between spirit and matter. Every great revolution of thought has touched that boundary. . . . The other breaks in the nature of things have turned out, one by one, to be optical illusions, or fences put there by ourselves for our own purposes: why not this one too?[35]

Hein and Griffin touch that boundary between spirit and matter to cross it. Instead of giving us a philosophical model, as Hilde Hein does, Griffin offers a story to free us from the allegiance to boundaries between mind and matter. In her poem, life is a continuum beginning and ending in the earth and progressing through generations of daughters—a continuum in which the blackbird is an indispensable and equal participant, and the sun shines both on us and in us as we burst the boundaries of ourselves in love. What we know, we know in relationship to matter—our bodies, the bodies of those who have gone before us, and those who will come after, whether they are human or

animal or mineral. This is so because we *are* matter. There is no
light outside the world of nature, no "reality" or "world of
forms" of which our lives are merely pale reflections; whatever
light there is is natural. We are composed of it, in the same way
that we are composed of water—the same water that makes
swamps and pools and rivers or supports the growth of moss and
heather. "We are nature seeing nature. . . . Nature speaking of
nature to nature."

Griffin's poem is mythic in two ways. It draws on the myth of
Demeter and Persephone as the daughter returns to the mother
and recovers her story. But there is no Hades in this story, nothing to separate mother from daughter from sister from earth any
more. To be sure, there were "those who had tried to keep us
apart" (p. 224), but they were unsuccessful. Neither the male nor
death are present in Griffin's revision. The underworld is just
another aspect of nature. On this level, the phrase "the light is in
us" is a feminist affirmation of the female's capacity for knowing
and speaking. On another level the poem is mythic in an even
more radical way. On that level it is a ritual gesture, an incanta-
tion, above all an image of an idea of self that is incandescent or
evanescent. "I have no boundary" (p. 227), the speaker says, and
with these words she undoes centuries of mythology. Light is
regenerated in our love for each other and for the earth, and it is
"dispersed over this earth . . . into the least hair on the deepest
root in this earth" (p. 227) to be recycled into the moss, the fern,
the cyclamen, the cosmos. Not only is there no *other*, there is no
darkness—only matter to become light to become knowledge,
and so on, endlessly. On that level, the "light" is in male and
female, plant and animal, earth and sky without reference to the
politics of Olympus or any other seat of power the human imagination has envisioned. On that level, the "center," the self that is
defined by its categorical differences from others, does not hold,
as Yeats predicted it would not.[36] But "things" do not fall apart,
nor does the human being relinquish consciousness. We merely
participate in reality differently—as one among equals.

Of course we do not yet know where this mythological impetus will lead. This will depend on how its images, stories, and
rituals are worked out in more conventional forms—and on how
widely they are shared outside of the relatively small feminist
"community" in which a myth is gaining shape and strength.

NOTES

INTRODUCTION

1. I find the following theorists essential: Roland Barthes, Ernst Cassirer, Mircea Eliade, Sigmund Freud, Northrop Frye, C. G. Jung, Claude Lévi-Strauss, and Philip Wheelwright. Relevant works by each are listed in the bibliography.

2. David Bidney, "Myth, Symbolism and Truth," in Thomas Sebeok, ed., *Myth: A Symposium*, is a contemporary example.

3. This argument is made most fully in Claude Lévi-Strauss, *The Savage Mind*.

4. Albert Cook, *Myth and Language*, pp. 1, 2.

5. Ibid., p. 266.

6. Eric Gould, *Mythical Intentions in Modern Literature*, p. 86.

7. Ibid., p. 63.

8. Ibid., p.177.

9. Ibid., p.86.

10. Also see Marjorie W. McCune *et al.*, eds., *The Binding of Proteus: Perspectives on Myth and the Literary Process;* John B. Vickery, "Literature and Myth," in Jean-Pierre Barricelli and Joseph Gibaldi, eds., *Interrelations of Literature,* pp. 67–89.

11. Cook, p. 2.

12. Gould, p. 84.

13. Robert Schwartz, "Imagery—There's More to It than Meets the Eye," in Ned Block, ed., *Imagery*, p. 129.

14. The most useful summaries of these developments occur in Roger Shattuck, *The Banquet Years*; Calvin Tompkins, *The Bride and Her Bachelors*.

15. Nancy Chodorow, *The Reproduction of Mothering*, pp. 166–169.

16. Mary Daly descibes a new space for women "on the boundary of the institutions of patriarchy" in *Beyond God the Father*, pp. 42–43; Edwin Ardener describes the relationship between "dominant" and "muted" cultures in "The 'Problem' Revisited," in Shirley Ardener, ed., *Perceiving Women*, pp. 22–25.

17. Cook, pp. 37–66.

18. Rosemary Ruether expressed this concern at the 1980 meeting of the National Women's Studies Association in response to Carol Christ, "Why Women Need the Goddess: Phenomenological, Psychological and Political Reflections," in Christ and Judith Plaskow, *Womanspirit Rising*.

19. See Edward Casey, *Imagining: A Phenomenological Study*, pp. 188–202.

20. In discussion following a presentation on medieval mystics at the American Academy of Religion meeting, November 1980.

21. Quoted by Karen Petersen and J. J. Wilson, *Women Artists: Recognition and Reappraisal*, pp. 15, 16.

22. I have in mind Julia Kristeva's insistence that there is no such thing as Woman with a capital W. "Women's Time," tr. Alice Jardin and Harry Blake, *Signs*, VII, 1 (Autumn 1981), p. 30.

23. Susan Friedman, *Psyche Reborn: The Emergence of H. D.*, p. 212.

24. Karen Elias-Button, "Journey into an Archetype: The Dark Woman in Contemporary Women's Poetry," *Anima* IV, 2 (Spring 1978), pp. 7, 8. Also see her "The Muse as Medusa," in Cathy N. Davidson and E. M. Broner, eds., *The Lost Tradition: Mothers and Daughters in Literature*, pp. 193–206.

25. Annis Pratt, *Archetypal Patterns in Women's Fiction*, p. 178.

26. Alicia Ostriker, "The Thieves of Language: Women Poets and Revisionist Mythmaking," *Signs* VIII, 1 (Autumn 1982), pp. 87–88.

27. Sandra M. Gilbert, "Confessional Mythology," p. 9; Special Session, "Myth in Comtemporary Women's Poetry," organized by Estella Lauter for the Modern Language Association convention in December 1980.

28. Rachel Blau DuPlessis, "To Begin Story," pp. 3, 4; Special Session cited in note 27. Also see her important essay, "The Critique of Consciousness and Myth in Levertov, Rich and Rukeyser," in Sandra M. Gilbert and Susan Gubar, *Shakespeare's Sisters*, pp. 280–300.

29. DuPlessis, "To Begin Story," p. 7.

30. Ibid., p. 2.

31. Alicia Ostriker, "The Thieves of Language: Women Poets and Revisionist Mythology," p. 5; Special Session cited in note 27.

32. Judith Kroll, *Chapters in a Mythology: The Poetry of Sylvia Plath*, pp. 2–3. Also see J. D. McClatchy, "Anne Sexton: Somehow to Endure," in J. D. McClatchy, ed., *Anne Sexton: The Artist and Her Critics*, pp. 279, 285, 287.

33. Christine Downing gives an experiential account of the relationship between "the goddess" and her many manifestations in *The Goddess: Mythological Images of the Feminine*, pp. 9–29.

34. Daly, p. 51.

35. David Bakan, *The Duality of Human Existence*, p. 15.

36. Diane Di Prima, *Loba*, p. 82.

1. ANNE SEXTON'S RADICAL DISCONTENT

1. The phrase "radical discontent" comes from a poem written in 1971 near the beginning of the period I describe here; it appears in Sexton's last posthumous collection, edited by Linda Gray Sexton, *Words for Doctor Y.*, p. 64. Hereafter page references to Sexton's works will appear in the text abbreviated as follows: *BF: The Book of Folly* (1972); *DN: The Death Notebooks* (1974); *AR: The Awful Rowing toward God* (1975); *45: 45 Mercy Street* (1976); *WDY: Words for Dr. Y.* (1978); *Letters:* Linda Gray Sexton and Lois Ames, eds., *Anne Sexton: A Self-Portrait in Letters* (1977). All of Sexton's books were published by Houghton Mifflin.

2. Perhaps a review of salient biographical information from the *Letters* and from J. D. McClatchy, ed., *Anne Sexton: The Artist and Her Critics* is in order. Anne Harvey was born in 1928 into an upper-middle-class family with roots in

Massachusetts and Maine. After attending public schools in Wellesley, Mass., and private schools in Lowell and Boston, she eloped with "Kayo" Sexton in 1948. She worked as a model while her husband served in the Korean War. She was first hospitalized for emotional disturbance in 1954, the year after her daughter Linda was born, and her psychological difficulties continued despite the help of at least eight therapists. Her first suicide attempt occurred a year after the birth of her second daughter, Joyce, in 1956, and she began writing poetry seriously in recuperation. She attended several writers' workshops in the following years, the most famous of which was Robert Lowell's seminar at Boston University in 1958, and she achieved almost immediate success, publishing her first book in 1960 and winning the Pulitzer Prize for her third in 1967. She won several awards and grants in the late 1960s and was the recipient of honorary doctorates from Tufts and Fairfield Universities in the seventies, becoming a full professor at Boston University in 1972. The year 1970 seems to have marked a psychological turning point as well as an aesthetic one: in a poem dated July 21, 1970, Sexton announced "My safe, safe psychosis is broken" (*WDY*, p. 31), apparently because of the "touch" of another human being. In that year, she wrote *Transformations* (1971), a book that may have opened up the transpersonal realm that she inhabited until her death. In the next four years, she wrote the five books that are the subject of this essay, as well as a few poems published for the first time in her *Complete Poems* (1981). In 1973 she obtained a divorce from her husband. Only two of her last five books were published during her lifetime: *BF* and *DN*; she read the galleys for *AR* on the day of her suicide, October 4, 1974.

3. From the *Letters* and the editor's notes for her posthumous books, I have tentatively established the dates of composition for her late works as follows: *Transformations* was written in the winter of 1970; *BF* in early 1971; most of *DN* in 1972, although in 1970 she said it was the book she would work on all her life (*Letters*, p. 368); *AR* in January 1973; and most of *45* between February 1973 and June 1974, although it charts the period from 1971 on. *WDY* spans her whole career, containing a poem sequence from 1960–70, another from 1971, a group from 1971–73, and three horror stories from 1974.

4. See James Hillman, *Re-Visioning Psychology*, pp. iv, x. 89.

5. See *AR* pp. 2, 17, 22, 28, 35, 41, 47, 76, and 85–86 for the various dimensions of this choice. Also see "The Bat or To Remember, To Remember" (*WDY*, pp. 93–101) for her story of a female crucifixion.

6. Mary Daly, *Beyond God the Father: Toward a Philosophy of Women's Liberation*; see esp. chapters II and III.

7. In a poem from 1969, Sexton had asked what the psychotics of the world were doing seeing their doctors when "the world's up for grabs" (*WDY*, p. 25). Apparently she was conscious of the world-making possibility in her exploration of her own deep images.

8. Suzanne Juhasz, *Naked and Fiery Forms: Modern Poetry by American Women, A New Tradition*, p. 127.

9. *Love Poems* (1968), pp. 23–25.

10. In this paragraph, I am indebted to Edward Casey, "Toward an Archetypal Imagination," *Spring* 1974, pp. 1–32, for his distinctions among conscious imagining, active imagination and archetypal imagination. Active imagination, the deliberate courting of fantasy images or waking dreams, is a mode of therapy in archetypal psychology. Also see J. D. McClatchy, "Anne Sexton: Somehow to Endure," in McClatchy, ed., *Anne Sexton*, for an interpretation of "The Boat" as a confessional poem, p. 283.

11. James Hillman, in his editorial comments on another version of this essay, notes that these are "important figures of a 'dying religion'; yet rat, for instance, is the New Year, the turning point, the survivor." I interpret Sexton's palindrome "Rats Live on No Evil Star (*DN*, pp. 18–19) in this light. Sexton chose the palindrome for her tombstone.

12. Juhasz contends that Sexton frequently makes myths (p. 133). I prefer to say that she frequently encounters archetypal images but that she rarely offers them as structures in whose terms we might live our lives, as she does here.

13. Ralph J. Mills, Jr., *Contemporary American Poetry*, pp. 231–233, noticed Sexton's identification with Christ as early as 1962 in "For God While Sleeping," *All My Pretty Ones*, 1962, p. 24.

14. Stephanie Demetrakopoulos, "Matrilinearity, The Demeter/Kore Archetype and the Feminine Quest for Consciousness in the Poetry of Anne Sexton," unpublished manuscript.

15. See Linda Gray Sexton's editorial notes in 45 and *WDY*.

16. Paul Friedrich, *The Meaning of Aphrodite*, pp. 187–191, 210. Many of the characteristics Friedrich emphasizes reverberate in Sexton's poetry: "Aphrodite's place is islands and mountains; she is associated with fruits and flowers, such as apples and roses, and with birds, such as the swan; she is the most golden and the most beautiful of the goddesses and the one most connected with sun and sunlight, but she is not connected to the moon; according to one story she was born from the water, according to another, from Zeus and Dione; she patronizes love within marriage and outside marriage and either emotional bond can cause much trouble; she is friendly, nearby, mobile, erotic, and sometimes intimate with gods or mortals; she was never a virgin; she is attended by the Graces, the Seasons and other nymphs; she is wily and guileful and wise about love and combines wild animal desire with artfulness and cultivation; she sometimes helps in war but is not warlike; she controls human and animal fertility and causes states of mind, such as longing and jealousy" (p. 73). Aphrodite's association with the dog correlates with Sexton's adoption of the dog as her *persona*.

17. Ibid., pp. 123–125, 128.

18. Ibid., p. 166. Also see p. 209 for a structuralist comparison of Demeter and Aphrodite, and p. 210 for an articulation of the hypothesis that the Greater Mysteries of Eleusis focused on the mystic unity of sexuality and maternalism.

19. Daly, p. 41.

20. Hillman in his address on "Concrete Psychology," C. G. Jung Conference, Notre Dame, April 1977.

21. *See Hillman, Re-Visioning Psychology*, pp. 89, 111.

22. Ibid., pp. 123–126.

23. Friedrich, pp. 129–148, esp. p. 136.

24. Ibid., pp. 187, 190–191.

25. See Nancy Chodorow, "Family Structure and Feminine Personality" in Michelle Z. Rosaldo and Louise Lamphere, eds., *Woman, Culture and Society*, pp. 43–66, esp. pp. 59–60, for a discussion of the difficulty women experience in maintaining ego boundaries.

26. Nothing in Sexton's biography suggests a more satisfactory reason for her capitulation. Her decision was made in *AR*, written in January 1973. Her divorce, her break with the last psychiatrist, and her overtly religious phase all came after the poems in question.

27. Daly, p. 50.

28. Ibid., p. 50.

29. Ibid., p. 51.
30. Ibid., p. 43.

2. KÄTHE KOLLWITZ: THE POWER OF THE MOTHER

1. See esp. Nancy Chodorow, "Family Structure and Feminine Personality," in Michelle Z. Rosaldo and Louise Lamphere, eds., *Woman, Culture and Society*, pp. 43–66; Stephanie Demetrakopoulos, "Anaïs Nin and the Feminine Quest for Consciousness: The Quelling of the Devouring Mother and the Ascension of the Sophia," *Bucknell Review* XXXIV (Spring, 1978), pp. 119–136; Adrienne Rich, *Of Woman Born*, pp. 240–246.

2. Erich Neumann, *The Great Mother*, offers the best-known articulation of archetypal images of the feminine. He sees the Good Mother, the Terrible Mother, the Anima or inspirational figure, and the Seductress as parts of one constellation of images called the Great Mother. Toni Wolff, in a little-known essay, *Structural Forms of the Feminine Psyche*, diagrams four "types" of woman: the Mother and the Hetaira, whose strengths lie in personal relationships with the child and the male lover; and the Amazon and the Medium, whose strengths lie in impersonal relationships. Nor Hall uses Wolff's schema as the basis for her explorations of the feminine psyche in *The Moon and the Virgin: Reflections on the Archetypal Feminine*. In addition, June Singer has argued for the existence of an archetype of the androgyne in her *Androgyny*. Mary Esther Harding's books, *The Way of All Women* and *Women's Mysteries: Ancient and Modern*, written in the 1930s, offer compelling explanations of the ways these theories work in the lives of women. Christine Downing's *The Goddess: Mythological Images of the Feminine*, performs a similar function from the vantage point of the new feminist scholarship on women in religion and psychology.

3. This self-portrait was the last of 84, according to Martha Kearns, *Käthe Kollwitz: Woman and Artist*, p. 221. Lucy Lippard, "Kollwitz: Chiaroscuro," in Renate Hinz, ed., *Käthe Kollwitz: Graphics, Posters and Drawings*, p. ix, confirms my sense of Kollwitz's emphasis on the female, calling Kollwitz a "woman-identified woman."

4. Among the few exceptions were her working women done around the turn of the century; see Kearns, pp. 82–83.

5. Her most moving statement of this intent to "distill," rather than to represent or express, is in the *Diary and Letters of Käthe Kollwitz*, ed. Hans Kollwitz, tr. Richard and Clara Winston, p. 85.

6. *Outbreak (Losbruch)*, 1903. Mixed technique etching, 20″ × 23¼″, Library of Congress, Washington. Carl Zigrosser, *Prints and Drawings of Käthe Kollwitz*, pl. 19; Mina C. and Arthur H. Klein, *Käthe Kollwitz: Life in Art*, p. 44; Hinz, pl. 39, 40.

7. *Uprising (Aufruhr)*, 1899. (Also called *Revolt* or *Rebellion*.) Etching and aquatint, 11⅝″ × 12½″, National Gallery of Art, Washington, Rosenwald Collection. Zigrosser, pl. 9; Klein p. 38; Hinz, pl. 29.

8. *The Carmagnole (Die Carmagnole)*, 1901. Etching and aquatint, 22½″ × 16⅛″, National Gallery of Art, Washington, Rosenwald Coll. Zigrosser, pl. 10; Klein, p. 42; Hinz, pl. 23, 24.

9. Kearns comments that Kollwitz's portrayal of strong female bodies, emphasizing their physical rather than their sexual aspect, and stressing the accompanying inner strength of character, was a pioneering accomplishment in the history of art; p. 105.

10. Kearns, p. 167, quotes Kollwitz's poignant realization of this in 1921 in her *Diary*, p. 100.

11. *Woman with Dead Child (Frau mit totem Kind)*, 1903. Etching, 16¾″ × 19⅛″, Library of Congress, Washington. Zigrosser, pl. 14.

12. *Woman with Child in Lap (Frau mit Kind im Schoss)*, 1916. Charcoal, 21½″ × 26½″, Coll. Erich Cohn. Zigrosser, pl. 1.

13. *Mother with Twins (Mutter mit Zwillingen)*, 1924–37. (Also called *Muttergruppe*.) Copies in bronze (in Krefeld), plaster (in Duisburg and the National Gallery–East Berlin). Height 30″. Klein, p. 117.

14. *Killed in Action (Gefallen)*, 1921. (Also called *Fallen*.) Lithograph, 12⅞″ × 14″, Philadelphia Museum of Art. Zigrosser, pl. 46; Klein, p. 77; Hinz, pl. 82.

15. *Death Seizes a Woman (Tod packt eine Frau)*, 1934. Lithograph, 20⅛″ × 14⅜″, Fogg Art Museum, Harvard University. Zigrosser, pl. 71; Klein, p. 125; Hinz, pl. 126.

16. *Seed Corn Must Not Be Ground (Saatfrüchte sollen nicht vermahlen werden)*, 1942. (Also called *Seed for the Planting Shall Not be Ground Up*.) Lithograph, 14½″ × 15½″. Zigrosser, pl. 64; Klein, p. 150; Hinz, pl. 132.

17. *After the Battle (Schlachtfeld)*, 1907. Etching on soft ground, 16¼″ × 20⅞″, National Gallery of Art, Washington, Rosenwald Coll. Zigrosser, pl. 20; Hinz, pl. 41.

18. *Woman Welcoming Death (Frau vertraut sich dem Tode an)*, 1934. (Also called *Woman Entrusts Herself to Death*.) Lithograph, 18½″ × 15½″, National Gallery of Art, Washington, Rosenwald Coll. Zigrosser, pl. 68; Hinz, pl. 123.

19. *Farewell (Abscheid)*, 1940. Bronze, height 6⅝″. Galerie St. Etienne, N.Y., controls photo. Klein, p. 146.

20. *Woman Thinking (Nachdenkende Frau)*, 1920. Lithograph, 11½″ × 10½″, Kunsthalle, Hamburg. Klein, p. 75. Kollwitz used a similar pose as early as 1897 in *Poverty* to define the mother's concern for the child. She uses it again for the mother in *Municipal Shelter* in 1926. Another essay could explore the relationships among these works and Kollwitz's avowed self-portraits that use the same gesture.

21. *Lament (Klage)*, 1940. Bronze relief, 10⅛″ square. Dr. Hans Kollwitz, Berlin. Klein, p. 141. The photograph shown was made from a tinted plaster model of the bronze relief.

22. *Mothers (Mütter)*, 1919. Lithograph, 17⅛″ × 23″, Philadelphia Museum of Art. Zigrosser, pl. 28. See comment by Kearns, pp. 155–156.

23. One exception comes to mind immediately: The prostitute in *Dive (Nachtasyl* or *Milieu)*, 1913 or 1914. Crayon drawing. Klein, p. 63.

24. *The Mothers (Die Mütter)* 1922–23. Woodcut, 13⅜″ × 15¾″, Kunsthalle, Hamburg and Philadelphia Museum of Art. Zigrosser, pl. 37; Klein, p. 82; Hinz, pl. 91.

25. *Tower of Mothers (Turm der Mütter)*, 1938. Bronze, 11″ sq. and 10½″ high. Coll. Hans Kollwitz, Berlin. Klein, p. 141; Kearns, p. 219.

26. Klein, p. 98.

27. *Greeting*, 1892, Zigrosser, pl. 1, Klein, p. 29, Hinz, pl. 2; *Self Portrait with Son Hans at the Table*, 1894, Klein p. 30; *Mother with Child in Arms*, 1910, Zigrosser, pl. 26, Hinz, pl. 62; *Mother with Child in Arms*, 1916, Zigrosser pl. 27, Klein, p. 68; *Woman with Sleeping Child*, 1927, Zigrosser, pl. 61; *Women Chatting*, 1930, Zigrosser, pl. 63, Klein, p. 105; *Mother with Boy*, 1931, Zigrosser, pl. 62, Klein, p. 106; *Maternal Happiness*, 1931. Klein, p. 107.

28. *Death and the Woman* (Tod und Frau) 1910. Etching and sand paper, soft ground, 17¾″ × 17½″. Kearns, p. 117.

29. Kearns, pp. 123–125, 131. Hinz finds a hiatus in Kollwitz's work from 1910–1918 and says it occurred partially because Kollwitz had exhausted her possibilities as an engraver, p. xxi.

30. *Diary and Letters*, p. 64. Quoted by Kearns, p. 135.

31. Kearns, pp. 171–172.

32. *Woman Reflecting (Nachdenkende Frau)*, 1920. Lithograph, 21¼″ × 14¾″, National Gallery of Art, Washington, Rosenwald Collection. Zigrosser, pl. 44. *Self Portrait (Selbstbildnis)*, 1921. Etching, 8½″ × 10½″. National Gallery of Art, Washington, Rosenwald Coll. Zigrosser, pl. 40.

33. *Death with Woman in Lap (Tod mit Frau im Schoss)*, 1921. Woodcut, 9⅜″ × 11⅜″. National Gallery of Art, Washington, Rosenwald Coll. Zigrosser, pl. 30. Described by Kearns, p. 167.

34. *Death with Girl in Lap (Tod hält Mädchen im Schoss)*, 1934. Lithograph, 17⅛″ × 14⅞″, National Gallery of Art, Washington, Rosenwald Collection. Zigrosser, pl. 69; Hinz, pl. 124.

35. *Death upon the Highway (Tod auf der Landstrasse, Tod des Landstreichers)*, 1934. Lithograph, 16⅛″ × 11½″. National Gallery of Art, Washington, Rosenwald Collection. Zigrosser, pl. 72; Hinz, pl. 127.

36. *Diary and Letters*, pp. 98–99. Quoted by Kearns, p. 165.

37. Ibid., pp. 161–162. Quoted by Kearns, p. 166.

38. Quoted by Kearns, p. 179.

39. Demetrakopoulos, pp. 127–130, sees Djuna's vision of a featureless doll rising from the sea at the end of *The Four-Chambered Heart* as a symbol of the successful outcome in Nin's long struggle with self-sacrifice reminiscent of her mother.

40. Barbara Rigney, final chapter of *Madness and Sexual Politics in the Feminist Novel*.

41. Annis Pratt, "*Surfacing* and the Rebirth Journey" in Arnold and Cathy N. Davidson, eds., *The Art of Margaret Atwood: Essays in Criticism*, pp. 139–157.

42. Chodorow, p. 51.

43. Ibid., p. 53.

44. Ibid., p. 65.

45. Ibid., pp. 59–60.

46. *Death Swoops (Tod greift in Kinderschar)*, 1934. Lithograph, 19¹¹/₁₆″ × 16½″, National Gallery, Washington, Rosenwald Coll. Zigrosser, pl. 70; Hinz, pl. 125.

47. David Bakan distinguishes masculine "agency" from feminine "communion" in *The Duality of Human Existence*, p. 15. It is interesting that Kollwitz's maternal image does not exemplify all the characteristics of agency described by Bakan: isolation; the urge to master; repression of thought, feeling, and impulse.

3. MARGARET ATWOOD: REMYTHOLOGIZING CIRCE

1. In *You Are Happy*, pp. 45–70. Page numbers given in the text refer to this book.

2. The term "remythologizing" comes from a lengthy discussion by Christian theologians beginning with Rudolf Bultmann's argument that the New Testament should be "demythologized," or stripped of all the trappings of its first-century world view. Bultmann's critics have suggested that although the Bible may need reinterpretation, it is impossible to deny all its mythic dimensions. Since reinterpreting myths perpetuates them, it makes more sense to speak of remythologizing. The discussion is by no means finished. I choose to

use the term because I think acts of mythmaking by contemporary women writers may prove significant in the theological discussion. See Rudolf Bultmann *et al., Kerygma and Myth,* ed. Hans Werner Bartsch; Karl Jaspers and Rudolf Bultmann, *Myth and Christianity.*

3. Richmond Lattimore, tr., *The Odyssey of Homer,* Book X, pp. 155–167. The words of "the dread goddess who talks with mortals" are reported as part of Odysseus' story told to Alkinoos.

4. See Erich Neumann, *The Great Mother,* p. 83, in which Circe is immortalized as the young witch, the negative anima figure, and priestess of the mysteries of drunkenness including ecstasy, madness, impotence, and stupor.

5. See Joseph Campbell's *The Hero with a Thousand Faces* for a persuasive argument that the quest is the monomyth of western culture.

6. Bultmann made a distinction between "kerygma" and myth that has been attractive to twentieth-century figures under the spell of science. He thought we could strip away mythology as if it were the husk covering the kernel of truth. See his essays, "New Testament and Mythology" and "A Reply to the Theses of J. Schiewind," in Bultmann *et al.,* pp. 1–44, 102–123.

7. Actually, there was an ancient ending of sorts in the cyclic Telegonia, in which Odysseus is shot by his son (by Circe), Telegonos, who then marries Penelope while Telemachos marries Circe. See H. G. Rose, *A Handbook of Greek Mythology,* p. 247. Apparently the story never exercised the influence of myth.

8. Atwood's strategies deserve comparison with those used by James Joyce in *Ulysses,* in which Joyce took on the bulkier task of revealing the way Homer's myth continued to operate in early twentieth-century Europe.

9. Atwood's strategy of reentering a dream or myth is similar to Ira Progoff's method of extending dreams instead of interpreting them. See his *The Symbolic and the Real.*

10. See W. B. Stanford, *The Ulysses Theme,* pp. 46–51, for a comparison of Circe and Calypso which gives the usual interpretation of Circe as a *femme fatale* or as *la belle dame sans merci.*

11. Sherrill Grace, *Violent Duality: A Study of Margaret Atwood,* p. 71.

12. Grace says that Circe demythologizes herself, p. 71.

13. Katherine Anne Porter, *A Defense of Circe.*

14. Ibid., p. 15.

15. Ibid., p. 9. The terms "creatix" and "aesthetic genius" appear on p. 16.

16. Ibid., p. 17.

17. Rachel Blau DuPlessis, "The Critique of Consciousness and Myth in Levertov, Rich and Rukeyser," pp. 280–300 in Sandra M. Gilbert and Susan Gubar, eds., *Shakespeare's Sisters,* opposes the concept of prototype to the concept of archetype because the prototype situates the poet's consciousness at a specific historical moment and "breaks with the idea of an essentially unchanging reality" (p. 299). Elsewhere, in my "Visual Art by Women: A Test Case for the Theory of Archetypes," Estella Lauter and Carol Schreier Rupprecht, eds., *Feminist Archetypal Theory,* forthcoming, I argue that the archetype is not an unchanging image but a tendency to form images in response to certain repeated experiences. In the present essay, I show that myths are not unchanging phenomena, even when they embody archetypal instead of historical figures.

18. *The Odyssey,* Book X, lines 333–335, p. 161.

19. Lilienfeld comments, "the metaphor of her baring herself to her lover is ugly and painful. . . . Heterosexuality depends on Circe's abandoning of moon power." "Circe's Emergence: Transforming Traditional Love in Margaret Atwood's *You Are Happy,*" *Worcester Review* V (Mar 1977), p. 34.

20. Linda W. Wagner, "The Making of *Selected Poems:* The Process of Sur-

facing," in Arnold and Cathy N. Davidson, eds., *The Art of Margaret Atwood,* pp. 93–94, makes the story of the mud woman the most important section of the Circe poems. She says, "The implicit question Circe poses is, does every man dream of a perfect experience that is entirely physical and entirely impersonal? Even after his lover has given him words, names, property, self, does her image pale beside his wormy fantasy?"

21. Wagner sees Penelope's "triumph" as a demonstration of Atwood's conviction that "verbal magic beats physical force," or "at the base of reality is the word," p. 94.

22. *The Odyssey,* Book X, lines 156–172, p. 156.

23. Rachel Blau DuPlessis, "To Begin Story," calls the ending sentimental. Paper presented at Modern Language Association convention, December 1980.

24. Virginia Woolf, *A Room of One's Own,* p. 90.

25. *Survival: A Thematic Guide to Canadian Literature,* p. 209.

26. Ibid., p. 209.

27. Grace does not agree, p. 77. I am indebted to Lilienfeld for starting this train of thought with her comment: "But the possibilities of Circe and Odysseus, fought through, transformed, have turned in the next sequence . . . into the possibilities for mortals," p. 36.

28. Annis Pratt, *Archetypal Patterns in Women's Fiction,* pp. 139–143.

29. Lilienfeld makes a wonderful interpretation of the "moonmarks" Circe notices on Odysseus' body: "By his sickle scars he is a marked man; he is bound by and to battle, to Penelope, to a relentless future. But the way the mark is shaped, like the moon . . . shows that Odysseus' being extends into the domain of women," p. 35.

30. Pratt, p. 141. Her analysis of *Surfacing,* pp. 157–161, beautifully illustrates the meaning of this "plunge" in the female quest.

31. Sandra Djwa, "The Where of Here: Margaret Atwood and a Canadian Tradition," in Davidson and Davidson, eds., p. 22, notes the descent pattern in Atwood's writing from her first book, *Double Persephone,* on.

32. Robert Lecker, "Janus through the Looking Glass: Atwood's First Three Novels," in Davidson and Davidson, eds., p. 194.

33. *Two-Headed Poems,* p. 105.

34. Robert Lecker is the most insistent about this idea that Atwood is duplicitous, pp. 177–204, but it runs through several of the essays in the Davidson and Davidson book. Atwood's wit and toughness apparently lead many critics to believe that her contradictions are purposeful attempts to engage her reader in her own wry "circle game." Eli Mandel seems to have begun this train of thought in his "Atwood Gothic," *Another Time,* pp. 137–145.

35. *Two-Headed Poems,* p. 97.

36. Wallace Stevens, *The Necessary Angel,* p. 142.

4. REMEDIOS VARO: THE CREATIVE WOMAN AND THE FEMALE QUEST

1. "El universo pictorico de Remedios Varo," in Octavio Paz and Roger Caillois, *Remedios Varo,* p. 26. I am indebted to Hugo Martinez-Serros, Lawrence University, for the translation of this essay.

2. See Paz and Caillois, p. 15. I see far more meaning in Varo's work than Caillois does.

3. The best articulation of the traditional models is still Joseph Campbell's *The Hero with a Thousand Faces.*

4. The following biographical information comes from "Nota Biográfica" in

Paz and Caillois, p. 168, and from Janet Kaplan, "Remedios Varo: Voyages and Visions," *Woman's Art Journal*, I, 2 (Fall 1980/Winter 1981), pp. 13–18.

5. Caillois has done a fine description of the substances, architecture, inhabitants, machines, and other marvels that hold Varo's world together; in Paz and Caillois.

6. *La revelación o el relojero*, 71 × 84 cm., plate 18, Paz and Caillois. Note on p. 174. Subsequent references to plates and notes will be to this edition. Paintings are in oil on canvas or on masonite unless otherwise noted.

7. *Armonía*, 74 × 93 cm., pl. 11, note on p. 173.

8. *Ermitaño*, 89 × 38 cm., pl. 36, note on p. 176.

9. *Música solar*, 91 × 61 cm., pl. 27.

10. *Simpatía*, pl. 67, note on p. 177.

11. As in *Tres destinos*, pl. 13, and *Retrato del Dr. Ignacio Chávez*, pl. 23, where Dr. Chávez only thinks he is in control.

12. *Flautista*, 75 × 93 cm., pl. 20. Varo says, "Half of the tower is transparent and only drawn because it was imagined by him who is constructing it," p. 175.

13. These works deserve the kind of reverie modelled by Gaston Bachelard in *The Poetics of Space*, tr. Maria Jolas.

14. Cf. Silvano Arieti, *Creativity: The Magic Synthesis*, Part I.

15. *La creación de las aves*, 52.5 × 62.5 cm., pl. 5.

16. *Naturaleza muerta resucitando*, 110 × 80 cm., pl. 1.

17. Campbell, pp. 30–38.

18. See Erich Neumann, *Amor and Psyche: The Psychic Development of the Feminine*.

19. *Ruptura*, 93 × 58 cm., pl. 10.

20. C. G. Jung's most helpful explanation of thinking, sensing, feeling, and intuiting as forms of conscious orientation toward the world is in his *Analytical Psychology: Its Theory and Practice*, pp. 11–25, 47–50.

21. *Cazadora de astros*, 48 × 34 cm., pl. 57, mixed media on paper.

22. *Papilla estelar*, 92 × 62 cm., pl. 68.

23. *Personaje*, 77 × 49 cm., pl. 33. See Mary Esther Harding, *Women's Mysteries: Ancient and Modern*, p. 133, for an account of Pan's relationship to the goddess.

24. *El minotauro*, 60 × 30 cm., pl. 51.

25. See Charlene Spretnak, *Lost Goddesses of Early Greece*, pp. 90-91.

26. *Encuentro*, 70 × 40 cm., pl. 72.

27. *Mimetismo*, 47 × 49 cm., pl. 66, note on p. 177.

28. Paz and Caillois, p. 21.

29. *Visita inesperada*, pl. 63, note on p. 177.

30. *Presencia inesperada*, pl. 75.

31. *Los caminos tortuosos*, 47 × 27.5 cm., pl. 71.

32. *Exploración de las fuentes del río Orinoco*, 44 × 39.5 cm., pl. 46.

33. *Nacer de nuevo*, 81 × 47 cm., pl. 60.

34. *La llamada*, 100 × 68 cm., pl. 58.

35. Juliana Gonzales, "Transmundo de Remedios Varo," in Paz and Caillois, tr. Hugo Martinez-Serros.

36. *Mujer saliendo del psicoanalista*, 71 × 41 cm., pl. 12, note on p. 174.

37. *Luz emergente*, 65 × 28 cm., pl. 61. She is Tara as described by Erich Neumann, *The Great Mother*, p. 334.

38. Ibid., pp. 310, 311 ff.

39. *Planta insumisa*, 84 × 62 cm. oval, title page, note on p. 173.

40. *Descubrimiento de un geólogo mutante,* pl. 21.
41. *Fenómeno de ingravedad,* 75 × 50 cm., pl. 17, note on p. 174.
42. *Vampiros vegetarianos,* 84 × 60 cm., pl. 54.
43. Annis Pratt, "Margaret Atwood's *Surfacing* and the Rebirth Journey," in Arnold and Cathy N. Davidson, eds., *The Art of Margaret Atwood.*
44. Annis Pratt, "Women and Nature in Modern Fiction," *Contemporary Literature* XIII, 4 (1972), pp. 476–490; see esp. 480, 483–484, 488.
45. See chapter 2.
46. Adrienne Rich, *Diving into the Wreck,* affords many examples of this schism which is so much more than a battle between the sexes. See "Trying to Talk with a Man," pp. 3–4.
47. Judy Chicago is only the most prominent of many visual artists who are exploring female sexuality. See also Annis Pratt, "Aunt Jennifer's Tigers: Notes toward a Pre-literary History of Women's Archetypes," *Feminist Studies* IV, 1 (February 1978), pp. 163–194. Also see Susan Gubar, "The Echoing Spell of H.D.'s *Trilogy,*" *Contemporary Literature* XIX, 2 (Spring 1978), pp. 196–218.
48. See Carol P. Christ, "Margaret Atwood: The Surfacing of Women's Spiritual Quest and Vision," *Signs* II, 2 (Winter 1976), pp. 316–330. Also see chapter 5.
49. O'Keeffe in the film *Georgia O'Keeffe,* WNET, 1976.

5. DIANE WAKOSKI: DISENTANGLING THE WOMAN FROM THE MOON

1. My approach is markedly different from that of Dianne F. Sadoff, "Mythopoeia, the Moon and Contemporary Women's Poetry," *Massachusetts Review* XIX, 1 (Spring 1978), pp. 93–110, who bases her argument about Wakoski on just one book of poems.
2. See Sherry B. Ortner, "Is Female to Male as Nature Is to Culture?" in Michelle Z. Rosaldo and Louise Lamphere, eds., *Woman, Culture and Society,* pp. 67–88.
3. Estella Lauter, "Diane Wakoski," in Lina Mainiero, ed., *American Women Writers,* p. 309. Diane Wakoski was born in Whittier, California, in 1937 to poor Polish-American parents. Little is known about her childhood. In 1962, she published the first of her 17 books of poems. She worked in a bookstore briefly, and then taught English at a junior high school until 1969. Since then, she has supported herself by her writing, poetry readings, workshops, and guest appointments at universities.
4. Carol P. Christ, "Margaret Atwood: The Surfacing of Women's Spiritual Quest and Vision," *Signs* II, 2 (Winter 1976), p. 329, asks "Is the traditional identification of women and nature a legacy of oppression or a source of power and vision?"
5. The history of women's relationship to nature is well-documented in several recent books: Susan Griffin, *Woman and Nature: The Roaring inside Her;* Annette Kolodny, *The Lay of the Land;* Carolyn Merchant, *The Death of Nature.*
6. Estelle Jelinek's collection *Women's Autobiography* is a promising step in this direction.
7. The well-known philosophers Susanne Langer, Simone Weil, Susan Sontag, and Hannah Arendt, with the single exception of Simone de Beauvoir, have chosen to address other issues. A book by Hilde Hein, *Half a Mind: Philosophy from a Woman's Point of View,* remains unpublished.
8. *Inside the Blood Factory,* pp. 71–73. Hereafter abbreviated *IBF.*

9. Mary Esther Harding, *Women's Mysteries: Ancient and Modern,* chapter 9.

10. Ibid., chapter 13.

11. Wakoski provides a list of her best poems in *Toward a New Poetry,* pp. ix, x.

12. *The Magellanic Clouds.* Hereafter abbreviated *MC.*

13. In reading the poems I discuss here, it is helpful to remember that the religion of Isis and Osiris, both moon deities, gave way to the worship of the sun god, Ra (whom Wakoski calls Atun-Re). Eventually Osiris, who because of his death and resurrection was Lord of the Underworld, was assimilated into the new religion and hailed as a sun god. See Harding, chapter 13, for a readable account of the story, including references to Horus (son of Isis and Osiris), the Dog Star (Sirius, the attendant or guardian of Isis), and the beheading of Isis, all of which figure in Wakoski's poems from this period.

14. In "Toward an Archetypal Imagination," Edward Casey distinguishes three types of imaginative experience (see note 10, chapter 1): conscious, every-day imagining is subject to immediate modification according to the imaginer's wishes, p. 17; active imagining discloses a world not entirely of our own mak-ing, where we become actors in a psychological play produced through the elaboration of fantasies, pp. 19–20; archetypal imagining discloses content rooted outside of human consciousness, p. 23. Wakoski records the second or third stages of imagining in the poems I describe here.

15. *The Motorcycle Betrayal Poems.* Hereafter *MBP.*

16. Sadoff takes Lady Bank Dick to be synonymous with Wakoski.

17. It is as if the moon had no existence apart from her, nor she from the moon. This is the precarious condition of being that Helen Vendler describes in Sylvia Plath's *Crossing the Water;* see *Part of Nature, Part of Us,* pp. 271–276.

18. *Smudging.* Hereafter abbreviated *S.*

19. *Dancing on the Grave of a Son of a Bitch.* Hereafter *DG.*

20. *Virtuoso Literature for Two and Four Hands.* Hereafter *VL.*

21. *Waiting for the King of Spain.* Hereafter *WKS.*

22. Margaret Atwood, *You Are Happy,* pp. 45–70.

23. *National Geographic* Map, 1969.

24. *The Man Who Shook Hands.* Hereafter *MSH.* Section III is called "Extend-ing the Moon's Complicated Geography," and the one poem in it is called "Looking for Bald Eagles in Wisconsin."

25. Compare my account of her development with that offered by James F. Mersmann, "Blood on the Moon: Diane Wakoski's Mythologies of Loss and Need," *Margins* (Jan., Feb., Mar., 1976), pp. 116–128. Perhaps because he em-phasizes her earlier books, Mersmann stresses the possibility that the poet's love will become devouring: "If Isis cannot be Isis, she will be Medusa" (p. 128). He sees her poetry, then, as a "moving vision of the terrible last stages of a disin-tegrating personality and a disintegrating society" (p. 128), whereas I see it as a step toward the new garden she hopes for in *Virtuoso Literature.*

6. LÉONOR FINI: RE-ENVISIONING *LA BELLE DAME SANS MERCI*

1. Léonor Fini's work has received little attention in this country. It is known mainly through the following articles and books: Silvio Gaggi, "Léonor Fini: A Mythology of the Feminine," *Art International* XXIII, 5–6 (September 1979), pp. 34–38, 49; Ann Sutherland Harris and Linda Nochlin, *Women Artists: 1550–1950,* pp. 329–331; Gloria Orenstein, "Women of Surrealism," *The*

Feminist Art Journal (Spring 1973), pp. 1, 15–21; Karen Petersen and J. J. Wilson, *Women Artists: Recognition and Reappraisal*, pp. 132–133, plates on pp. 7, 133 and 141; Nina Winter, "Léonor Fini," *Interview with the Muse*, pp. 48–59; Rozsika Parker and Griselda Pollock, *Old Mistresses: Women, Art and Ideology*, pp. 137–143.

2. Fini lists her birthdate as 1918 in the *International Who's Who*.

3. Xavière gauthier, *Léonor Fini, p.* 88. I rely heavily on her biographical account; in turn, she relies heavily on Marcel Brion, *Léonor Fini et son oeuvre*.

4. Winter, p. 55.

5. Gauthier, p. 88. Apparently Fini was more rebellious than her interview with Winter implies.

6. Nochlin estimates that she arrived in Paris as early as 1932; both Gauthier and Winter say that it was 1937. The resolution of this issue will be of special interest to those who want to chart the development of female creativity, since she would have been only fourteen in 1932. Harris and Nochlin, p. 329.

7. Gauthier, p. 133.

8. Winter, pp. 57–58.

9. In the theatre, she did scenery or costumes for works written or produced by Balanchine, Anouilh, Britten, Audiberti, Menotti, Genêt and many others. Fellow artists Eluard, Genêt, Cocteau, Ernst, and Audiberti published essays, poems, and comments on her work, and de Chirico and Eluard sponsored an exhibit in New York as early as 1937. The critics Edmund Wilson and Mario Praz wrote about her in the mid-forties. In the fifties and sixties, she became famous for her illustrations of Genêt, Baudelaire and Poe.

10. Jean Genêt, "Mademoiselle: A Letter to Léonor Fini," tr. Bernard Frechtman, *Nimbus* III, 1 (1955), p. 37. This essay was orginally published as *Lettre à Léonor Fini*.

11. Orenstein, p. 6.

12. Ibid., pp. 15, 16; Gaggi, p. 38.

13. Genêt, p. 35.

14. Gaggi, p. 34.

15. Erich Neumann, *The Great Mother*, p. 275. Marcel Brion repeated his well-known statement that Fini's subject is "the realm of the mothers" as late as 1964 in *Léonor Fini*, the exhibit catalogue of the Eighteenth Belgian Summer Festival (ed. André de Rache). The comment is accurate in a general way, but recent scholarship concerning the goddesses encourages us to be more precise.

16. Neumann, p. 260.

17. Petersen and Wilson, p. 141.

18. Orenstein, p. 16.

19. Mary Esther Harding, *Women's Mysteries*, pp. 117–126.

20. Ibid., p. 184.

21. W. B. Yeats, *Collected Poems*, pp. 211–212.

22. Gauthier, p. 118.

23. Ibid., pp. 118–119. Gaggi, p. 35, provides the following (incomplete) translation of Victor Brauner's description of Fini's artistic process, cited in Constantine Jelenski, *Léonor Fini*, p. 28: "On the white surface of the canvas, you throw colours by apparent chance. They are guided by an unconscious automism that begins to establish the material kinship of your props. Next you see the emergence of the first home-ports of the construction, and they are still nebulae of an infinitely transformable kind, like so many crossroads where the imagination can hang its selection of what is to be. We are present at the birth of a chaos of colours, of a giddy chemical-mineral swirl. . . . The whole thing

slowly takes the form of a tragic royal personage, forcefully manifesting a contortion, seized in time, yet changing. On its body or its envelope, the tiny forms of unknown matter grow, inventions, sometimes precious stones, sometimes life-giving liquors, or molten metals, changing to tears, drops of blood or of dew. . . . This painting is the story of matter and life beyond the present and the past." Jelenski identifies the painting Brauner saw as *Vespertilia*, dated 1960. Thus, the description pertains to Fini's creative process in her third stage.

24. Gaggi, p. 35.
25. Ibid., p. 38.
26. Gaggi to the contrary, p. 38.
27. Gauthier, p. 124.
28. See Monique Wittig, *Les Guérillères*, tr. David LeVay, p. 27, for another reference to a sun goddess by a contemporary French writer. The "dora" portion of the name means "gift," and "Heliodora" may mean "Gift of Sun." The vision of a woman "clothed with the sun" is biblical (Revelation of John, 12: 1–6). Images of a sun goddess appear in contemporary American poetry as well and deserve further study.
29. Gaggi, p. 38.
30. In Jelenski, pp. 14, 15.
31. Victor Turner's well-known analysis of "liminal" or threshold experiences has been applied to the subject of goddesses and goddess religions by Paul Friedrich, *The Meaning of Aphrodite*, pp. 132–149.
32. Gauthier, p. 126, uses the term "guérillères" for all the women in Fini's fourth stage.
33. Ibid., p. 130.
34. Ibid.
35. Quoted by Jelenski, p. 37.

7. MYTHIC PATTERNS IN CONTEMPORARY VISUAL ART BY WOMEN

1. In alphabetical order, these are the collections I used: A.I.R. Gallery (New York), slides of members' work; A.R.C. Gallery (Chicago), slides of members' work; Artemesia Gallery (Chicago), slides of members' work; Boston Visual Artists Union, slides of members' work (men and women); the California State College at Sonoma Collection of works by women artists from the medieval period to the present, chosen by Karen Petersen and J. J. Wilson; The D.C. Slide Registry of Women Artists; the Hatch-Billops Collection: Archives of Black American Cultural History (New York); the artist file at the New Museum (New York), maintained by the staff for future shows or as records of previous shows; The Northern California Women's Caucus for Art slide registry; the Ryerson Library file of Chicago artists and artists who have graduated from the Art Institute School; The Southeast Women's Caucus for Art slide registry; the SOHO 20 Gallery (New York), slides of members' works; The Women's Art Registry of Minnesota (W.A.R.M.) slides, including several slide-tape "essays": on the self-image, the W.P.A. in Minnesota, the figure, non-objective art and American Abstract Artists of the Thirties; The Women's Caucus for Art: Houston, slide registry; slides from an exhibit called "Women-in-Sight: New Art in Texas," selected by Marcia Tucker (Austin, 1979) for a group called "Women and Their Work"; Women in the Arts (New York), slide registry of member artists from the early 1970s to the present. Typically, the work in the small galleries (A.I.R., A.R.C., Artemesia, SOHO 20, W.A.R.M.) is juried by members, whereas the work in the registries is not juried.

2. Lucy Lippard, *From the Center: Feminist Essays on Women's Art*, pp. 49, 81, 86. Also see her "Sweeping Exchanges: The Contribution of Feminism to the Art of the 1970s,"*Art Journal* (Fall/Winter 1980), pp. 362–365; and my "Moving to the Ends of Our Own Rainbows: Steps toward a Feminist Aesthetic," in Patricia Werhane, ed., *Philosophy and Art*.

3. Eleanor Munro, *Originals: American Women Artists*, pp. 21–23.

4. Claude Lévi-Strauss *Myth and Meaning*.

5. As evidenced by recent shows at the New Museum, the Ingbar Gallery, Brooke Alexander, Inc., and the Rosa Esman Gallery.

6. Lewis Thomas, *The Lives of a Cell*, p. 122.

7. See Rosemary Ruether, *New Woman/New Earth*; Carolyn Merchant, *The Death of Nature*; Susan Griffin, *Woman and Nature*.

8. Judy Chicago, in an interview with Lippard, *From the Center*, p. 230, feared women were not making this kind of contribution.

9. Lippard, "Sweeping Exchanges," p. 362.

10. Ibid., p. 363.

11. Ibid., p. 364.

12. As in *Everglades*, lithograph, 30" × 22", 1975.

13. *The Deceptive Change Bag*, pictured in the brochure for *Wonder Production*, Vol. I.

14. *Wonder Production* brochure.

15. Statement provided by Lanyon in meeting with author.

16. "Ellen Lanyon in Conversation with Ruth Iskin," p. 10. Provided by Lanyon.

17. M.F.A. statement, p. 1 (University of California at Berkeley, 1980). *Ascending, Descending* was made into a postcard and is available in a set from the Northern California Women's Caucus for Art for $10.00.

18. Mixed media on paper, 51" × 51", in "Women-in-Sight" exhibit.

19. Artist's statement, W.A.R.M. Gallery.

20. Women in the Arts file.

21. Benson's work is featured in the W.A.R.M. Gallery's slide-tape presentation: "Self-Portrait in Change: Eleven Women Artists."

22. Quoted by Mary Stofflett in the notes for *American Women Artists: The Twentieth Century* (Harper and Row Audiovisual Dept., 1980).

23. *The Veil of Isis*, mixed-media sculpture-cradle, 4'2" × 2'6" × 5'6", Northern California Women's Caucus for Art.

24. Handmade paper with bark paper, stones, print collage, wood, 27" × 22". Artist's file, A.R.C. Gallery.

25. Artist's file, W.A.R.M. Gallery.

26. The sculpture is part of the travelling exhibit of black women artists, *Forever Free*, organized by Arna and Jacqueline Bontemps and David Driskell. I have written about this piece at greater length in "Visual Images by Women: A Test Case for the Theory of Archetypes," in Estella Lauter and Carol S. Rupprecht, *Feminist Archetypal Theory*, chapter 3.

27. From a note on her 1977 show at Artemesia Gallery.

28. Artist's statement, Artemesia Gallery.

29. Artist's statement, W.A.R.M. Gallery.

30. Joanna Frueh, "The Psychological Realism of Ellen Lanyon," *Feminist Art Journal* VI, 1 (Spring 1977), p. 21.

31. As Lippard claims in "Sweeping Exchanges," p. 362.

32. Pencil, 28" × 24", D.C. Slide Registry of Women's Art.

33. They are included in the W.A.R.M. Gallery slide-tape show, "Self-Portrait in Change."

34. *Magic Sam* is in Karen Petersen and J. J. Wilson, *Women Artists: Images, Themes, and Dreams* (Harper and Row Audiovisual Dept., 1975).

35. Each painting is 24″ × 36″, acrylic. Exhibited at the Frumkin Gallery, New York, February 1981.

36. Artist's statement, Artemesia Gallery.

37. See Eleanor Tufts, *Our Hidden Heritage* pp. 223–232.

38. Kate Horsfield and Lynn Blumenthal. Interview wih June Leaf, Video Data Bank, Art Institute School of Chicago.

39. Paul Waggoner Gallery, Chicago.

40. "Paintings on Paper," a guest exhibit, Artemesia Gallery, November 1980.

41. Lewis Thomas, pp. 147–148.

42. *Literary Women* p. 246.

43. Statement in her catalogue, "What I Love: Paintings, Poetry and a Drawing," 1970.

44. LaDuke is an Oregon artist; I first saw her work in the slides at California State College, Sonoma.

45. Harris is a member of the Women's Caucus for Art: Houston. The best introduction to Saar's work is *Spirit Catcher: The Art of Betye Saar*, in the series *Originals: Women in Art* (Wilmette: Ill.: Films Inc., 1978).

46. This imagery occurs in the work of two Wisconsin artists: the well-known illustrator of children's books, Nancy Eckholm Burkert, and Costa Rican-born Flora Langlois, now a resident of Door County.

47. See especially the work of three Washington D.C. artists, Wendy Eisenberg, Helen Hole and Rebeckah Hoffsommer, included in the D.C. Slide Registry of Women Artists.

48. SOHO 20 brochure, 1979.

49. Margaret Aspinwall, ed., *The Painterly Print: Monotypes from the 17th to the 20th Centuries*. Entry on Mary Frank.

50. See her "Head in Ferns" in Eleanor Munro's excellent chapter on her work, *Originals: American Women Artists*, pp. 289–308.

51. Artist's statement and brochure, A.I.R. Gallery, 1978.

52. SOHO 20 brochure.

53. Artist's statement, W.A.R.M. Gallery, 1978.

54. Yvonne Pickering Carter, "Morphological Transcription of Forms in Nature: Rocks and Water as the Subject of Abstract Painting," Howard University, 1968.

55. *Patricia Johanson: Plant Drawings for Projects*, note for #12.

56. Ibid., note for #1.

57. *Patricia Johanson Drawings for the Camouflage House and Orchid Projects*.

58. Artist's file, A.I.R. Gallery.

59. William Zimmer, *Soho Weekly* (May 1979). In addition to saying that the works were "really vaginas," he said that "The Abstract Expressionists wished to identify their bodies with the earth, but as men couldn't come this close."

60. Reprinted in Lippard, *From the Center*, p. 111.

61. Ibid.

62. *Georgia O'Keeffe*, 1939 exhibit catalogue, quoted by Laurie Lisle, *Portrait of an Artist: A Biography of Georgia O'Keeffe*, p. 192.

63. *From the Plains I* (1919) is reproduced in Georgia O'Keeffe, *Georgia O'Keeffe*, pl. 2.

64. Quoted by Lisle, pp. 133–134.

65. Ibid., p. 98.

66. Ibid., p. 190.
67. Ibid., p. 140.
68. See *Black Iris* (1926), in *Georgia O'Keeffe*, pl. 30.
69. Ibid. See *Pelvis III* (1944), pl. 74; *Red Hills and Bones* (1941), pl. 97.
70. Lisle, p. 212.
71. Moers, p. 257, 259.
72. Ibid., p. 262.
73. Ibid., p. 259.
74. Artist's statement, A.I.R. Gallery.
75. Artist's statement, W.A.R.M. Gallery.
76. Artist's statement, W.A.R.M. Gallery.
77. "Women-in-Sight" exhibit.
78. California State College, Sonoma.
79. Artist's statement, Northern California Women's Caucus for Art registry.
80. Donna Byars, *Private Icons* (Bronx Musuem of Art). In artist's file, A.I.R. Gallery.
81. A complete set of slides of the show is in the collection at California State College, Sonoma.
82. D.C. Slide Registry of Women's Art.
83. W.A.R.M. Gallery.
84. Women's Caucus for Art: Houston.
85. Ibid.
86. Quoted by the artist from Carl Sagan, *The Cosmic Connection: An Extraterrestrial Perspective,* p. 52; found in the artist's statements, SOHO 20 Gallery.
87. *Seven Cycles: Public Rituals* (New York: AIR Gallery, 1980), p. 17.
88. Ibid., p. 24.
89. Ibid.
90. Ibid., p. 53.
91. Kate Horsfield and Lyn Blumenthal, Interview with Nancy Graves (March 1978), Video Data Bank, Art Institute School of Chicago.
92. Merlin Stone, *Ancient Mirrors of Womanhood,* Vol. 1, p. 58.
93. Henry Beston, *The Outermost House,* p. 25; quoted by Lippard, *From the Center,* p. 283.
94. Graves in Jay Belloi, *Nancy Graves,* n.p.
95. Quoted by Brenda Richardson, "Nancy Graves: A New Way of Seeing," *Arts* 46, 6 (April 1972), p. 61.
96. The work is called *Variability of Similar Forms* (1970) in *Nancy Graves: A Survey, 1969–1980* (Buffalo: Albright-Knox Gallery, 1981), pl. 5.
97. Emily Wasserman, "A Conversation with Nancy Graves," *Artforum* IX, 2 (Oct. 1970), p. 43.
98. Ibid., p. 46.
99. Linda Cathcart in *Nancy Graves: A Survey,* p. 21.
100. Ibid., p. 22.
101. I am thinking in particular of her fragmentation of subjects into dots, her presentation of spatial layers in terms of curvilinear forms and "central" images, and her use of soft flesh tones in pigmentation.
102. Graves in an interview with Paul Cummings, Archives of American Art, Smithsonian Institution (August 1972), discusses her struggle for independence from her family and from her husband, Richard Serra.
103. In *Nancy Graves: A Survey,* p. 22, she says, "It is only possible for me to see an image if I have a way of interpreting it."

104. *Dorothy Hood: Recent Paintings* (Houston: Contemporary Arts Museum, 1970).

105. Irene Rice Pereira, interview with Forest Selvig, Archives of American Art, Smithsonian Institution (August, 1968), pp. 8, 9.

106. Ann McCoy, "Alice Baber: Light as Subject," *Art International* (Sept./Oct. 1980), p. 140.

107. Northern California Women's Caucus for Art.

108. *Flowers of Form* (Fisk University, 1974), n.p. *Memories* is in Karen Petersen and J. J. Wilson, *Women Artists: Third World* (Harper and Row Audiovisual, 1975).

109. Saar's work can be seen in the film *Spirit Catcher: The Art of Betye Saar*.

110. Artist's statement, The New Museum.

111. The Boston Visual Artists Union.

112. Southeast Women's Caucus for Art.

113. *Cosmicide* is in Mary Stofflett, *American Women Artists: The Twentieth Century* (Harper and Row Audiovisual, 1980).

114. Commentary provided by June Wayne in a letter, June 6, 1983.

115. Mary W. Baskett, *The Art of June Wayne*, pp. 64–76.

116. Lewis Thomas, pp. 123–124.

117. See earlier discussion, pp. 00–00. *Cosmos* is pictured in Karen Petersen and J. J. Wilson, *Women Artists, Recognition and Reappraisal*, p. 16.

8. "WOMAN AND NATURE" REVISITED IN POETRY BY WOMEN

1. Joseph Campbell lists four general functions of myth in his "Mythological Themes in Creative Literature and Art," in Joseph Campbell, ed., *Myths, Dreams and Religion*, pp. 138–175. Briefly, these are metaphysical reconciliation with the conditions of existence; the formulation of a cosmological image in keeping with the science of the time; the validation of some specific social order; and preparation of the individual for the psychological passages from birth to death.

2. Susan Griffin, *Woman and Nature*, p. 219.

3. Rozsika Parker and Griselda Pollock, *Old Mistresses: Women, Art and Ideology*, see esp. pp. 145–151.

4. Griffin, p. 226.

5. May Sarton, *A Grain of Mustard Seed*, p. 66.

6. Ibid., p. 68.

7. "Less and Less Human, O Savage Spirit," *The Collected Poems of Wallace Stevens*, p. 327.

8. *The Twelve-Spoked Wheel Flashing*, p. 5.

9. *Living in the Open*, p. 16.

10. All the lines quoted here come from the following poems in *Living in the Open*: "Homesick," p. 4; "Cod Summer," p. 13; "Healing of Weariness," p. 21.

11. "Shadows of the Burning," in *The Moon Is Always Female*, p. 103.

12. "Tumbling and with Tangled Mane," *The Moon Is Always Female*, pp. 109–110.

13. See also poems: Denise Levertov, "The Pulse" in *The Sorrow Dance*, p. 77; "Cancion," in *The Freeing of the Dust*, p. 49; Adrienne Rich, "The Knot," *Necessities of Life*, p. 41; Lisel Mueller, *Voices from the Forest*, p. 31; Linda Pastan, "Hurricane Watch," *Aspects of Eve*, p. 41.

14. Robert Bly, *News of the Universe: Poems of Twofold Consciousness*, p. 210.

15. Helen Vendler, *Part of Nature, Part of Us*, p. 274.

16. William Carlos Williams, *Paterson*, p. 30.

17. The images come from May Swenson's "Ocean Whale-Shaped," "A Bird's Life," and "Out of the Sea Early," in *Half Sun Half Sleep*, pp. 72, 29, 81; and "Stony Beach," in *To Mix with Time*, p. 172.

18. *Half Sun Half Sleep*, pp. 64–65.

19. *Coal*, p. 6.

20. *Waiting for My Life*, p. 12.

21. *The Wooing of Earth*, p. 68.

22. *Against Nature: Wilderness Poems*, p. 8.

23. Ibid., p. 27. Also see her "The Summer Woman," pp. 50–51. Cf. Sarton's "Beyond the Question," *A Grain of Mustard Seed*, p. 69, and Lisel Mueller's "The Mermaid," in *Dependencies*, p. 14.

24. "When There Were Trees," *Carpenter of the Sun*, reprinted in Paul Feroe, ed., *Silent Voices*, p. 77.

25. *The Witch and the Weather Report*, p. 45.

26. Bly, p. 286.

27. Susan Astor, "The Farmer Lost a Child," in Feroe, p. 4.

28. Besmilr Brigham, "Mountains," in Laura Chester and Sharon Barba, *Rising Tides*, pp. 120–121.

29. Griffin, p. 217.

30. *Rites of Ancient Ripening*, p. 52.

31. Lewis Thomas, *The Lives of a Cell*, p. 124.

32. Ibid., p. 125.

33. Feroe, p. 3.

34. *The Bible of the Beasts of the Little Field*, p. 44. At least in some parts of the poem (pp. 42–47) the speaker seems to be a tree. Also see Denise Levertov, "Animal Rights," in *Footprints*, p. 28.

35. Feroe, p. 57.

36. "Mistress," *Alphabet for the Lost Years*, Part II, n.p.

37. *The Jacob's Ladder*, p. 21.

38. *The Sorrow Dance*, p. 26. Also see Colette Inez, "The Woman Who Loved Worms," in Chester and Barba, p. 198.

39. *O Taste and See*, p. 3.

40. *Footprints*, pp. 43–44.

41. Serena Sue Hilsinger and Lois Brynes, eds., *Selected Poems of May Sarton*, p. 180.

42. "A Village Tale," Ibid., pp. 181–182, is another poem in which an animal redeems the human, this time by digging a buried dog out of his grave.

43. Ibid., p. 176.

44. *A Grain of Mustard Seed*, p. 69.

45. Ibid., p. 70.

46. Ibid., p. 71.

47. *New Heaven/New Earth*, p. 111.

48. Ted Hughes, ed., *The Collected Poems: Sylvia Plath;* p. 57. The poem was written in 1956.

49. Ibid., p. 130. The poem was written in 1959.

50. Frances McCullough, ed., *The Journals of Sylvia Plath*, p. 28.

51. *Geography III*, p. 22–31.

52. "The Fish," *The Complete Poems*, pp. 48–50.

53. "For a Shetland Pony Brood Mare Who Died in her Barren Year," *Up Country*, pp. 40–41.

54. "The Totems," *The Animals in That Country*, p. 22.

55. "Elegy for the Great Tortoises," Ibid., p. 23.

56. Ibid., p. 10.

57. Carl Sagan, *The Dragons of Eden*, p. 114.

58. "Songs of the Transformed," *You Are Happy*, pp. 30–42.

59. Ibid., p. 39.

60. Ibid., pp. 43–44.

61. Roy Willis, *Man and Beast*, p. 128: "The distinctive peculiarity of animals is that, being at once close to man and strange to him, both akin to him and unalterably not-man, they are able to alternate, as objects of human thought, between the contiguity of the metonymic mode and the distanced, analogical mode of the metaphor. This means that, as symbols, animals have the convenient faculty of representing both existential and normative aspects of human experience, as well as their interrelation; what is beyond society, the ultimate ends of action, and the incorporation of such values in the structure of social perception and relations. At this level of abstraction, human diversity and human identity are coterminous."

62. "Bestiary U.S.A.," in *45 Mercy Street*, pp. 25–45.

63. Ibid., p. 41.

64. Ibid., p. 40. See Chapter 1 for my interpretation of her identification with Jesus.

65. Ibid., p. 45.

66. Ibid., p. 42.

67. Ibid., p. 44.

68. *A Grain of Mustard Seed*, p. 20.

69. Ibid., p. 23.

70. Diane di Prima's reason for identifying the Loba as the overarching goddess figure may be to include not only our animal origins but also our Native American heritage in an image of the deity.

71. *Loba*, p. 38.

72. Ibid., p. 59.

73. Ibid., p. 82.

74. Ibid., pp. 11–12.

75. Ibid., pp. 179–180.

76. Ibid., pp. 188–189.

77. Ibid., p. 190.

78. Ibid., p. 58.

79. In addition to the poems I have quoted, see pp. 41, 42-43, 57–60, 62–64, 67–68, 81–82, 83–90, 141, 171, 179, 184–185.

80. *Lady of the Beasts*, p. 130.

81. Susan Griffin; all quotations are from pp. 223–227.

82. Julia Penelope Stanley and Susan J. Wolfe (Robbins), "Toward a Feminist Aesthetic," *Chrysalis: A Magazine of Women's Culture* 6 (1978), p. 67.

CONCLUSION: THE LIGHT IS IN US

1. I refer to the following paintings: *La Bergère des sphinx* (1942); *Divinité chthonienne guettant le sommeil d'un jeune homme* (1947); *Le Bout du monde* (1948).

2. Mary Esther Harding, *Women's Mysteries*, pp. 117–126.

3. Rosemary Ruether's chapter on "The Descent of Woman" in her *New Woman/New Earth*, pp. 3–35, overlooks Chaucer's revival of the goddess who represents "natural fertility and social order and wisdom" (p. 12).

4. See Sylvia Brinton Perera, *The Descent of Inanna*.

5. I refer to the following paintings: *La Chambre descellée* (1964); *L'Autre Côté* (1964); *Le Retour des absents* (1965); *La Fête secrète* (1964).

6. I refer to the following paintings: *Il s'agit sans doute d'Azraël* (1967); *Le Fait accompli* (1967).

7. Julia Kristeva, "Women's Time," pp. 23–25.

8. Alicia Ostriker, "The Thieves of Language," *Signs* VII, 1 (Autumn 1982), p. 87.

9. I refer her to Fini's *La Pensierosa* (1954).

10. The concept of the "muted culture" was articulated by Edwin Ardener in Shirley Ardener, ed., *Perceiving Women;* pp. 23–25.

11. Erich Gould, *Mythical Intentions in Modern Literature*, p. 10.

12. Carol Christ, *Diving Deep and Surfacing*, p. 13.

13. Martha Kearns, *Käthe Kollwitz*, p. 165; Käthe Kollwitz, *Diary and Letters*, pp. 98–99.

14. Kearns, p. 166; Kollwitz, pp. 161–162.

15. Christ, pp. 13–18.

16. Cited by Carol S. Rupprecht in her report on the First International Interdisciplinary Conference on Women's Studies, *The Women's Studies Quarterly: International Supplement* (July 1982), pp. 43–44.

17. Joseph Campbell, *The Masks of God: Creative Mythology*, pp. 677, 90.

18. Campbell describes the process of mythmaking as a transcendence of categories, p. 90.

19. See Hilde Hein, "Knowledge and the Model of Mind" in her unpublished book manuscript, *Half a Mind: Philosophy from a Woman's Point of View*, pp. 466–469 for an analysis of the role light imagery plays in western epistemology.

20. Nancy Chodorow, *The Reproduction of Mothering*, pp. 166–169.

21. My method represents a deliberate "misreading" of Claude Lévi-Strauss, "The Structural Study of Myth," in Richard and Fernande De George, eds., *The Structuralists from Marx to Lévi-Strauss*, p. 176.

22. Margaret Atwood, *Two-Headed Poems*, pp. 96–97.

23. Julia Stanley and Susan Wolfe (Robbins), "Toward a Feminist Aesthetic," *Chrysalis* 6 (1978), p. 67.

24. Lucy Lippard, *From the Center*, p. 49.

25. Ibid., p. 69.

26. Lippard, "Sweeping Exchanges," p. 365.

27. Adrienne Rich, *The Dream of a Common Language* p. 59. The theme of female enclosure extends from Rich's earliest poems to her latest. See "Aunt Jennifer's Tigers," *A Change of World* and "The Lioness," *The Dream of a Common Language*, pp. 21–22.

28. Paul Friedrich, *The Meaning of Aphrodite*, pp. 73, 146, 187–191, 210. Margaret Atwood also describes the powers of Venus as maternal and sexual, *Survival*, p. 210.

29. See Carol P. MacCormack, "Nature, Culture and Gender: A Critique," in MacCormack and Marilyn Strathern, eds., *Nature, Culture and Gender*, pp. 1–21, for a critique of Lévi-Strauss's ideological categories.

30. Hein, pp. 480, 481, 482.

31. Erik Erikson, "Womanhood and the 'Inner Space'," in his *Identity, Youth and Crisis;* reprinted in Jean Strouse, ed., *Women and Analysis*, pp. 333–390.

32. Hein, pp. 483, 484–485, 486.

33. Ibid., p. 490. Mary Jane Gormley, in her reading of this manuscript, suggests that Hein's interpenetrative model has affinities with the philosophies

of Jacques Maritain: "Love unites us to another insofar as it becomes one with us" (*Réflexions sur l'intelligence;* Paris, Desclée de Brouwer, 1938, p. 110); and Thomas Aquinas: "Love is a more unifying force than is knowledge" (S.T. 1a.2ae. 28, 1 ad 3).

34. Ibid., pp. 487–488.

35. Mary Douglas, "In the Nature of Things," in her *Implicit Meanings,* p. 210.

36. William Butler Yeats, "The Second Coming," *Collected Poems,* p. 184.

BIBLIOGRAPHY

I. Women's Studies, Feminist Theory

Abel, Elizabeth, ed. *Writing and Sexual Difference*. A Special Issue of *Critical Inquiry* 8, 2 (Winter 1981).

Ardener, Edwin. "Belief and the Problem of Women." In Shirley Ardener, ed., *Perceiving Women*. London: J. M. Dent and Sons, 1975; pp. 1–18.

———. "The 'Problem' Revisited." In Shirley Ardener, ed., *Perceiving Women*. London: J. M. Dent and Sons, 1975; pp. 19–27.

Ardener, Shirley, ed. *Perceiving Women*. London: J. M. Dent and Sons, 1975.

Chodorow, Nancy. "Family Structure and Feminine Personality." In Michelle Z. Rosaldo and Louise Lamphere, eds., *Woman, Culture and Society*. Stanford: Stanford University Press, 1974; pp. 43–66.

———. *The Reproduction of Mothering*. Berkeley: University of California Press, 1978.

Christ, Carol P. "Margaret Atwood: The Surfacing of Women's Spiritual Quest and Vision." *Signs* II, 2 (Winter 1976), pp. 316–330.

———. "Why Women Need the Goddess: Phenomenological, Psychological, and Political Reflections." In Carol P. Christ and Judith Plaskow, eds., *Womanspirit Rising: A Feminist Reader in Religion*. San Francisco: Harper and Row, 1979; pp.273–287.

———. *Diving Deep and Surfacing: Women Writers on Spiritual Quest*. Boston: Beacon Press, 1980.

——— and Judith Plaskow, eds., *Womanspirit Rising: A Feminist Reader in Religion*. San Francisco: Harper and Row, 1979.

Cixous, Hélène. "The Laugh of Medusa." Tr. Keith and Paula Cohen. *Signs* I, 4 (Summer 1976), pp. 875–894.

———. "Castration or Decapitation?" Tr. Annette Kuhn. *Signs* VII, 1 (Autumn 1981), pp. 41–55.

Daly, Mary. *Beyond God the Father: Toward a Philosophy of Women's Liberation*. Boston: Beacon Press, 1973.

———. *Gyn/Ecology: The Metaethics of Radical Feminism*. Boston: Beacon Press, 1978.

Davidson, Cathy N. and E. M. Broner, eds. *The Lost Tradition: Mothers and Daughters in Literature*. NewYork: Frederick Ungar, 1980.

de Castillejo, Irene Claremont. *Knowing Woman: A Feminine Psychology*. New York: Harper and Row, 1973.

Demetrakopoulos, Stephanie. *Listening to Our Bodies: The Rebirth of Feminine Wisdom*. Boston: Beacon Press, 1983.

Diner, Helen. *Mothers and Amazons: The First Feminine History of Culture*. Garden City, N.Y.: Doubleday, 1973.

Downing, Christine. *The Goddess: Mythological Images of the Feminine*. New York: Crossroad Press, 1981.

DuPlessis, Rachel Blau. "Psyche, Or Wholeness." *The Massachusetts Review*, XX, 1 (1979), pp. 77–96.

———. "To Begin Story." Paper presented at the Modern Language Association Convention, December 1980.

———. "The Critique of Consciousness and Myth in Levertov, Rich, and Rukeyser." In Sandra M. Gilbert and Susan Gubar, eds., *Shakespeare's Sisters*. Bloomington: Indiana University Press, 1979.

Elias-Button, Karen. "Journey into Archetype: The Dark Woman in Contemporary Women's Poetry." *Anima* IV, 2 (Spring 1978), pp. 5–11.

Friedman, Susan. "Creating a Woman's Mythology: H. D.'s *Helen in Egypt*." *Women's Studies* V, 2 (1977), pp. 163–197.

Gilbert, Sandra M. "Confessional Mythology." Paper presented at the Modern Language Association Convention, December 1980.

Gilbert, Sandra M., and Susan Gubar. *The Madwoman in the Attic*. New Haven: Yale University Press, 1979.

Goldenberg, Naomi. *The Changing of the Gods*. Boston: Beacon Press, 1979.

Griffin, Susan. *Pornography and Silence: Culture's Revenge against Nature*. New York: Harper and Row, 1981.

Griscom, Jane L. "On Healing the Nature/History Split in Feminist Thought." *Feminism and Ecology*. Special Issue of *Heresies* IV, 1, Issue 13 (1981), pp. 4–9.

Hall, Nor. *The Moon and the Virgin: Reflections on the Archetypal Feminine*. New York: Harper and Row, 1980.

Harding, Mary Esther. *The Way of All Women*. New York: Harper and Row, 1971.

———. *Women's Mysteries: Ancient and Modern*. New York: Harper and Row, 1971.

Hein, Hilde. "Half a Mind: Philosophy from a Woman's Point of View." Manuscript.

Janeway, Elizabeth. *Man's World, Women's Place*. New York: Dell, 1971.

——— *Between Myth and Morning: Women Awakening*. New York: William Morrow, 1974.

Jelinek, Estelle C., ed. *Women's Autobiography: Essays in Criticism*. Bloomington: Indiana University Press, 1980.

Keohane, Nannerl O., *et al.*, eds. *Feminist Theory: A Critique of Ideology*. Chicago: University of Chicago Press, 1982.

King, Ynestra. "Feminism and the Revolt of Nature." *Feminism and Ecology*. Special issue of *Heresies* IV, 1, Issue 13 (1981), pp. 12–16.

Kristeva, Julia. "Women's Time." Tr. Alice Jardin and Harry Blake. *Signs* VII, 1 (Autumn 1981), pp. 13–35.

Lauter, Estella. "Moving to the Ends of Our Own Rainbows: Steps Toward a Feminist Aesthetic." In Patricia Werhane, ed., *"Philosophical Issues in Art."* Engelwood Cliffs: Prentice Hall, 1983.

——— and Carol Schreier Rupprecht. "Feminist Archetypal Theory: Interdisciplinary Re-Visions of Jungian Thought." Knoxville: University of Tennessee Press, forthcoming, 1984.

MacCormack, Carol, and Marilyn Strathern, eds. *Nature, Culture and Gender*. Cambridge: Cambridge University Press, 1980.

Marks, Elaine, and Isabelle de Courtivron, eds. *New French Feminisms*. New York: Schocken, 1981.

Merchant, Carolyn. *The Death of Nature: Women, Ecology and the Scientific Revolution*. San Francisco: Harper and Row, 1980.

Moers, Ellen. *Literary Women*. Garden City, N.Y.: Doubleday, 1976.

Monaghan, Patricia. *Women in Myth and Legend*. London: Junction Books, 1981.

Ochshorn, Judith. *The Female Experience and the Nature of the Divine*. Bloomington: Indiana University Press, 1980.

Ortner, Sherry B. "Is Female to Male As Nature Is to Culture?" In Michelle Z. Rosaldo and Louise Lamphere, eds., *Woman, Culture and Society*. Stanford: Stanford University Press, 1974.

Ostriker, Alicia. "The Thieves of Language: Women Poets and Revisionist Mythology." Paper presented at the Modern Language Association Convention. December 1980.

———. "The Thieves of Language: Women Poets and Revisionist Mythmaking." *Signs* VIII, 1 (Autumn 1982), pp. 68–90.

———. *Writing Like A Woman*. Ann Arbor: University of Michigan Press, 1983.

Perera, Sylvia Brinton. *The Descent of Inanna*. Toronto: Jung Society, 1981.

Pomeroy, Sarah. *Goddesses, Whores, Wives and Slaves*. New York: Schocken, 1975.

Pratt, Annis. *Archetypal Patterns in Women's Fiction*. Bloomington: Indiana University Press, 1981.

Rich, Adrienne. *Of Woman Born*. New York: W. W. Norton, 1976.

———. "When We Dead Awaken: Writing as Re-Vision." In *On Lies, Secrets and Silence: Selected Prose, 1966–1978*. New York: W. W. Norton, 1979.

Rigney, Barbara. *Madness and Sexual Politics in the Feminist Novel*. Madison: University of Wisconsin Press, 1978.

Rosaldo, Michelle Z., and Louise Lamphere, eds. *Woman, Culture and Society*. Stanford: Stanford University Press, 1974.

Ruether, Rosemary. *New Woman/New Earth*. New York: Seabury, 1975.

Rupprecht, Carol. "The First International Interdisciplinary Conference on Women's Studies." *Women's Studies Quarterly: International Supplement* I, 1 (July 1982), pp. 43–44.

Spacks, Patricia. *The Female Imagination*. New York: Knopf, 1975.

Spretnak, Charlene. *Lost Goddesses of Early Greece: A Collection of Pre-Hellenic Mythology*. Berkeley: Moon Books, 1978.

Stewart, Grace. *A New Mythos*. St. Albans, Vermont: Eden Press, 1979.

Stone, Merlin. *When God Was a Woman*. New York: Harcourt Brace Jovanovich, 1978.

———. *Ancient Mirrors of Womanhood*. 2 vols. New York: New Sibylline Books, 1979.

Strouse, Jean, ed. *Women and Analysis*. New York: Dell, 1974.

Washbourn, Penelope. *Becoming Woman: the Quest for Wholeness in Female Experience*. New York: Harper and Row, 1979.

Wolff, Toni. *Structural Forms of the Feminine Psyche*. Zurich: C. G. Jung Institute, 1956.

II. *Myth Studies*

Bachofen, Johann Jacob. *Myth, Religion and Mother Right*. Tr. Ralph Mannheim. Princeton: Princeton University Press, 1967; rpt. of 1926 version of *Das Mutterrecht*. Germany: 1861, original publication.

Barbour, Ian G. *Myths, Models and Paradigms: A Comparative Study in Science and Religion*. New York: Harper and Row, 1974.

Barthes, Roland. *Mythologies*. Tr. Annette Lavers. New York: Hill and Wang, 1972.

Briffault, Robert. *The Mothers*. George Allen & Unwin Ltd., 1959.

Bullfinch's Mythology. New York: Avenel, 1978.

Bultmann, Rudolf, *et al. Kerygma and Myth: A Theological Debate*. Ed. Hans Werner Bartsch. New York: Harper and Row, 1961.

Campbell, Joseph.*The Hero with a Thousand Faces*. New York: Pantheon, 1949.

———. *The Masks of God: Occidental Mythology*. New York: Viking Press, 1964.

———. *The Flight of the Wild Gander: Explorations in the Mythological Dimension*. New York: Viking, 1969.

———. *The Masks of God: Primitive Mythology*. New York: Viking, 1969.

———. *The Masks of God: Creative Mythology*. New York: Viking, 1970.

———, ed. *Myths, Dreams and Religion*. New York: Dutton, 1970.

Cassirer, Ernst. *Language and Myth*. Tr. Susanne K. Langer. New York: Dover, 1946.

———. *Philosophy of Symbolic Forms*. Vol. II. Tr. Susanne Langer. New Haven: Yale University Press, 1955.

Cook, Albert. *Myth and Language*. Bloomington: Indiana University Press, 1980.

DeGeorge, Richard and Fernande, eds. *The Structuralists from Marx to Lévi-Strauss*. Garden City, N.Y.: Doubleday Anchor Books, 1972.

Douglas, Mary. *Natural Symbols: Explorations in Cosmology*. New York: Random House, 1973.

———. *Rules and Meanings*. Harmondsworth, Middlesex: Penguin, 1973.

———. *Implicit Meanings*. London: Routledge and Kegan Paul, 1975.

Eliade, Mircea. *Myths, Dreams and Mysteries*. Tr. Philip Mairet. New York: Harper and Row, 1960.

———. *Images and Symbols*. Tr. Philip Mairet. New York: Sheed and Ward, 1961.

———. *Myth and Reality*. Tr. Willard Trask. New York: Harper and Row, 1963.

Ellmann, Richard, and Charles Feidelson, Jr., eds. *The Modern Tradition*. New York: Oxford University Press, 1965.

Freud, Sigmund. *Moses and Monotheism*. Tr. Katherine Jones. New York: Knopf, 1939.

———. *Totem and Taboo*. Tr. James Strachey. New York: W. W. Norton, 1950.

———. *Civilization and Its Discontents*. Tr. James Strachey. New York: W. W. Norton, 1961.

Friedrich, Paul. *The Meaning of Aphrodite*. Chicago: University of Chicago Press, 1978.

Frye, Northrop. *Anatomy of Criticism*. Princeton: Princeton University Press, 1957.

———. *Fables of Identity: Studies in Poetic Mythology*. New York: Harcourt, Brace and World, 1963.

———. *Spiritus Mundi*. Bloomington: Indiana University Press, 1976.

———. *The Great Code: The Bible and Literature*. New York: Harcourt, Brace, Jovanovich, 1982.

Gimbutas, Marija. *The Gods and Goddesses of Old Europe*. Berkeley: University of California Press, 1974.

Gould, Eric. *Mythical Intentions in Modern Literature*. Princeton: Princeton University Press, 1982.

Graves, Robert. *The White Goddess*. New York: Creative Age Press, 1948.
――――. *Greek Myths*. 2 vols. Harmondsworth, Middlesex: Penguin, 1955.
Harrison, Jane Ellen. *Mythology*. New York: Harcourt, Brace and World, 1963; rprt. Longmans, Green and Co., 1924.
――――. *Prolegomena to the Study of Greek Religion*. New York: Meridian, 1957.
Heyob, Sharon. *The Cult of Isis among Women*. Leiden: E. J. Brill, 1975.
James, E. O. *The Cult of the Mother Goddess*. New York: Barnes and Noble, 1959.
Jaspers, Karl, and Rudolph Bultmann. *Myth and Christianity: An Inquiry into the Possibility of Religion without Myth*. New York: Noonday Press, 1958.
Jung, Carl Gustav. *Man and His Symbols*. Garden City, N.Y.: Doubleday, 1964.
――――. *The Spirit in Man, Art, and Literature*. Vol. 15 of *The Collected Works of C. G. Jung*. Princeton: Princeton University Press, 1966.
――――. *Analytical Psychology: Its Theory and Practice*. New York: Random House, 1968.
――――. *The Archetypes and the Collective Unconscious*. Vol. 9.1 of *The Collected Works of C. G. Jung*. 2nd ed. Princeton: Princeton University Press, 1968.
――――. *Psychology and Alchemy*. Vol. 12 of *The Collected Works of C. G. Jung*. Princeton: Princeton University Press, 1968.
――――. *Mysterium Coniuntionis*. Vol. 14 of *The Collected Works of C. G. Jung*. 2nd ed. Princeton: Princeton University Press, 1970.
――――. *The Structure and Dynamics of the Psyche*. Vol. 8 of *The Collected Works of C. G. Jung*. 2nd ed. Princeton: Princeton University Press, 1972.
Jung, Carl Gustav and C. Kerenyi. *Essays on a Science of Mythology: The Myth of the Divine Child and the Mysteries of Eleusis*. Tr. R. F. C. Hull. Princeton: Princeton University Press, 1950.
Lehner, Ernst and Johanna. *A Fantastic Bestiary*. New York: Tudor, 1969.
Lévi-Strauss, Claude. *The Savage Mind*. Chicago: University of Chicago Press, 1959.
――――ム *Myth and Meaning*. New York: Schocken, 1979.
Maranda, Pierre, ed. *Mythology*. Harmondsworth, Middlesex: Penguin, 1972.
McCune, Marjorie W., *et al.*, eds. *The Binding of Proteus: Perspectives on Myth and the Literary Process*. Lewisburg, Pa.: Bucknell University Press, 1980.
Neumann, Erich. *Art and the Creative Unconscious*. Tr. Ralph Manheim. New York: Bollingen Foundation, 1959.
――――. *Amor and Psyche: The Psychic Development of the Feminine*. Tr. Ralph Manheim. New York: Bollingen, 1960.
――――. *The Great Mother*. New York: Bollingen, 1963.
New Larousse Encyclopedia of Mythology. London: Hamlyn, 1968.
Rose, H. G. *A Handbook of Greek Mythology*. London: Methuen & Co., Ltd., 1928.
Sebeok, Thomas, ed. *Myth: A Symposium*. Bloomington: Indiana University Press, 1974.
Singer, June. *Androgyny*. Garden City, N.Y.: Doubleday, 1976.
Slater, Philip. *The Glory of Hera*. Boston: Beacon Press, 1968.
Slote, Bernice, ed. *Myth and Symbol*. Lincoln: University of Nebraska Press, 1963.
Turbayne, Colin Murray. *The Myth of Metaphor*. Rev. ed. New Haven: Yale University Press, 1962.
Vickery, John B. "Literature and Myth." In Jean-Pierre Barricelli and Joseph Gibaldi, eds., *Interrelations of Literature*. New York: Modern Language Association, 1982.

——, ed. *Myth and Literature: Contemporary Theory and Practice*. Lincoln: University of Nebraska Press, 1966.

Wheelwright, Philip. *Metaphor and Reality*. Bloomington: Indiana University Press, 1962.

——. *The Burning Fountain: A Study in the Language of Symbolism*. Bloomington: Indiana University Press, 1968.

III. Poetry and Literary Criticism

Atwood, Margaret. *The Circle Game*. Toronto: Anansi, 1966.

——. *The Animals in That Country*. Boston: Little, Brown and Co., 1968.

——. *The Journals of Susanna Moodie*. Toronto: Oxford University Press, 1970.

——. *Procedures for Underground*. Toronto: Oxford University Press, 1970.

——. *Power Politics*. New York: Harper and Row, 1971.

——. *Surfacing*. New York: Popular Library, 1972.

——. *Survival: A Thematic Guide to Canadian Literature*. Toronto: Anansi, 1972.

——. *You Are Happy*. New York: Harper and Row, 1974.

——. *Two-Headed Poems*. Toronto: Oxford University Press, 1978.

——. *True Stories:* New York: Simon and Schuster, 1981.

Barnstone, Aliki and Willis, eds. *A Book of Women Poets from Antiquity to Now*. New York: Schocken, 1980.

Beeler, Janet N. *Dowry*. Columbia, Missouri: University of Missouri, 1978.

Bernikow, Louise. *Among Women*. New York: Harper and Row, 1981.

——, ed. *The World Spilt Open: Four Centuries of Women Poets in England and America,* 1552–1950. New York: Vintage, 1974.

Bishop, Elizabeth. *The Complete Poems*. New York: Farrar, Strauss and Giroux, 1969.

——. *Geography III*. New York: Farrar, Strauss and Giroux, 1976.

Bly, Robert. *News of the Universe: Poems of Twofold Consciousness*. San Francisco: Sierra Club Books, 1980.

Bodkin, Maude. *Archetypal Patterns in Poetry*. New York: Oxford University Press, 1978. rprt. 1934.

——. *Studies of Type-Images in Poetry, Religion and Philosophy*. Folcroft, Pa.: Folcroft, 1951.

Brigham, Besmilr. *Heaved from the Earth*. New York: Knopf, 1969.

Brooks, Gwendolyn. *Selected Poems*. New York: Harper and Row, 1963.

——. *In the Mecca*. New York: Harper and Row, 1968.

Chester, Laura, and Sharon Barba, eds. *Rising Tides: 20th Century American Women Poets*. New York: Washington Square Press, 1973.

Conron, John. *The American Landscape: A Critical Anthology of Prose and Poetry*. New York: Oxford University Press, 1974.

Davidson, Arnold and Cathy N., eds. *The Art of Margaret Atwood: Essays in Criticism*. Toronto: Anansi, 1981.

Demetrakopoulos, Stephanie. "Anaïs Nin and the Feminine Quest for Consciousness: the Quelling of the Devouring Mother and the Ascension of the Sophia." *Bucknell Review* XXXIV (Spring 1978), pp. 119–136.

——. "Matrilinearity, the Demeter/Kore Archetype and the Feminine Quest for Consciousness in the Poetry of Anne Sexton." Manuscript.

di Prima, Diane. *Selected Poems 1965–1975*. Plainfield, Vermont: North Atlantic Books, 1975.

——. *Loba*. Parts I-VIII. Berkeley: Wingbow Press, 1978.

DuPlessis, Rachel Blau. *Wells*. New York: Montemora, 1980.

Feroe, Paul, ed. *Silent Voices*. St. Paul, Minn.: Ally Press, 1978.

Fisher, Dexter. *The Third Woman: Minority Women Writers of the United States*. Boston: Houghton Mifflin Co., 1980.

Friedman, Susan. *Psyche Reborn: The Emergence of H. D.* Bloomington: Indiana University Press, 1981.

Gelpi, Barbara Charlesworth and Albert. *Adrienne Rich's Poetry*. New York: W. W. Norton, 1975.

Gilbert, Sandra, and Susan Gubar. *Shakespeare's Sisters*. Bloomington: Indiana University Press, 1979.

Gluck, Louise. *The House on Marshland*. New York: Ecco Press, 1975.

——. *Descending Figure*. New York: Ecco Press, 1980.

Grace, Sherrill. *Violent Duality: A Study of Margaret Atwood*. Montreal: Vehicule Press, 1980.

Griffin, Susan. *Woman and Nature: The Roaring inside Her*. New York: Harper and Row, 1978.

Gubar, Susan. "The Echoing Spell of H. D.'s Trilogy." *Contemporary Literature* XIX, 2 (Spring 1978), pp. 196–218.

H. D. *Selected Poems*. New York: Grove Press, 1957.

——. *Helen in Egypt*. New York: New Directions, 1961.

——. *Hermetic Definition*. New York: New Directions, 1972.

——. *Trilogy*. New York: New Directions, 1973.

——. *Sea Garden*. New York: St. Martin's Press, 1975.

Hacker, Marilyn. *Presentation Piece*. New York: Viking, 1974.

——. *Separations*. New York: Knopf, 1976.

——. *Taking Notice*. New York: Knopf, 1980.

Howe, Florence, and Ellen Bass, eds. *No More Masks! An Anthology of Poems by Women*. Garden City, N.Y.: Doubleday, 1973.

Iverson, Lucille, and Kathryn Ruby, eds. *We Become New: Poems by Contemporary Women*. New York: Bantam, 1975.

Jong, Erica. *Here Comes and Other Poems*. New York, New American Library, 1975.

——. *Loveroot*. New York: Holt, Rinehart and Winston, 1975.

——. *At the Edge of the Body*. New York: Holt, Rinehart and Winston, 1979.

——. *Witches*. New York: New American Library, 1981.

Jordan, June. *New Days: Poems of Exile and Return*. New York: Emerson Hall, 1974.

——. *Things That I Do in the Dark*. New York: Random House, 1977.

——. *Civil Wars*. New York: Harper and Row, 1983.

Juhasz, Suzanne. *Naked and Fiery Forms: Modern Poetry by American Women, A New Tradition*. New York: Harper and Row, 1976.

Keith, W. J. *The Poetry of Nature: Rural Perspectives in Poetry from Wordsworth to the Present*. Toronto: University of Toronto Press, 1980.

Kolodny, Annette. *The Lay of the Land*. Chapel Hill: University of North Carolina, 1975.

Kroll, Judith. *Chapters in a Mythology: The Poetry of Sylvia Plath*. New York: Harper and Row, 1976.

Kumin, Maxine. *Up Country*. New York: Harper and Row, 1972.

——. *To Make a Prairie: Essays on Poets, Poetry, and Country Living*. Ann Arbor: University of Michigan Press, 1979.

——. *Our Ground Time Here Will Be Brief: New and Selected Poems*. New York: Viking, 1982.

Lattimore, Richmond, tr. *The Odyssey of Homer*. New York: Harper and Row, 1965.

Lauter, Estella. "Diane Wakoski." In Lina Mainiero, ed. *American Women Writers IV*. New York: Frederick Ungar, 1982, pp. 309–310.

Lecker, Robert. "Janus through the Looking Glass: Atwood's First Three Novels." In Arnold and Cathy N. Davidson, eds., *The Art of Margaret Atwood: Essays in Criticism*. Toronto: Anansi, 1981, pp. 177–204.

LeSueur, Meridel. *Rites of Ancient Ripening*. Minneapolis: Vanilla Press, 1975.

Levertov, Denise. *The Jacob's Ladder*. New York: New Directions, 1961.

———. *O Taste and See*. New York: New Directions, 1964.

———. *The Sorrow Dance*. New York: New Directions, 1968.

———. *Relearning the Alphabet*. New York: New Directions, 1970.

———. *To Stay Alive*. New York: New Directions, 1971.

———. *Footprints*. New York: New Directions, 1972.

———. *The Poet in the World*. New York: New Directions, 1973.

———. *The Freeing of the Dust*. New York: New Directions, 1975.

———. *Life in the Forest*. New York: New Directions, 1978.

———. *Light Up the Cave*. New York: New Directions, 1981.

———. *Candles in Babylon*. New York: New Directions, 1982.

Lilienfeld, Jane. "Circe's Emergence: Transforming Traditional Love in Margaret Atwood's *You Are Happy*." *Worcester Review* 5 (March 1977), pp. 29–37.

Lorde, Audre. *From a Land Where Other People Live*. Detroit: Broadside Press, 1973.

———. *Coal*. New York: W. W. Norton, 1976.

———. *The Black Unicorn*. New York: W. W. Norton, 1978.

———. *The Cancer Journals*. Argyle, N.Y.: Spinsters, Ink 1980.

Macpherson, Jay. *Poems Twice Told: The Boatman and Welcoming Disaster*. Toronto: Oxford University Press, 1981.

Mandel, Eli. "Atwood Gothic." In *Another Time*. Erin, Ontario: Press Porcepic, Ltd., pp. 137–145.

McClatchy, J. D., ed. *Anne Sexton: The Artist and Her Critics*. Bloomington: Indiana University Press, 1978.

McCombs, Judith. "Atwood's Nature Concepts: An Overview." *Waves* VII, 1 (Fall 1978), pp. 68–77.

———. *Against Nature: Wilderness Poems*. Paradise, California: Dustbooks, 1979.

Mersmann, James F. "Blood on the Moon: Diane Wakoski's Mythologies of Loss and Need." *Margins* (Jan., Feb., Mar. 1976). pp. 116–128.

Mills, Ralph J. *Contemporary American Poetry*. New York: Random House, 1966.

Morgan, Robin. *Monster*. New York: Vintage, 1972.

———. *Lady of the Beasts*. New York: Random House, 1976.

———. *Depth Perception*. Garden City, N.Y.: Doubleday, 1982.

Mueller, Lisel. *Dependencies*. Chapel Hill: University of North Carolina, 1965.

———. *Life of a Queen*. La Crosse, Wis.: Northeast/Juniper Books, 1970.

———. *The Private Life*. Baton Rouge: Louisianna State Univ. Press, 1976.

———. *Voices from the Forest*. LaCrosse, Wis.: Juniper Press, 1977.

Oates, Joyce Carol. *New Heaven/New Earth*. New York: Faucett Crest, 1974.

Olson, Ed, ed. *Symposium on Diane Wakoski*. *Margins* (Jan., Feb., Mar. 1976).

Ostriker, Alicia. *The Mother/Child Papers*. Santa Monica: Momentum Press, 1980.

———. *A Woman under the Surface*. Princeton: Princeton University Press, 1982.

Pastan, Linda. *A Perfect Circle of Sun*. Chicago: The Swallow Press, 1971.

———. *Aspects of Eve*. New York: Liveright, 1975.

———. *The Five Stages of Grief*. New York: W. W. Norton, 1978.

———. *Waiting for My Life*. New York: W. W. Norton, 1981.

Piercy, Marge. *Breaking Camp*. Middletown, Conn.: Wesleyan University Press, 1968.

———. *Hard Loving*. Middletown, Conn.: Wesleyan University Press 1969.

———. *To Be of Use*. Garden City, N.Y.: Doubleday, 1973.

———. *Living in the Open*. New York: Knopf, 1976.

———. *The Twelve-Spoked Wheel Flashing*. New York: Knopf, 1978.

———. *The Moon Is Always Female*. New York: Knopf, 1980.

———. *Circles on the Water: Selected Poems of Marge Piercy*. New York: Knopf, 1982.

Plath, Sylvia. *The Collected Poems*, ed. Ted Hughes. New York: Harper and Row, 1981.

———. *The Journals of Sylvia Plath*, ed. Frances McCullough. New York: Dial Press, 1982.

———. *Letters Home*, ed. Aurelia Schober Plath. New York: Harper and Row, 1975.

Porter, Katherine Anne. *A Defense of Circe*. New York: Harcourt. Brace and Co., 1954.

Pratt, Annis. "Women and Nature in Modern Fiction," *Contemporary Literature* XIII, 4 (1972). pp. 476–490.

———. "Aunt Jennifer's Tigers: Notes toward a Pre-literary History of Women's Archetypes." *Feminist Studies* IV, 1 (February 1978), pp. 163–194.

———. "*Surfacing* and the Rebirth Journey." In Arnold and Cathy N. Davidson, eds., *The Art of Margaret Atwood: Essays in Criticism*. Toronto: Anansi, 1981, pp. 139–157.

Rich, Adrienne. *A Change of World*. New York: W. W. Norton, 1951.

———. *Necessities of Life*. New York: W. W. Norton, 1966.

———. *Diving into the Wreck*. New York: W. W. Norton, 1973.

———. *Poems: Selected and New, 1950–1974*. New York: W. W. Norton, 1975.

———. *The Dream of a Common Language*. New York: W. W. Norton, 1978.

———. *A Wild Patience Has Taken Me This Far*. New York: W. W. Norton, 1981.

Rukeyser, Muriel. *The Speed of Darkness*. New York: Random House, 1971.

———. *Breaking Open*. New York: Random House, 1973.

———. *The Gates* New York: McGraw-Hill, 1974.

———. *The Life of Poetry*. New York: William Morrow, 1974.

Sadoff, Dianne F. "Mythopoeia, The Moon, and Contemporary Women's Poetry." *Massachusetts Review* XIX, 1 (Spring 1978), pp. 93–110.

Sandler, Linda, ed. *Margaret Atwood: A Symposium*. *The Malahat Review* (Jan. 1977). University of Victoria.

Sarton, May. *A Grain of Mustard Seed*. New York: W. W. Norton, 1971.

———. *Collected Poems: 1930–1973*. New York: W. W. Norton, 1974.

———. *Selected Poems of May Sarton*. Eds. Serena Sue Hilsinger and Lois Brynes. New York: W. W. Norton, 1978.

Schaeffer, Susan Fromberg. *The Witch and the Weather Report*. New York: Seven Woods Press, 1972.

———. *Granite Lady*. New York: Collier, 1974.

———. *Alphabet for the Lost Years*. San Francisco: Gallimaufry, 1976.

———. *The Bible of the Beasts of the Little Field*. New York: Dutton, 1980.

Sexton, Anne. *To Bedlam and Part Way Back*. Boston: Houghton Mifflin, 1960.

———. *All My Pretty Ones*. Boston: Houghton Mifflin, 1962.

———. *Live or Die*. Boston: Houghton Mifflin, 1966.

———. *Love Poems*. Boston: Houghton Mifflin, 1969.

————. *Transformations*. Boston: Houghton Mifflin, 1971.

————. *The Book of Folly*. Boston: Houghton Mifflin, 1972.

————. *The Death Notebooks*. Boston: Houghton Mifflin, 1974.

————. *The Awful Rowing toward God*. Boston: Houghton Mifflin, 1975.

————. *45 Mercy Street*. Boston: Houghton Mifflin, 1976.

————. *Words for Doctor Y*. Boston: Houghton Mifflin, 1978.

————. *The Complete Poems*. Boston: Houghton Mifflin Co., 1981.

Sexton, Linda Gray, and Lois Ames, eds. *Anne Sexton: A Self-Portrait in Letters*. Boston: Houghton Mifflin Co. 1977.

Shange, Ntozake. *For Colored Girls Who Have Considered Suicide When the Rainbow Is Enuf*. New York: Macmillan, 1977.

————. *Nappy Edges*. New York: St. Martin's, 1978.

Sherwin, Judith Johnson. *Uranium Poems*. New Haven: Yale University Press, 1969.

————. *Impossible Buildings*. Garden City, N.Y.: Doubleday, 1973.

Stanford, Ann, ed. *The Women Poets in English*. New York: McGraw-Hill, 1972.

Stanford, W. B. *The Ulysses Theme*. New York: Barnes and Noble, 1968.

Stanley, Julia Penelope and Susan J. Wolfe (Robbins). "Toward a Feminist Aesthetic." *Chrysalis: A Magazine of Women's Culture* 6 (1978), pp. 57–71.

Stetson, Erlene, ed. *Black Sister: Poetry by Black American Women, 1746–1980*. Bloomington: Indiana University Press, 1981.

Stevens, Wallace. *The Collected Poems of Wallace Stevens*. New York: Knopf, 1955.

Swenson, May. *To Mix with Time*. New York: Charles Scribner's Sons, 1963.

————. *Poems to Solve*. New York: Charles Scribner's Sons, 1966.

————. *Half Sun Half Sleep*. New York: Charles Scribner's Sons, 1967.

Van Duyn, Mona. *To See to Take*. New York: Atheneum, 1973.

Vendler, Helen. *Part of Nature, Part of Us*. Cambridge: Harvard University Press, 1980.

Wagner, Linda W. "The Making of Selected Poems: the Process of *Surfacing*." In Arnold and Cathy N. Davidson, eds. *The Art of Margaret Atwood: Essays in Criticism*. Toronto: Anansi, 1981, pp 81–94.

Wakoski, Diane. *Inside the Blood Factory*. Garden City, N.Y.: Doubleday, 1968.

————. *The Motorcycle Betrayal Poems*. New York: Simon and Schuster, 1971.

————. *Smudging*. Los Angeles: Black Sparrow Press, 1972.

————. *Dancing on the Grave of a Son of a Bitch*. Los Angeles: Black Sparrow Press, 1974.

————. *The Magellanic Clouds*. Los Angeles: Black Sparrow Press, 1974.

————. *Trilogy*. Garden City, N.Y.: Doubleday, 1974.

————. *Virtuoso Literature for Two and Four Hands*. Garden City, N.Y.: Doubleday, 1975.

————. *Waiting for the King of Spain*. Santa Barbara: Black Sparrow Press, 1976.

————. *The Man Who Shook Hands*. Garden City, N.Y.: Doubleday, 1978.

————. *Toward a New Poetry*. Ann Arbor: University of Michigan Press, 1980.

Walker, Alice. *Goodnight Willie Lee, I'll See You in the Morning*. New York: Dial Press, 1979.

Willard, Nancy. *Carpenter of the Sun*. New York: Liveright, 1974.

Williams, William Carlos. *Paterson*. New York: New Directions, 1963.

Wittig, Monique. *Les Gúerillères*. Tr. David Le Vay. New York: Avon Books, 1969.

Woolf, Virginia. *A Room of One's Own*. Harmondsworth, Middlesex: Penguin, 1928.

Yeats, W. B. *Collected Poems*. New York: Macmillan, 1956.

IV. Visual Art, Art History, Art Criticism

Aspinwall, Margaret, ed. *The Painterly Print: Monotypes from the 17th to the 20th Centuries.* New York: Metropolitan Museum of Art, 1980.

Baskett, Mary W. *The Art of June Wayne.* New York: Harry N. Abrams, 1969.

Belloi, Jay. *Nancy Graves.* La Jolla, Calif.: La Jolla Musuem, 1973.

Berger, John. *Ways of Seeing.* New York: Penguin, 1977.

Bontemps, Arna Alexander, Jacqueline Fonvielle-Bontemps and David C. Driskell. *Forever Free: Art by African American Women, 1862–1980.* Alexandria, Va.: Stephenson, 1980.

Brion, Marcel. *Léonor Fini et son oeuvre.* Paris: J. J. Pauvert, 1955.

Broude, Norma, and Mary D. Garrard, eds. *Feminism and Art History: Questioning the Litany.* New York: Harper and Row, 1982.

Caldwell, Susan Havens. "Experiencing The Dinner Party." *The Woman's Art Journal* I, 2 (Fall 1980/Winter 1981), pp. 35–37.

Carter, Yvonne Pickering. "Morphological Transcription of Forms in Nature: Rocks and Water as the Subject of Abstract Painting." M. F. A. Thesis. Howard University, 1968.

Channing, Richard. "Nancy Graves: Map Paintings." *Art International* XVIII, 9 (Nov. 1974), pp. 26–7, 62.

Cummings, Paul. *Interview with June Wayne.* August 4, 1970. Archives of American Art.

———. *Interview with Nancy Graves.* August 18, 1972. Archives of American Art.

Curry, Elizabeth. "Käthe Kollwitz as Role Model for the Older Woman." *Chrysalis: A Magazine of Women's Culture* VII (1979), pp. 55–69.

Dorothy Hood: Recent Paintings. Houston: Contemporary Art Museum, 1970.

Edelson, Mary Beth. *Seven Cycles.* New York: A.I.R. Gallery, 1980.

Fine, Elsa. *Women and Art.* Montclair, N.J.: Allanheld & Schram, 1978.

Frueh, Joanna. "The Psychological Realism of Ellen Lanyon," *Feminist Art Journal* VI, 1 (Spring 1977), pp. 17–21.

Gaggi, Silvio. "Léonor Fini: A Mythology of the Feminine," *Art International* XXIII, 5–6 (September 1979), pp. 34–38, 49.

Garner, Gretchen. *A.R.C. Past and Present.* Chicago: A.R.C. Education Foundation, 1979.

Gauthier, Xavière. *Léonor Fini.* Paris: Le Musée de Poche, 1973. 2nd edition, 1979.

Genêt, Jean. "Mademoiselle: Letter to Léonor Fini." Tr. Bernard Frechtman. *Nimbus* III, 1 (1955), pp. 30–37; orig. *Lettre à Léonor Fini.* Paris: Loyeau, 1950.

Harris, Ann Sutherland, and Linda Nochlin. *Women Artists: 1550–1950.* New York: Knopf, 1976.

Hinz, Renate, ed. *Käthe Kollwitz: Graphics, Posters, Drawings.* Tr. Rita and Robert Kimber. New York: Pantheon Books, 1981.

Hoag, Betty Lochrie. *Interview with June Wayne.* June 14, 1965. Archives of American Art.

Horsfield, Kate, and Lyn Blumenthal. *Interview wth Nancy Graves.* March 1978. Video Data Bank. Art Institute School of Chicago.

———. *Interview with Michelle Stuart.* June 1978. Video Data Bank. Art Institute School of Chicago.

———. *Interview with Lucy Lippard.* January 1979. Video Data Bank. Art Institute School of Chicago.

————. *Interview with Joan Brown.* April 1979. Video Data Bank. Art Institute School of Chicago.

Hughes, Robert. *The Shock of the New.* New York: Knopf, 1981.

Jaguer, Édouard. *Remedios Varo.* Mexico City: Ediciones Era, 1980.

Jelenski, Constantine. *Léonor Fini.* Lausanne: La Guilde du Livre et Clairefontaine, 1968.

Kaplan, Janet. "Remedios Varo: Voyages and Visions." *Woman's Art Journal* I, 2 (Fall 1980/Winter 1981), pp. 13–18.

Käthe Kollwitz. St. Paul, Minn.: Minnesota Museum of Art, 1973.

Kearns, Martha. *Käthe Kollwitz: Woman and Artist.* Old Westbury: Feminist Press, 1976.

Kistler, Bernard. "The Tapestries of June Wayne." *Craft Horizons* XXXIV, 6 (Dec. 1974), pp. 36–39, 80–81.

Klein, Mina C. and Arthur. *Käthe Kollwitz: Life in Art.* New York: Schocken Books, 1975.

Kollwitz, Käthe. *Diary and Letters of Käthe Kollwitz,* ed., Hans Kollwitz. Tr. Richard and Clara Winston. Chicago: Henry Regnery Co., 1955.

Lanyon, Ellen. *Wonder Production,* Vol. I. Chicago: Landfall Press, 1971.

Lauter, Estella. "Visual Art by Women: A Test Case for the Theory of Archetypes." In Estella Lauter and Carol Schreier Rupprecht, eds., "Feminist Archetypal Theory: Interdisciplinary Re-Visions of Jungian Thought." Knoxville: University of Tennessee Press, forthcoming, 1984.

Lippard, Lucy. "Distancing: The Films of Nancy Graves." *Art in America* 63, 6 (Nov.-Dec. 1975), pp. 78–82.

————. *From the Center.: Feminist Essays on Women's Art.* New York: Dutton, 1976.

————. "A New Landscape Art: Four Contemporary Artists Go 'Back to Nature'." *Ms.* 5 (April 1977), pp. 68–73.

————. "Sweeping Exchanges: The Contribution of Feminism to the Art of the 1970s." *Art Journal* (Fall/Winter 1980), pp. 362–365.

————. "Kollwitz Chiaroscuro." In Renate Hinz, ed., *Käthe Kollwitz: Graphics, Posters, Drawings.* Tr. Rita and Robert Kimber. New York: Pantheon Books, 1981.

————. *Overlay: Contemporary Art and the Art of Prehistory.* New York: Pantheon Books, 1983.

Lisle, Laurie. *Portrait of an Artist: A Biography of Georgia O'Keeffe.* New York: Seaview Books, 1980.

McCoy, Ann. "Alice Baber: Light as Subject." *Art International* 24 (Sept.-Oct. 1980), pp. 135–140.

Miller, Lynn F., and Sally S. Swenson. *Lives and Works: Talks with Women Artists.* Metuchen, N.J.: Scarecrow Press, 1981.

Moore, Sylvia. "Dorothy Hood." *Woman's Art Journal* I, 2 (Fall 1980/Winter 1981), pp. 51–54.

————. "Alice Baber." *Woman's Art Journal* III, 1 (Spring/Summer 1982), pp. 40–43.

Munro, Eleanor. *Originals: American Women Artists.* New York: Simon and Schuster, 1979.

Nancy Graves: A survey, 1969–1980. Buffalo: Albright-Knox Gallery, 1981.

Nemser, Cindy. *Art Talk.* New York: Scribner's, 1975.

O'Keeffe, Georgia. *Georgia O'Keeffe.* New York: Penguin, 1976.

Orenstein, Gloria Feman. "Women of Surrealism." *The Feminist Art Journal* (Spring 1973), pp. 1, 15–21.

———. "Reemergence of the Archetype of the Great Goddess in Art by Contemporary Women." *The Great Goddess.* Special Issue of *Heresies* 2, 1 (Spring 1978), pp. 74–85.

Originals: Women in Art. Georgia O'Keeffe, Wilmette, Ill.: Films, Inc., 1978.

Originals: Women in Art. Spirit Catcher–The Art of Betye Saar. Wilmette, Ill.: Films Inc., 1978.

Parker, Rozsika and Griselda Pollock. *Old Mistresses: Women, Art and Ideology.* New York: Pantheon Books, 1981.

Patricia Johanson: Plant Drawings For Projects. Rosa Esman Gallery, 1978.

Patricia Johanson: Drawings for the Camouflage House and Orchid Projects. Rosa Esman Gallery, 1979.

Patricia Johanson: Landscapes, 1969–1980. Rosa Esman Gallery, 1981.

Paz, Octavio, Roger Caillois, and Julia Gonzalez. *Remedios Varo.* Mexico City: Ediciones ERA, 1966.

Petersen, Karen and J. J. Wilson. *Women Artists: Recognition and Reappraisal.* New York: Harper and Row, 1976.

Poggioli, Renato. *The Theory of the Avant-Garde.* Tr. Gerald Fitzgerald. Cambridge: Harvard University Press, 1968.

Pollock, Griselda. "Women, Art and Ideology: Questions for Feminist Art Historians." *Woman's Art Journal.* IV, 1 (Spring/Summer 1983), pp. 39–47.

Pratt, Annis. "Aunt Jennifer's Tigers: Notes Toward A Pre-literary History of Women's Archetypes." *Feminist Studies* IV, 1 (February 1978), pp. 163–194.

de Rache, André, ed. *Léonor Fini.* XVIII Festival Belge d'Eté. Uitgever, 1965.

Rabinovitz, Lauren. "Issues of Feminist Aesthetics: Judy Chicago and Joyce Wieland." *Woman's Art Journal* I, 2 (Fall 1980/Winter 1981), pp. 38–42.

Ratcliffe, Carter. "On Contemporary Primitivism." *Artforum* XIV (Nov. 1975), pp. 57–66.

Remedios Varo. Mexico City: Ediciones ERA, 1966. Texts by Octavio Paz, Roger Caillois, and Juliana Gonzalez.

Richardson, Brenda. "Nancy Graves: A New Way of Seeing." *Arts* 46, 6 (April 1972), pp. 57–61.

Rubenstein, Charlotte S. *American Women Artists: From Early Indian Times to the Present.* Boston: G. K. Hall, 1982.

Russell, H. Diane. "Art History." *Signs* V, 3 (Spring 1980), pp. 468–481.

Schwartz, Barry. *The New Humanism: Art in a Time of Change.* New York: Praeger, 1974.

Selvig, Forrest. *Interview with I. Rice Pereira.* August, 1968. Archives of American Art.

Shattuck, Roger. *The Banquet Years.* New York: Vintage, 1968.

Snyder, Carol. "Reading the Language of the Dinner Party." *Woman's Art Journal,* I, 2 (Fall 1980/Winter 1981), pp. 30–34.

Snyder-Ott, Joelynn. *Women and Creativity.* Millbrae, Calif.: Les Femmes Publishing, 1978.

Stowens, Susan. "June Wayne: 'The Dorothy Series.'" *American Artist* 43 (May 1979), pp. 50–55, 92–100.

Tompkins, Calvin. *The Bride and Her Bachelors.* Harmondsworth, Middlesex: Penguin, 1968.

Tufts, Eleanor. *Our Hidden Heritage.* New York: Paddington Press, 1974.

Van Wagner, Judith K. "I. Rice Pereira: Vision Superceding Style." *Woman's Art Journal* I, 1 (Spring/Summer 1980), pp. 33–38.

Wasserman, Emily. "A Conversation with Nancy Graves." *Artforum* IX, 2 (Oct. 1970), pp. 42–47.

Wayne, June. "The Creative Process: Artists, Carpenters and the Flat Earth Society." *Craft Horizons* XXXVI, 5 (Oct. 1976), pp. 30–31, 64–67.
Weisman, Celia. "O'Keeffe's Art: Sacred Symbols and Spiritual Quest." *Woman's Art Journal* III, 2 (Fall 1982/Winter 1983), pp. 10–14.
Winter, Nina. *Interview with the Muse*. Berkeley: Moon Books, 1979.
Women's Traditional Arts: The Politics of Aesthetics. Special issue of *Heresies* I, 4 (Winter 1978).
Zigrosser, Carl. *Prints and Drawings of Käthe Kollwitz*. New York: Dover, 1969.

V.   *General*

Arieti, Silvano. *Creativity: The Magic Synthesis*. New York: Basic Books, 1976.
Bachelard, Gaston, *The Poetics of Space*. Tr. Maria Jolas. New York: The Orion Press, 1964.
Bakan, David. *The Duality of Human Existence: An Essay on Psychology and Religion*. Chicago: Rand McNally, 1966.
Beston, Henry. *The Outermost House*. New York: Viking, 1956.
Block, Ned, ed. *Imagery*. Cambridge, Mass.: M.I.T. Press, 1981.
Casey, Edward, "Toward an Archetypal Imagination." *Spring: An Annual of Archetypal Psychology and Jungian Thought*. New York: Spring Publications, 1974.
――――. *Imagining: A Phenomenological Study*. Bloomington: Indiana University Press, 1976.
Dubos, René. *The Wooing of Earth*. New York: Scribner's, 1980.
Erikson, Erik H. *Childhood and Society*. 2nd Ed. New York: W. W. Norton, 1963.
――――. *Identity, Youth and Crisis*. New York: W. W. Norton, 1968.
Hillman, James. *The Myth of Analysis*. New York: Harper and Row, 1972.
――――. *Re-Visioning Psychology*. New York: Harper and Row, 1975.
――――. *Suicide and the Soul*. Zurich: Spring Publication, 1976.
――――. "Concrete Psychology." Address given at the C. G. Jung Conference, Notre Dame University, April 1977.
――――. "An Inquiry Into Image." *Spring: An Annual of Archetypal Psychology and Jungian Thought*. Zurich: Spring Publications, 1977.
――――. "Further Notes on Images." *Spring: An Annual of Archetypal Psychology and Jungian Thought*. Irving, Texas: Spring Publications, 1978.
――――. "Image-Sense." *Spring: An Annual of Archetypal Psychology and Jungian Thought*. Irving, Texas: Spring Publications, 1979.
Progoff, Ira. *Depth Psychology and Modern Man*. New York: McGraw-Hill, 1959.
――――. *The Symbolic and the Real*. New York: McGraw-Hill, 1963.
――――. *Jung, Synchronicity, and Human Destiny*. New York: Dell, 1973.
Rothenberg, Albert, and Carl B. Hausman, eds. *The Creativity Question*. Durham, N.C.: Duke University Press, 1976.
Sagan, Carl. *The Cosmic Connection: An Extraterrestrial Perspective*. Garden City, N.Y.: Doubleday, 1973.
――――. *The Dragons of Eden*. New York: Ballantine, 1977.
――――. *Cosmos*. New York: Random House, 1980.
Thomas, Lewis. *The Lives of a Cell: Notes of a Biology Watcher*. New York: Bantam, 1974.
――――. *The Medusa and the Snail: More Notes of a Biology Watcher*. New York: Bantam, 1979.
Willis, Roy. *Man and Beast*. New York: Basic Books, 1974.

INDEX